# NORTH AMERICAN
## ODYSSEY

ALSO BY AMY AND DAVE FREEMAN

*A Year in the Wilderness*

# NORTH AMERICAN
# ODYSSEY

12,000 MILES Across

the CONTINENT

by KAYAK, CANOE,

and DOGSLED

## AMY AND DAVE FREEMAN

MILKWEED EDITIONS

Published 2024 by Milkweed Editions
Printed in Canada
Cover design by Mary Austin Speaker
Cover photo by Amy Freeman
Author photo by Nate Ptacek
24 25 26 27 28   5 4 3 2 1
*First Edition*

Library of Congress Cataloging-in-Publication Data

Names: Freeman, Amy, author. | Freeman, Dave (Wilderness guide), author.
Title: North American odyssey : 12,000 miles across the continent by kayak,
    canoe, and dogsled / Amy and Dave Freeman.
Other titles: Twelve thousand miles across the continent by kayak, canoe,
    and dogsled
Description: First edition. | Minneapolis, Minnesota : Milkweed Editions,
    2024. | Summary: "In 2010, experienced wilderness travelers Amy and Dave
    Freeman married and set out on an unusual honeymoon: a 12,000 mile,
    human-powered journey across North America"-- Provided by publisher.
Identifiers: LCCN 2024012801 (print) | LCCN 2024012802 (ebook) | ISBN
    9781571311689 (hardback ; acid-free paper) | ISBN 9781639550340 (ebook)
Subjects: LCSH: Outdoor life. | Honeymoons. | Kayaking. | Canoes and
    canoeing. | Dogsledding.
Classification: LCC GV191.6 .F736 2024  (print) | LCC GV191.6 (ebook) |
    DDC 796.5--dc23/eng/20240429
LC record available at https://lccn.loc.gov/2024012801
LC ebook record available at https://lccn.loc.gov/2024012802

Milkweed Editions is committed to ecological stewardship. We strive to align our book
production practices with this principle, and to reduce the impact of our operations in
the environment. We are a member of the Green Press Initiative, a nonprofit coalition of
publishers, manufacturers, and authors working to protect the world's endangered forests
and conserve natural resources. *North American Odyssey* was printed on acid-free 100%
postconsumer-waste paper by Friesens Corporation.

*To the people in all the remote northern communities that we paddled and dogsledded through. Your kindness and knowledge enriched us in countless ways. You taught us to listen to the land. We hope that this book will encourage others to listen as well.*

# Contents

## Introduction

A MIST HUNG over the Wintergreen dog yard in the early morning light, caused by the humidity of rapidly melting snow. It obscured the upper reaches of white pines, sentinels that shaded the seventy Canadian Inuit sled dogs and provided perches for ravens on the lookout for an easy meal of spilled kibble. The sled dogs knew the end of winter was upon them; their days of running through Minnesota's Northwoods pulling tourists on sleds would soon be over for the year. The sun was rising earlier each day, and their coats were beginning to blow out the downy layer of underfur that had kept them warm all winter. But the energy in the air was different today, and they could sense it.

All the guides were there, plus the gradually accumulating smells of new people. On the day after the spring equinox of 2010, guides were harnessing every dog and attaching corsages to the collars of three of them. The dogs of honor belonged to us: Daisy, Fennel, and Thistle were our pets in the summer but earned their room and board just like us at Wintergreen Dogsled Lodge, near Ely, Minnesota, all winter.

Did the dogs know the cause for the occasion? It didn't matter really; they were just happy to go for one last run, with paws gripping lake ice and smells of the forest emerging after the stasis of winter. But the occasion was significant to us—this was our wedding day. Soon the dogs would be transporting our loved ones a mile and a half down White Iron Lake to a point of land blanketed in fragrant red and white pine needles. The folk musicians would strike up, their joyful notes mingling in the air with the laughter of loved ones and excited howls of sled dogs.

Spring had struck northern Minnesota well before anyone expected. Plans made far in advance had rapidly changed in the few days before our wedding—and they were quite different from the typical concerns about flowers, seating arrangements, and music. We had to relocate the site of the ceremony due to melting, unsafe ice near the mouth of the South Kawishiwi River. Skis and snowshoes were no longer appropriate for trails and the lake's surface of glare ice. People would be canoeing on this lake within a week.

Everyone arrived at a rocky sun-glazed point on White Iron Lake mostly by foot and dogsled, and a brave few by ice skate and ski. We walked down the duff-covered aisle that had been a dogsledding trail just a week before. We exchanged our vows in a cathedral of red pines surrounded by a hundred of our closest friends and family. Straw bales served as pews. No scripture was read; rather the words of Sigurd Olson were shared by our friend, mentor, and boss: Paul Schurke. Dave's first partner in adventure and our dear friend, Eric Frost (Frosty), had been ordained online to marry us. Sunlight filtered through the pine branches, casting a glow on the faces of those near and dear to us. They were dressed in mukluks, wool sweaters, and down vests instead of suits, ties, dresses, and heels. All these people we loved were here in a place that was beloved and sacred to us. Siblings, uncles, nieces and nephews, friends from high school and college that were all scattered across the country had converged in this place to see why we loved it and each other so much.

\* \* \*

LAKE COUNTRY IN northeastern Minnesota is a triangle of Laurentian mixed forest framed by Lake Superior, the Iron Range, and the Canadian border. The land is wild, untrammeled, and filled with interconnected waterways. The water from bogs, lakes, streams, and rivers flows either north toward Hudson Bay or south to Lake Superior. Black spruce, tamarack, Labrador tea, and cranberries can be found in the bogs while white and red pine, jack pine, birch, aspen, and blueberries grow in the thin covering of soil atop granite, gabbro, and basalt. Wild rice, bullhead lilies, and cattails thrive in the clean water. Gray wolves still hunt moose and whitetail deer in the forest, while bald eagles, osprey, and loons live off abundant fish in the lakes. This land was scoured and shaped by glaciers, resulting in shorelines of exposed bedrock that are often reflected perfectly on still, dark water. Within the 3-million-acre Superior National Forest, 1.1 million acres of rugged landscape is federally managed as the Boundary Waters Canoe Area Wilderness, or BWCAW. Those who wish to know this place travel the waterways by canoe in the summer and dog team, ski, or snowshoe in the winter. No roads, artificial lights, or even signposts interrupt one's gaze.

The expansive wild vistas and formidable experiences of this "canoe country," as Sigurd Olson called it, made a lasting impression on both of us during childhood trips with our families. Time spent in this place could challenge your physical abilities while canoeing across a storm-tossed lake or slogging through a rocky, meandering portage. Yet at the same time, the view from atop a granite cliff or a sunset at a lake's edge, accentuated by the reedy call of a loon across its surface, could leave you content with the world and your place in it. Even when we were young and lived hundreds of miles to the south, it evoked a feeling of home. So we both spent more and more time there, independently pursuing livelihoods that revolved around wilderness adventures until a love for paddling and chance meeting in the summer of 2005 brought us together along the shore of Lake Superior.

At first it appeared we would be friends and temporary paddling partners in our free time during Lake Superior's all-too-short summer: one a dirtbag living in a wall tent deep in the woods between international expeditions while trying to get the Wilderness

Classroom, a fledgling nonprofit, off the ground; the other in Grand Marais for one last summer during a short respite from an intense graduate program at the School of the Art Institute of Chicago, heading toward a career in academia.

As we paddled after work, the horizon beckoned, more and more with each short outing. Lake Superior has many moods, from cotton candy clouds reflecting off its mirror-smooth surface to steep, frothing waves whipped up by winds that tear at kayak paddles and throw cold, stinging spray into exposed faces. This urge to continue grew from a shared desire to see what lay ahead, past the ever-changing line where the water and sky meet. It was satisfying and exhilarating to have found someone else who shared this innate drive.

We had been inseparable ever since, spending five years living and working together. Our shared life mostly occurred on trails and in a tent as we spent our summers guiding kayak or canoe trips, winters guiding dogsledding trips, and the rest of the time on Wilderness Classroom learning adventures—human-powered expeditions that we broadcast online to elementary and middle school classrooms through the website and educational nonprofit that Frosty and Dave founded back in 2002.

Our first learning adventure together began on the last day of August 2006, a little over a year after we met. The dream of discovering what lay over the horizon together had finally come to fruition. After sliding our heavily loaded kayaks off the smooth, familiar pebbles of Grand Marais's East Bay beach into Lake Superior's cold, clear water, we pointed our bows to the northeast to follow the shore in a clockwise direction. Kayaking around the largest freshwater lake in the world as summer's warmth and calm transitioned into autumn's darkness, freezing temperatures, and gales revealed not only Lake Superior's secrets but also our true, unvarnished selves. Upon our return we learned that our friends had taken bets on whether or not we would stay together. Luckily, the journey had cemented our bond rather than shattering it.

Within a year of circumnavigating Lake Superior together, we embarked on an even grander learning adventure across South America with Frosty and three other team members. In three two-month-long stages, we bicycled from the Pacific Coast through the Andes and canoed the Amazon River to the Atlantic. All the while we documented the journey to share photos, videos, scientific data, guided reading exercises, lesson plans, and other educational materials with thousands of students back in the United States.

* * *

AFTER WE SAID "I do" every sled dog (that had remarkably sat silently in its harness on the ice through the entire ceremony) howled in unison—one joyful howl that ended as abruptly as it started. In a whirlwind of cheers, hugs, and cameras clicking, we hopped on the first dogsled and took off down the smooth lake ice under a cloudless blue sky.

Our wedding was soon overshadowed by the launch of our most ambitious journey yet, which had begun to take shape in our heads even before the notion of getting married. On Earth Day of 2010, we would embark on a nearly twelve-thousand-mile human-powered journey across North America. From Bellingham, Washington, we would kayak, canoe, dogsled, and hike our way up to the Arctic Ocean and then down to Key West. As this was to be the Wilderness Classroom's tenth learning adventure, twelve hundred teachers and sixty-five thousand students were ready to learn along with us. The North American Odyssey, as we called it, would also be our honeymoon.

The month between our wedding and departure was filled with frenzied preparation that had begun more than a year before. We had written grant proposals and sought sponsors while Frosty helped to put the finishing touches on the curriculum guide and web resources. We drove around the Midwest conducting school assemblies for the students who would soon be following our progress and learning throughout the journey. The Wilderness Classroom's board helped with the educational content, recruiting schools, and PR. A lot of our equipment and some of our food was donated by outdoor companies, but instead of registering for kitchen appliances and linens, we had registered for things like a tent, sleeping pads, and organic mac and cheese to help fill in the gaps. Most of our donated equipment was sponsored by outdoor companies that we had built a relationship with during our previous expeditions. Our canoes (a Royalex Cascade and Kevlar Itasca) were from Wenonah, our kayaks (two expedition layup Solstices) from Current Designs, paddles from Mitchell, clothing from ExOfficio, bars from GoMacro and Clif Bar, and life jackets from MTI Adventurewear.

We had the details planned out and food packed for only the first stage of the journey—1,400 miles by sea kayak from Bellingham, Washington, to Skagway, Alaska. These boxes were ready to be sent general delivery to various post offices in British Columbia and Alaska. The rest of the route was a vague squiggly line connecting waterways and trails on a map. Although we had done enough research to know the rest of the route was doable, each stage would require more thorough planning that could be accomplished during the preceding stage and the brief pauses in travel while we waited for freeze-up or thaw.

The route was our unique contrivance, but it was rooted in historic routes and previous expeditions. As pieces came together, our reading grew more focused on things like guidebooks for kayaking the Inside Passage, the history of the Klondike Gold Rush, and the journals of Alexander Mackenzie and Charles Camsell.

We were lucky enough to glean firsthand information from people who had paddled or dogsledded portions of our route. Glenn Charles shared his experience of kayaking the Inside Passage over the phone. Polar explorer Will Steger invited us to his homestead for tea. He and Paul Schurke led the first confirmed dogsled journey to the North Pole without resupply in 1986, and in 1990 Will led the seven-month, 3,741-mile International Trans-Antarctica Expedition. We struck up an email conversation with Valerie Fons who, with Verlen Kruger, paddled the Mississippi River in a record-setting twenty-three days in 1984 and in the late 1980s paddled 21,000 miles from the Arctic to Cape Horn in the Two Continent Canoe Expedition.

We also made countless calls to locals in remote Canadian Indigenous communities we would pass through, which were helpful and frustrating in equal measure. The local Environment and Natural Resources (ENR) offices were often our first contact, and sometimes the Royal Canadian Mounted Police (RCMP). These calls typically resulted in offers for places to stay or store our resupplies but were lacking in descriptors of what we could expect for trail or waterway conditions. For example, when trying to determine whether or not our desired route between Deline and Gameti in the Northwest Territories was traveled by hunters on snowmobiles in the winter, the answer was "It depends on the caribou."

If there is one thing we have learned about expedition planning it's that you will never have every last duck in a row before you leave home—and that's okay. Remaining flexible and not nailing down our entire route was beneficial because it allowed us to make changes as we went. We approached our route planning with an open mind and a certain degree of humility and deference to advice from locals. Would there be enough water in the Tazin River? Would we find old, seldom-used portage trails? Would there be a trail packed by snowmobiling caribou hunters or four feet of powder between Great Bear Lake and Great Slave Lake?

We would just have to see when we got there.

# NORTH AMERICAN

# ODYSSEY

# Kayaking the Inside Passage

## *Bellingham, Washington, to Skagway, Alaska*

### 1,400 MILES

WE ARRIVED IN Bellingham, Washington, a couple of days before the launch, having driven from Minnesota in our station wagon with an old, rickety kayak trailer in tow. The journey began to feel real upon reaching Larrabee State Park the evening before the launch of our three-year odyssey. We were newlyweds about to embark on a nearly twelve-thousand-mile journey by kayak, canoe, foot, and dogsled across North America. Our destination was Key West, Florida.

We caught our first glimpse of the Pacific Ocean right at the onset of golden hour. The air was damp and heavy—so much so that we could feel its moisture content deep in our lungs with each inhalation. We followed a moss-lined trail that emerged from the dark, temperate rainforest out onto a point and along the way found half a dozen banana slugs that were ten times the size of any slug we had ever seen. One glance into the salt water revealed more life than the total of what we had seen in Lake Superior. Purple sea stars, anemones, urchins, and barnacles clung to the dark rocks. Long, olive-green strands of kelp indicated the direction of the ocean's current. The sun dipped low and orange behind the San Juan Islands.

Earth Day (April 22) of 2010 was our self-appointed start date, and two friends—John and Clayton—had joined us to kayak 1,400 miles up the Inside Passage during the first several months of our "honey-moon." In many ways John, with his sandy-blond hair and shy smile, was responsible for our introduction. He owned Superior Coastal Sports in Grand Marais, Minnesota. We both worked for him as kayak guides but during different years, until our fateful overlap in 2005. John had given each of us a solid foundation of basic sea kayaking skills and inadvertently brought us together. His quiet and gentle de-meanor, combined with tremendous paddling skills built while white water kayaking and slalom racing in the 1980s, made him an excellent teacher. We had never seen him show any signs of fear or apprehension as we pushed to improve our paddling skills on Lake Superior under his watchful eye. His long, lean frame made kayaking look effortless, and in a way, having both him and Clayton join us for the first few months of our journey felt like a safety net.

Clayton, smaller in stature than John and with his brown hair in a tidy bowl cut, had recently retired from a corporate job in human re-sources. He had grown up in Grand Marais, the son of a commercial fisherman who wanted an easier life for his children and encouraged Clayton to study hard and find his own opportunities outside the small town where he was raised. In his retirement Clayton guided for John just for fun. He was nearly twice our age, but a constant regimen of running, skiing, and paddling allowed him to paddle circles around us. A few years prior, he had kayaked—unsupported and without resupply—around Lake Superior in just over a month. He was driven by the sheer joy and challenge of paddling. He had sea kayaked in Baja and the Pacific Northwest and had firsthand experience with tides and currents, which the rest of us lacked. John and Clayton were both bachelors at a crossroads in life: Clayton free from his corporate career, and John having just sold his kayak busi-ness. They were both trying to figure out what to do next.

We set up our three tents on the moist ground between mas-sive trunks of Douglas fir, under the dense canopy created by their branches. After one last huddle at a picnic table with the map spread between us, we climbed into our tents just in time for raindrops to pelt the nylon and drench the forest floor. Any anxiety about the up-coming journey melted away as this comforting and familiar sound lulled us to sleep.

We were up before dawn on Earth Day. A smattering of clouds soon dissipated, and the ocean was kind to us, with light wind and minimal waves. A brief but chaotic scene on the beach was inevitable as we stuffed dry bag after dry bag into our four kayaks. Amy's dad was there to see us off and we wondered what he thought of the disarray. The clothing, camping gear, and couple weeks' worth of food fit in easily. But we still had to carefully stow an assortment of electronics that seemed incongruous with a water-based wilderness trek: the satellite terminal, laptop, digital camera, and foldable solar panels that would enable us to share the journey with classrooms across the country. With the final bits of tech gear stowed, we had won the game of Tetris within the hatches of our sea kayaks, happily sealing them and looking at watches. Although awkward at first, this was a ritual that would soon become second nature to us, along with sliding our boats into the water, cramming our feet onto the foot pegs, and sealing our spray skirts over the cockpit coaming.

We waved at the lone silhouette standing on the beach and pointed our bows toward Cypress Island and then to Obstruction Pass. An established campsite on Orcas Island was our destination for the day—only fifteen miles away. The stress from months of preparation sloughed from our minds and bodies as we settled into the rhythm dictated by our double-bladed paddles and headed for the San Juan Islands. We were putting into practice something we had learned from years of conducting human-powered journeys and observations of various successful and unsuccessful expeditions. Start slow and easy; work up to longer, harder days. It is nearly impossible to log the necessary training hours in a kayak, canoe, or on skis to achieve peak physical shape prior to an expedition. Planning to paddle thirty to forty miles per day at the beginning of our journey could be a recipe for tendonitis or carpal tunnel syndrome. This was a marathon, not a sprint, and our goal was to share the journey, not rush through it.

The students following our adventure didn't care how far we went each day; what mattered most was that we had the time and energy to share the experience with them and answer the questions they sent. We knew the students cared more about things like giant banana slugs slithering along the dark, dank forest floor and purple sea stars clinging to rocks along the intertidal zone than daily mileage. Our work with the Wilderness Classroom had always been motivated by an understanding that "in the end we will conserve only what we love; we will love only what we understand; and we will understand only what we are taught," as Baba Dioum says.

During these lower-mileage days we made progress, but we were far from spent at the end of the day. On windy, rainy days lunch breaks were short because we would get chilled quickly once we stopped paddling, but on sunny days, we soaked in the dry warmth and let our muscles rest for an hour or more as we read, ate, talked, and relaxed, all the while observing the dense forests, rugged shores, and dramatic seascapes that were never in short supply. As our bodies adjusted to the steady rhythm of paddling and the rigors of hauling our one-hundred-plus-pound loaded kayaks across the intertidal zone each morning and afternoon, our minds were slowly figuring out the most efficient camp routine. Each day we shaved a few minutes off, and before long everyone set about their delegated chores with little need for debate because we all knew our role in making our home each night and breaking it down in the morning, leaving nothing but a few patches of trampled underbrush where our bodies had lain.

As we settled into the rhythm of travel dictated by the sun and tides, it became apparent that about a third of our stuff was unnecessary. Why did we bring it? Because we were habituated to using it—accustomed to accumulating. It is so hard to let go of these things. We hoped that by the time we reached Key West we would truly be whittled down to the bare necessities.

* * *

NONE OF OUR freshwater paddling experience prepared us for the twice daily rise and fall of the ocean tide, changing as much as eight feet every six hours. We would come to learn the synchrony between the size of the tide and the lunar cycle. For now, we were content to paddle smarter by responding to the currents as water rushed around islands and through constricted channels. We began to view our passage between islands as that of paddling a river—albeit an ever-changing river that would reverse directions every six hours.

When the current was in our favor, we took advantage of it by paddling out in the middle of the channel where the flow was at its strongest. Our perspective would be molded by where we positioned our kayaks. Out in mid-channel we were viewing the landscape from a distance. This afforded us the opportunity to study the topography of our surroundings and appreciate the grandeur of this place. Variegated shades of green contained within the steep forested hillsides dropped to the water. And behind lay the occasional shimmer of a snowcapped mountain. We were four small beings afloat in an intricate maze of countless channels of water coursing, pulsing, like blood through capillaries.

Our free ride would eventually lessen in intensity and then shift to flow against us. A noticeable drop in our speed or newly formed swirls of an eddy off a point would indicate it was time to hightail it from the middle of the "river" to the edge. As we worked our way against the current we would hug the shore, hopping eddies and taking in the minutiae. No longer pondering the vast expanse between us and distant peaks, our focus shifted to close observations of the details found on the seam where land met sea. If the tide was low, we would contemplate the precarious situation of countless orange and purple sea stars and translucent pink anemones left exposed, clinging awkwardly to rocks like boogers. Looking down into the clear, cool water revealed tentacles of anemones fully expanded and fluttering in the current, contrasted with the ominous dark spikes of sea urchins. Here and there, the telltale line of white dots on an abalone or the bizarre, otherworldly sea cucumber could be glimpsed slinking along the bottom. When our pace slowed, our experience of the intricacies of life at the water's edge became richer.

We followed a water trail through the San Juan Islands. Late one afternoon, while we were poking along the shore to look for a campsite on Posey Island, a man emerged from a cottage and began talking to us with the aid of a megaphone. "Hello kayakers!" his deep voice bellowed. He proceeded to ask us half a dozen questions as we took turns shouting responses to him.

We eventually found the campsite, which was posh enough to have a picnic table—and it happened to be directly across from megaphone man. It was raining, of course, so we set up camp in the way we would almost every night until reaching Skagway, Alaska, in early July. We hung a tarp first. Then we carefully set up each tent under the tarp so as not to get its interior soaked before the tent's rainfly was attached. Once constructed, we relocated each tent to a semilevel spot for the night. The tarp would remain over the patch of ground that would become our cooking area.

Just before twilight John decided to stretch his legs by exploring the island's shoreline. Only a few yards from the campsite, he slipped on a damp tree root and fell. He reappeared with his sandy gray hair tussled, a frown on his face, and his left arm held closely to his side. The fall had tweaked his shoulder, and judging by the grimace on his weathered face, it was causing a great deal of pain. We dug out the first aid kit for anti-inflammatories and a sling as John expressed his dismay. This could potentially end the trip for him, but it was too soon to tell. We were all worried and frustrated by how such a silly thing as slipping on a leisurely walk could result in an injury.

A small craft advisory kept us from paddling the next day. Megaphone man invited us over to the cottage, so we paddled across as he and another man sauntered down to the beach to greet us. Adriel was a sturdily built, dark-haired, megayacht designer. As we might have surmised from the megaphone conversation, he was the most outgoing of the group and immediately began asking questions about our journey as we climbed out of our boats. Stu was a wiry individual with a graying blond ponytail. His wry smile and piercing blue-gray eyes gave the impression that he didn't take life too seriously, yet enjoyed everything it had to offer. A prestigious kinetic artist (think of sculptures that move like Alexander Calder's giant mobiles), his pieces worked perfectly on the yachts Adriel designed. They lived in Seattle and had come here to recharge and contemplate a career change.

Stu handed John a bag of ice for his shoulder and stoked the fire in a woodstove attached to an outdoor hot tub. Our new acquaintances were on a mission to dive for crabs for dinner and soon donned wet suits in the hot tub to brace themselves against the cold Pacific water. Then it was our turn for a good soak in the cedar tub while woodsmoke wafted out the stovepipe above our heads.

That evening we feasted on crab and oysters while learning more about the megayacht scene in Seattle. Adriel had designed some astoundingly large and opulent boats, a statement reinforced by photos of a two-hundred-foot-long megayacht dwarfing all the other boats around it. In photos of a lavish interior full of woodwork, windows, and chandeliers, he pointed out Stu's handiwork. We quizzed Adriel on fuel consumption and costs of these decadent behemoths, and his answers left our heads spinning, shocked that there were people in this world who possessed enough money to commission these things and hire a captain and crew to whisk them off to exotic locales. The resources consumed by one megayacht in a week would basically fund our entire three-year journey. Two people exploring an entire continent for three years versus a week on a floating mansion that burns five hundred liters of fuel per hour. We were eager to head off in the morning to see where these eighteen-foot boats propelled by our own bodies would take us.

* * *

WHILE THE UNDERWATER creatures of the intertidal zone continued to mesmerize us as we made steady progress north and crossed into British Columbia, there were much larger creatures in the water that attracted our attention. Sea otters curiously peeked at us from patches of bull kelp before diving down to retrieve some tasty morsel, only to reappear, floating on their backs as their dexterous little paws opened a clam or dug into a sea urchin. Sometimes they even used rocks as anvils resting on their bellies, slamming their prey against the rock to get at the meat inside. We oftentimes felt as if we were being watched and would turn to see a small, slick, dark head bobbing just above the water's surface, peering at us with wide eyes. Harbor seals were our constant companions. While these small pinnipeds shyly kept their distance, their larger relatives—sea lions—were bolder. On one occasion a two-thousand-pound male Steller's sea lion slid off his rock and charged straight at John and Clayton with such speed that they frantically backpaddled away from him and his harem.

Past Lund, British Columbia, we left the Sunshine Coast, which sees much less rainfall than the rest of the British Columbia coast because it is in the rain shadow of Vancouver Island's towering mountains. From here on out, we soon learned what makes a temperate rainforest a rainforest. In many ways we felt as if we were living the same gray, rainy day over and over again. Opportunities to dry out soggy tents diminished. Mildew flourished on the constantly damp exteriors of our dry suits. A trend in the wind direction disheartened all of us: the rainy days provided us with a tailwind, while the rare sunny days coincided with a strong headwind that prevented us from going anywhere. In other words, whenever we paddled it was raining. At least the rare days when headwinds forced us to stay onshore allowed us to dry out our tents, clothing, and dry suits, and hike around in the sunshine.

We tried to not let the weather get us down. It was, after all, partially responsible for the vibrant mossy green carpet on the forest floor and the towering western red cedars, Douglas firs, and Sitka spruces. Though we soon learned that it was one thing to camp below the shelter of their branches and quite another to navigate waterways and constantly misjudge distances because the trees were so much bigger than anything any of us was accustomed to. We often found ourselves looking across a channel and mentally estimating the time it would take to get there, thinking, *Half an hour, tops*, only to find ourselves still paddling two hours later—tricked again by the arboreal giants that surrounded us.

One unexpected consequence of paddling through this forested landscape was encountering areas eerily devoid of trees. The topography was such that hillsides and mountains rose up out of the water, giving us viewsheds that extended for dozens of miles in either direction. The lush green of tall conifers seemed to always be there, sandwiched between the stark white of snow-dusted mountains and mottled shadows of the intertidal zone—until it wasn't. Irregular patches of brown earth stood out among the remaining intact deep green forest, like a poorly trimmed Chia Pet. These massive clear-cuts far from civilization were a stark reminder of humanity's ever-lengthening grasp.

According to the World Wildlife Fund, "Temperate conifer forests sustain the highest levels of biomass in any terrestrial ecosystem." North America's temperate rainforest extends approximately 2,500 miles between California and the Gulf of Alaska and provides an important habitat for many species, not to mention its significant role in global carbon sequestration. However, "this forest has been beset by logging over the last century, with little unprotected old growth remaining." In fact, more than half of this coastal temperate rainforest—one of the most endangered forest types on the planet—has been destroyed.

Our first view of brown, naked hillsides in British Columbia would haunt us for years to come. Occasionally we would hear a distant mechanical drumbeat of a helicopter growing steadily louder and catch a glimpse of these insect-like machines hauling impossibly large logs. It took our breaths away. The timber was so valuable in these inaccessible mountains that it was economical to drop in crews and machinery, and then later fly the crews, machinery, and timber out. Seeing a helicopter in action provided a new understanding for the scale of the bald patchwork on the hills we passed. Quietly, we each wondered what this place had looked like before the aerial human intrusion.

Some of these trees were likely over one thousand years old, already reaching for the sky when Columbus sailed. But these giants are just the backbone of an astoundingly diverse web of life found nowhere else on Earth. As Robin Wall Kimmerer writes, "Native peoples of the coastal Pacific Northwest made rich livelihoods here for millennia, living with one foot in the forest and one on the shore, gathering the abundance of both." Here we were, guided by the sun, stars, winds, and tides, trying to leave nothing more than a few footprints on the beach that would be washed away by the next high tide, but we couldn't escape threads that connected us to clear-cut hillsides.

With the scent of fresh-cut wood wafting into our nostrils and the sound of chain saws buzzing in our brains as we paddled north, each of us wrestled with the pang of guilt. We contributed to the loss by being part of a society that valued the trees' use as building materials and paper products over the abundant life they once supported, from the uppermost branches to the microbes and rhizomes in the soil surrounding their roots and the shade and shelter their canopy created.

\* \* \*

A HUNDRED-MILE WILDERNESS labyrinth of rugged passages, lined with glistening white peaks, separates the Strait of Georgia and Johnstone Strait. Every twelve hours and twenty-five minutes the gravitational pull of the moon sends trillions of gallons of water surging through these passages like clockwork. As high tide ebbs it exposes a kaleidoscope of sea stars, urchins, kelp, and mussels, clinging to the seaweed-covered rocks where sea and land collide. Along with the weather, the tides dictated our movements and constantly reminded us that we were dwarfed by the earth and the heavens, which rumble on, guided by the ocean's metronome-like cadence, in-out, in-out. The ocean rises and drops about fourteen feet in this never-ending cycle.

In the tight constrictions tidal rapids formed impassable white water gauntlets for much of the day, forcing us to carefully navigate these passages at slack tide, the precious few minutes when the water stops flowing in either direction. After months of pouring over maps and reading about Yuculta Rapids, Gillard Passage Rapids, Dent Rapids, and Greene Point Rapids, we were finally entering the Cordero Channel and anxiously approached our first tidal rapid.

After a brief break on the rocky shore, we launched our kayaks into perfectly slack water. We warily, but hastily, paddled through a steep-sided, forest-lined channel that had recently been a raging rapid and soon would be again. The current began to flow against us, increasing in strength at alarming speed. With a hundred yards to go, we dug our paddles in with all we had. In a matter of minutes we would no longer be able to paddle against the incoming tide and would be flushed back the way we'd come. At its peak these tidal rapids flow at more than twelve miles an hour, causing standing waves and whirlpools that have sunk much larger vessels. Inch by inch we clawed our way forward to the giant eddy formed by Big Bay. Resting in calm water, we were all smiles watching the white water intensify with each passing minute. "Time and tide wait for no man," John muttered. We had passed through only the first half mile of tidal rapids, and it would be six hours before the tide turned and we could continue on our way through the remaining three and a half miles of treacherous waters.

By carefully timing our passages, the remaining tidal rapids were easier to navigate, and gentle currents propelled us northward toward the open expanse of Johnstone Strait. A curious seal appeared every few minutes to stare at us with its glassy black eyes before slipping below the surface. As the sun edged toward the horizon our paddles felt heavy, but we pushed on. Rafted together, peering at the map, we noticed a shallow cove with a small stream running into it, which appeared to be a perfect spot to camp.

The bows of our kayaks connected with the soft sand, but what had appeared to be a pristine beach deep in the Canadian coastal wilderness from a distance soon transformed into an eerie scene. This remote cove was filled with colorful man-made detritus. How could this be? We were miles from the nearest road or town. Sifting our fingers through the sand revealed a mixture of pulverized plastic and Styrofoam over which were strewn lighters, tangled fishing nets, weathered Croc shoes, tampon applicators, soda bottles, and thousands of other pieces of plastic garbage slowly being degraded by the sun, wind, sand, and water. It took us five minutes to clear a garbage-free spot large enough for a two-person tent. John set up his tent on a huge eight-inch-thick flat piece of Styrofoam rather than trying to clear a mound of trash.

Somehow the water flushing through the Cordero Channel was depositing tons of plastic on this beach as billions of gallons of water ebbed and flowed with the same steady rhythm that has governed the tides for millennia. How long had this beach been like this? Where did all this garbage come from? Why here? Where this plastic came from was most likely as varied as the waste itself; some of it likely reached the ocean from the closest communities or boaters passing through, but some could have traveled thousands of miles in the vast Pacific Ocean's winds and currents from as far away as Asia. All we could grasp at the time was that the tides and currents, wind, waves, storms, and calms had turned this quarter-mile-long beach into a repository. We were shocked, saddened, and abruptly catapulted from a state of wilderness bliss into humanity's darkest recesses. Once the shock wore off, we pulled out our camera to document this horrific scene and share photos and video clips with the students who were following our journey. They would be as appalled as we were; none of us would ever look at a soda bottle or plastic shopping bag in the same way.

The sheer volume of plastic in use worldwide and the environmental disaster it represents slapped us in the face. While the snow-capped peaks towering to our west on Vancouver Island left us with a sense of isolation and wonder, our home for the night in this garbage patch left us questioning our place in the world and the choices that we made every day. Talking softly in our tent, unable to sleep, we realized that as much as we loved wild places, we were part of the industrial society that had turned this remote pristine beach into a garbage dump.

This problem has been slowly building for decades. In 1950, 2.5 billion people produced about 1.5 million tons of plastic, but by 2016, with more than 7 billion people on the planet, we were generating more than 300 million tons of plastic. The fact that 14 million tons of plastic find their way into our oceans each year, to join the more than 5 trillion pieces of plastic already floating there, makes it a little easier to understand how this beach became smothered in plastic. With numbers so vast and abstract it is hard to fathom their volume, just as it is hard to contemplate stars in the sky or the millions of light-years between galaxies, but as we tried to sleep surrounded by garbage, the immense problem caused by our plastic addiction left us unable to turn away.

The irony was not lost on us that most of our food was wrapped in plastic and our tent, tarp, dry suits, life jackets, and many other items that seemingly made this wilderness journey possible were made of petroleum products. Plastic was woven into the modern, wasteful world we were trying to shed for a simpler way of being. Food, water, shelter, and companionship were the simple elements that combined with the wind, weather, and tide to guide us as we inched northward. We were left with a confused, hollow feeling in our guts. Much like after an unresolved argument with a loved one, we wanted to make things right and cause the friction, or in this case the garbage, to go away. We knew it wasn't that easy, so we stared at the thin nylon covering overhead until finally drifting off to sleep. Eliminating the plastic in our lives seemed more intimidating than the thousands of miles that lay ahead.

By the time we approached Port Hardy, British Columbia, a mere three weeks into a three-year journey, it was apparent that even our eighteen-foot kayaks carried more than we really needed. We were already making a mental list of needless items to give away or mail home once we reached Alaska. Leaving the "plastic beach" in our wake, the need to pare down seemed even more urgent, but deep down we knew that in the next grocery store we would buy food, batteries, and other seemingly necessary odds and ends wrapped in plastic. How long would we use these things before throwing them away, and where would the discarded items go after they left our hands? We were, of course, following leave-no-trace principles, collecting our trash to dispose of once we reached the handful of towns along our route. But what would happen to it once we dropped it in the trash can or recycling bin? We were choosing to buy things that, though we used them for a blink of an eye, would remain on Earth, buried in a landfill, floating in the ocean, or washed up on a beach for centuries.

Our days took on a comfortable rhythm despite the ever-changing landscape and lengthening hours of daylight. After a brief struggle to open sleepy eyes, the daily routine began—stuffing our sleeping bags and deflating our pads before emerging from our tents to boil water for coffee and prepare a breakfast of oatmeal or granola. We packed damp tents as quickly as possible to minimize the discomfort of cold, wet hands. Launching the kayaks was sometimes a group effort. It seemed more often than not we would finish our day on a relatively high tide, and when we were ready to go in the mornings, our kayaks were twenty feet or more from the water's edge. Fully loaded, it took all four of us to carry each kayak down the irregular, slippery slope of the shore. Peeing and then zipping ourselves into our dry suits were the final steps of the morning ritual before we clambered into the cockpits of our boats and sealed up our spray skirts.

We would then shove off from shore and enter our own little worlds as we began to paddle in our varied styles and paces. Clayton was usually in the lead, setting a pace that the rest of us couldn't comfortably maintain. We would focus on the expanding *V* left in his wake. But eventually, we would get to chatting or looking around at a sea otter or densely packed arrangement of purple and orange sea stars just a few feet below our bows, causing us to forget the constant exertion and any residual muscle soreness.

Most days were filled with hours of silent meditation, or to the outside observer, relative boredom punctuated by adrenaline and extreme focus when storms, waves, surf landings, or challenges appeared. The rhythmic motion of muscles flexing, relaxing, and stretching as paddle blades bit the water often induced a meditative state. Push, catch, lift, push, catch, lift, around and around, always one blade in the water. Those peaceful hours have merged together in our memories of the mist rising from the layered silhouettes of Douglas firs or the mesmerizing ovoid water surface before the wind picked up. This rhythm allowed the mind to slowly chew on an idea. The clear-cuts and plastic beach would often resurface within an ever-growing and cycling mental list of environmental concerns in the days, weeks, and years of wilderness travel ahead.

* * *

EVERY PADDLE STROKE pulled us toward grander vistas and deeper wilderness, leaving us in a constant state of wonder. Otters, bald eagles, seals, crabs—we were surrounded by so much life. Long ago we had learned that long journeys are much more of a mental than physical challenge. Discipline, grit, and sound judgment are worth far more than bulging muscles and athleticism. Our schedule of relatively minimal mileage and frequent rest days had been effective; John's shoulder injury had improved and none of us felt any symptoms of overuse injuries. We had all grown stronger and more confident with each passing day, and it was time for the training wheels to come off.

On May 21 we left Port Hardy and the shelter of Vancouver Island behind. For the next 50 miles we would be exposed to the full force of the Pacific Ocean. Swells originating thousands of miles away roamed unimpeded before colliding on the rugged coastline. A mixture of nerves and excitement churned in our guts as we progressed northward. On the first day out of Port Hardy we still gained some protection from Hope, Nigei, and Hurst Islands, but as we approached Skull Cove after 20 miles, we found ourselves staring west at a watery horizon line. Gulls rode the wind, gliding effortlessly over the menacing white-tipped rollers that thundered onto land. Shore birds scurried up and down the beach in a delicate dance with the water's ebb and flow, constantly in search of nourishment delivered by each crashing wave.

The innumerable islands stretching the length of British Columbia and Southeast Alaska bore the brunt of the Pacific's wind and waves, allowing us to meander through passageways on the inside—hence the route's name, the Inside Passage. There were, however, two substantial gaps in the string of barrier islands, the first of which lay before us. Once we left the protection of Skull Cove, we would be paddling along thirty miles of exposed coastline. To make matters worse, there were two headlands to get around—Cape Caution and Kelp Head. Having interviewed several people who had paddled the Inside Passage, we knew that weather windows when the waves and wind subsided enough to safely kayak out and around were brief and infrequent. We had heard of people waiting as long as a week for good weather. Cape Caution, we knew, would be especially tricky because of shoals extending out from land. The swell of the open ocean travels rather smoothly until a shallow, irregular bottom riles up unpredictable waves. We were a long way from help—thirty-five miles from Port Hardy to the south and forty-eight miles from Namu to the north.

We estimated the crossing would take us seven to eight hours, and as far as we knew, there would be no opportunity to land along this inhospitable, wave-pummeled, rocky stretch of coast. Even in the most benign conditions, eight hours is a long time for one's body to be wedged in a sea kayak while keeping up continuous aerobic output. Pile on top of that the threat of capsize from the irregular waves, in water of 48 degrees Fahrenheit. Immersion at that temperature means you have fewer than five minutes of dexterity and thirty to sixty minutes before being overcome with exhaustion or passing out. Our dry suits and life jackets would give us more time, but none of us wanted to take a swim in the middle of the crossing.

We had trained for this, each of us proficient at bracing, rolling, self-rescue, and rescuing someone else, further decreasing the potential time someone would spend in the water if they capsized. When thrown off-balance by a wave, our first line of defense was to use our paddle to brace on that wave and keep the kayak from flipping over. If, despite our best efforts, the wave were to flip the kayak upside down, we could use legs, hips, torso, shoulders, and a sweep of the paddle in a carefully choreographed motion to roll the heavily laden kayak back upright—all while holding our breath and resisting the growing sense of panic as our bodies screamed for air. The variables weighed heavily on our minds. If the conditions were substantial enough to tip one or more of us over, how likely would we be to successfully roll back up again? What if someone got separated from the group and capsized—would one of us be able to reach that person in time? What if the swimmer got separated from their boat? How well could we perform a rescue in building waves and wind? Needless to say, none of us slept well the night before rounding Cape Caution.

We left our camp at five o'clock in the morning, knowing the wind would increase throughout the day, and we wanted to get past Cape Caution before that happened. Bobbing through six-foot rolling swells, we headed north toward the cape. The rocky shelf of a shoreline was devoid of vegetation fifty feet back from the water's edge because any plant trying to cling to land so close to the sea had been swept away by an inevitable gale.

Heading into the swells felt like paddling uphill, then reaching the top only to take a second to get a good look around before dropping down into the trough, losing sight of the horizon. In a sea kayak, you are essentially sitting at water level, so wave heights are easy to gauge relative to your body. One-foot waves are about naval height, two-foot waves just below the shoulder, and three-foot waves are at eye level or the top of your head, depending on your height. Any bigger than that and you're estimating based on how long the horizon line or your traveling companions disappear from view. At first the swells felt foreign, and we were tempted to tense our muscles and fight the motion, but after several hours the same rhythmic trance that washed over us in calm, protected waters made the time pass quickly.

A blur of dark gray snapped us into the moment. Three Pacific white-sided dolphins broke the surface at the crest of the swell in front of us before plunging into the trough. We marveled at their speed and grace, their ability to be totally at home in the open ocean. Most of the other boats we had met during our journey were forty- or fifty-foot sailboats and motor yachts who warned us about the heavy seas and dangerous shoals off Cape Caution. We had learned to take people's warnings and advice with a grain of salt, but we still felt vulnerable as we traversed what many had warned us was the crux of the Inside Passage, whether sailing, motoring, or kayaking. Our brief encounter with the dolphins, appearing so at ease, lightened our mood.

The swells grew larger and more irregular as we rounded Cape Caution—and right at the cape's apex, a fifth kayak appeared briefly when we all crested a swell at the same time. How funny to find ourselves bobbing up and down during the most challenging part of our route, greeting a cheery couple in a tandem Folbot folding kayak that had left from Juneau, Alaska, forty-five days earlier, heading for Seattle. In many ways kayaking is like riding a bicycle; when you are moving forward you are quite stable, but when you stop it is hard to balance. It was difficult to visit with our fellow paddlers for long as they appeared and disappeared in the six-to-eight-foot swell. Our brief encounter made clear that both parties had many beautiful vistas and challenges ahead. Far too quickly we had to wish them fair winds and continue around Cape Caution into what we hoped would be slightly calmer waters.

With the headland of Cape Caution disappearing behind us and the swell subsiding, our party converged to discuss our options. We had paddled sixteen miles since launching our kayaks at five o'clock, and our bladders were starting to complain. John polled the group to see if anyone else wanted to search for a place to stop. "I have to pee," he said, "but if there's nowhere to land or no one else wants to stop, I'm willing to go in my dry suit." The rest of us laughed nervously and sincerely hoped peeing our pants wouldn't be necessary. After a few more minutes of paddling, a gentle curving white-sand beach to our right appeared to be protected from the surf by a series of boulders. It would be the only plausible lunch/pee stop for miles. John surfed through a rocky opening, and we all soon joined him in the calm waters off the beach. After more than five hours in our kayaks our legs felt like Jell-o as we wobbled around on land.

As we scarfed down handfuls of trail mix and slabs of summer sausage and cheese, we weighed our options. Although beautiful, our current location was quite exposed and a gale was forecast to arrive overnight, bringing thirty-knot winds and heavy seas. If we could push on another fourteen miles around Kelp Head we would enter the next section of protected channels leading north. Everyone agreed we should go for it while the weather held, so after fifteen minutes of blissful freedom of movement, we crammed our legs back into our cockpits and returned to the Pacific's rhythmic heartbeat.

The wind switched to the southwest and slowly increased as the front drew near. After nearly thirty miles of paddling our arms felt like rubber and lack of movement in our legs had put our feet to sleep. Fortunately the building tailwind helped speed us up as we rounded Kelp Head and tucked into a protected bay. We made it into the shelter of the bay just as the winds began in earnest. A hundred-yard sliver of sand welcomed our tired party, and we silently began our evening ritual of setting up camp. Violent storms had flung several massive Douglas fir trunks onto the beach like a giant game of pick up sticks. After unloading our kayaks we lifted them up on top of the tree trunks and lashed them down, out of reach of all but the most ferocious tides and wind-driven waves. It felt good to push ourselves and have our longest and most challenging day behind us. Relief and a sense of accomplishment made our conversation that evening light and happy.

Gale force winds built overnight, and we awoke in the morning to the distant rhythmic roar of surf pounding on Kelp Head. The gale showed no signs of abating, so we spent the day exploring the beach and resting. A pair of Pacific loons and a curious seal bobbed out in the bay. Down the beach we followed two sets of fresh wolf tracks that meandered along the high tide line. A gentle swell lapping the beach reminded us of the maelstrom unfolding just outside our protected cove.

In the afternoon the rain stopped, and the sun broke through the clouds for the first time in several days. Sitting on the sand, savoring the feeling of sun warming our faces, filled us with contentment; there was no place else we would rather be. Schedules, deadlines, emails, news flashes, and commercials were slowly losing meaning and sloughing away, being replaced by the often challenging and uncomfortable but simple realities of a life dictated by wind, weather, tide, food, water, and shelter.

The kitchen-related wedding gifts we'd received would have filled every nook and cranny of one of our kayaks, yet here we were debating whether we should get rid of our second pot because we never used it. The four gallons of fresh water we gathered from mountain-fed streams tumbling into the sea lasted the two of us three days—four if we pushed it—but at home we would flush far more clean water down the toilet each day without a second thought. How could a shelter just tall enough for us to sit up and just enough square footage for us to lay down feel like all the room we needed, when we grew up in houses one hundred times this size? Would we remain fulfilled and content with this simple existence, or was this a rush of bliss that would eventually collide with reality and a desire for everything we left behind? If more people felt the simplicity of a nomadic journey, could it turn the tide for plastic-covered beaches, clear-cut forests, and the harsh realities of our modern lives?

* * *

STOPPING IN COMMUNITIES along our route was typically something we looked forward to. These stops provided an opportunity for us to buy some fresh fruits and vegetables, meet new people, have our senses overwhelmed for a brief period, and maybe even rustle up a cold beer, warm shower, or a coin-operated laundry before returning to our rhythmic and predictable routine of paddling, pitching camp, and cooking a meal.

As we paddled into Bella Bella (or Wáglísla, a Heiltsuk descriptive place name referring to the way the nearby creek mouth fans out and disappears into the beach) we saw a massive traditional dugout canoe a few yards from where we landed. Ocean canoes carved out of massive cedar logs and paddled by about a dozen paddlers are the traditional means of travel from community to community, providing strong cultural links all along the Inside Passage from Alaska to Washington. We had read about these traditional canoes but had never seen one before. On this day we were on a mission to interview local students and teachers, as requested by the students we were working with online. As we walked through town people greeted us with smiles and pointed us toward the school.

The school was a commanding structure and appeared to be one of the community's newest buildings. Rows and rows of bicycles decorated with brightly colored streamers were parked out front and all the classrooms were empty. A woman with a warm smile and inquisitive eyes came over and explained that she was the vice principal. "You came on a special day," she said. "Today is our annual sports day. You just missed the bicycle parade. Now, as you can see, all the children are in the field, which is divided into stations, so teams of students can rotate through all sorts of activities. We have soccer, shot put, high jump, balloon popping, nail pounding, long jump, and face painting. Would you like a quick tour of the school?"

As we toured the beautiful, modern facility she explained that all the teachers work to blend Heiltsuk traditions with their teaching and that the Heiltsuk have a very strong connection to the ocean, rivers, and forests. "The school is currently monitoring a sandhill crane nest. We get live video in the classrooms from a camera near the nest. The students are so excited; the eggs should hatch any day now. We are also planning to set up a camera near a river, so students can observe the grizzly bears feeding during the salmon run—right in their classrooms."

Inquiries about the traditional voyaging canoe led us to the Koeye Café, which was a hub for community members working to stop a proposed oil pipeline. Wáglísla is in the heart of the Great Bear Rainforest and the traditional territory of the Heiltsuk Nation. With steaming beverages in hand we listened as the young woman who was running the café explained that her father was the canoe builder. She was petite, in her early twenties, with long, sleek black hair and a welcoming smile.

"The canoe over by your kayaks is called a glwa and was made out of western red cedar. It is twenty-five feet long," she explained as she escorted us outside to take a closer look at its black hull, prominent bow, and elegant swooping shape. "My father [Frank] raised the money to build the canoe and then organized other people from our community to embark on a 350-mile journey from Bella Bella to Vancouver in 1986 for the World Exposition." The canoe's unique shape, honed by generations of people intimately familiar with these waters, looked like it would ride the waves with ease. Three years after the World's Fair Expo '86, Frank Brown led a group that included five other ocean-going nations paddling canoes to Seattle. At his journey's culmination Frank issued a challenge to others: make a canoe and paddle to Bella Bella in 1993 for the Qatuwas (People Gathering Together) Festival. More than thirty canoes answered, and some three thousand people gathered to celebrate.

After peppering her with questions about the canoe, the town, and Heiltsuk culture, we learned how the community was in the middle of a long fight to stop the Enbridge Northern Gateway pipeline, which would carry oil from the Alberta tar sands to the British Columbia coast, where it would be loaded on large tankers and transported to markets all over the world. In 2010 the fight against the pipeline was just ramping up, and First Nations bands were beginning to sign the Save the Fraser Declaration in opposition, hoping to protect the Fraser River watershed. By 2014 the Northern Gateway pipeline would be approved by the federal government, subject to conditions. Upon taking office in 2015, Canadian prime minister Justin Trudeau imposed a ban on oil tanker traffic along the northern coast of British Columbia, then the Federal Court of Appeal officially rejected plans for the pipeline in 2016. By that time more than 130 First Nations bands had signed the declaration.

For the people of Bella Bella fighting to stop the pipeline, the concern wasn't if a tanker would spill vast amounts of oil in their sacred homeland—it was when. "Do you remember the Exxon Valdez oil spill?" asked a welcoming elder we met while walking around town. "That was a big one, but there have been others. If the pipeline is built there will be more. The otters and birds are covered in oil. It kills the fish and the shoreline gets coated with disgusting black tar. This place is sacred; it sustains us. We must protect it. For us, fighting to protect this place is as necessary as breathing; it is something we have to do and will keep doing until there are no more breaths to take." The *Deepwater Horizon*, which exploded two days before our journey began, was still spewing oil into the Gulf of Mexico. It was destined to become the largest oil spill in the history of the United States, ultimately spilling "more than 300 Olympic-sized swimming pools of oil into the Gulf's waters" (twelve times more oil than the Exxon Valdez spill).

During our paddle, which was six years prior to the Standing Rock protests and the movement to stop pipelines throughout North America as a means to slow climate change, we caught a glimpse of a

First Nation community fighting to protect the land and sea, which formed the backbone of their culture, from a multinational energy company's pipeline. The wild lands and waters where their ancestors had lived for millennia were too precious to risk. We were moved, inspired, and sad to paddle away from this remarkable community. Although remote and wild, these vast tracts of land and water were the ancestral home of people who have been gathering seaweed, kelp, herring eggs, salmon, medicines from trees and plants, and building materials for homes and canoes for centuries. The concept of wilderness as land devoid of humans is erroneous. Although we spent our days paddling through undeveloped waterways surrounded by rugged shoreline and towering trees, there was a rich human history all around us fused in the rocks, entangled in the roots, and underneath the lush green carpet of moss.

* * *

FINDING A CAMPSITE for the night was often challenging once we left the relative ease and comfort of towns. We had to factor in the rise and fall of the tide; what looked like an ideal beach at low tide might be underwater at high tide, or an easy access at high tide might result in a precarious carry of gear and boats over yards of slime-covered, wobbling boulders to launch our kayaks at low tide. Plus we often had to hunt for places to squeeze our tents in. The underbrush of this forest was not as friendly as that of northern Minnesota. Here we were forced to battle a nasty, spiky plant called devil's club, and we all developed differing strategies. John and Clayton seemed to prefer living on the edge, often setting up their tents on a sliver of beach, hoping that high tide would not flood their tents. The trade-off for some sleepless hours in the middle of the night was ease of setup and complete devil's club avoidance. We preferred to tuck into the woods. Perhaps we had to do a little more work to find a spot for our tent that was free of our thorny nemesis, but we would sleep easy knowing that high water certainly would not reach us. Plus we were newlyweds, so a little extra privacy and a secure nest for the night was welcome.

The beach dwellers were often camped closer to our cooking area. However, us forest dwellers were often a bit closer to the spot we had chosen to hang our food. We were in brown bear territory, which made us particularly wary with our food or when wandering into the woods alone. Having grown up camping and canoeing in the Northwoods of Minnesota, where the creatures are all quite innocuous—no poisonous snakes or insects, no raccoons, and no particularly dangerous mammals (of black bear, gray wolf, Canada lynx, and moose, the latter is probably the most dangerous)—we were all genuinely afraid of brown bears and wanted to do everything possible to avoid having a disastrous encounter.

We had asked several others who paddled this route what they did. Some just kept their food in their kayak hatches overnight. Some stashed their food in the woods away from camp. One person even told us he kept his food in his tent. In the end we determined that the protocol we were used to in the Boundary Waters (hanging the food), although labor-intensive, was our best option. Keeping our food inside our kayaks sounded like a bad idea because if a bear did get into our food, it meant our means of transportation would also be destroyed. So we'd be stranded, without food, near a potentially dangerous bear who had just associated us with an easy meal. Stashing food in the woods had merits, but the drawback was that if anything did get into our food, we most likely wouldn't hear the burglary happening. We would resort to stashing on occasion after receiving resupplies because the volume of food we had was simply too great to hang, so we would hang as much as we could and stash the rest. Sleeping with the food in our tents was not worth the risk in our minds.

Since we kept our food in dry bags small enough to fit into our kayak hatches, each evening we amassed a collection of bags, like a bunch of giant multicolored grapes. Our objective was to suspend this heavy and awkward bundle at least twelve feet off the ground and six feet from the nearest tree or limb. The whole time we were in brown bear territory, we operated with a heightened sense of awareness. The faintest sound at night would wake us. We each carried a canister of bear spray at all times. When we selected our campsites we looked for signs of bear activity and would pass up a site if we found multiple tracks or piles of scat. On occasion we'd select a campsite, set up our tents and, only after wandering down the beach, spot a track the size of a dinner plate in the sand, which generally led to a fitful night's sleep.

During our entire trek up the British Columbia coast, we didn't see a single brown bear. There were two instances when we spotted a black bear, however. The first sighting was just a bear picking its way below the high tide line, finding something to eat among the slimy rocks as we paddled by. The second was in the long, narrow Princess Royal Channel shortly after leaving Wáglísla. We had just entered Fraser Reach and stopped to stretch our legs and explore an abandoned fish cannery at Butedale. We walked around the surreal, postapocalyptic setting of the abruptly abandoned, decaying buildings slowly returning to their natural surroundings. This cannery had operated from 1911 through 1967 and in its heyday had a workforce of five hundred people processing salmon, halibut, and herring. These abandoned canneries, we learned, oftentimes have a caretaker—because it is cheaper to pay one or two people to look after a place than completely decommissioning it and paying for all the environmental cleanup costs. We didn't see anyone else around, just one small house with a sign that warned us we were being filmed. As we picked our way down the overgrown path back to the dilapidated dock, we spotted a rotund black bear ambling along the ridge above us. Each time we saw a bear, a surge of adrenaline quickened our pulses, but once we identified the creature as a black bear, we calmed down and continued on with our day.

A drizzle ensued shortly after we began paddling again. Perhaps not finding the caretaker at the cannery added to the feeling of desolation as we worked our way up Fraser Reach under mottled gray skies. There was no other development, just steep, rocky, forested hillsides punctuated by the occasional cliff face. This was the most remote we had felt so far, with the last town we stopped in, Bella Bella, being about a hundred miles behind and the next town, Prince Rupert, lying about a hundred miles ahead. As we slowly perceived the light level dropping, we began to look for a campsite. Puzzling about where to stop, we eyed the inhospitable and steep shoreline. Our guidebook offered no help here, basically stating that there were no places to camp and landing was nearly impossible for most of Fraser Reach.

We pressed on until near darkness. Then we passed a waterfall and came up with an idea as we scanned a nearby high rocky ledge. The tide was at midcycle; it would fall another five feet. At this moment, another ledge presented itself just a foot above the water. Climbing out here would be just like climbing onto a dock. The only feasible spot to set up our tents was on top of the original high ledge we spotted next to the waterfall, which was about fifteen feet above the water. We noted the time, because we would have to leave exactly twelve hours later when the water level would be the right height for us to safely launch our kayaks again. After climbing out of our boats and heaving them up onto the lower ledge, we scrambled up a rough, brushy trail and formed a fire line for passing all our equipment up.

Earlier in the journey this situation would have felt overwhelming, but by now our team had gelled, our muscles toned, and most importantly, we were brimming with confidence. The challenges, both physical and mental, associated with setting camp in this unconventional and slightly precarious spot now seemed novel and funny, rather than daunting. During the first few weeks every sore muscle or extra challenge caused glimpses of doubt or worry that flashed momentarily in our brains. But as our bodies hardened and our spirits melded with land and water, our confidence in reaching Skagway blossomed. And if we could make it to Skagway, then why not Key West?

We set up our tents on the cool, damp rock protruding from the cliff that rose up behind us, and used rocks to secure the tents because there was no dirt to pound stakes into. Dinner was a quick affair, eaten under a tarp while we were all still dressed in our dry suits, with the din of the waterfall preventing much conversation. Even when water stopped falling from the sky, we realized we were well within range of the mist of the falls. Everything was wet, rapidly cooling us, so there was nothing worthwhile to do besides wash dishes and get into our tents as soon as possible. Sleep came quickly, after a moment of savoring the deep satisfaction of climbing into a warm, dry sleeping bag, while the sound of the falls rumbled in our ears.

At some point in the night, John slipped out of his tent to pee. The rain had stopped and the sky was clear; the stars were a welcome sight. He peered over the edge expecting to see reflections of the stars in the calm water but was instead witness to a much brighter ethereal glow. Below our camp lay what looked like a portal into another dimension. Where the rushing water entered the ocean, it excited a plume of bioluminescent plankton. "Get up, get up," he called, "you have to see this!" Millions of miniature creatures in the water emitted a glow when agitated by the falling water. Looking down into that pulsing, glowing plume was like viewing the Milky Way from above. In that moment, we no longer had sore muscles or frustrations. Watching an ocean of life churning and swirling in the glowing depths left us completely in awe, as if glimpsing into a hidden world that had lain in wait just under us this whole time.

When had the last human perched here on a moonless night to witness this phenomenon? How can we place a value on this natural wonder or calculate the cost of an oil spill that destroys the tiny plankton pulsing and glowing in the depths? They brought joy and wonder to our hearts, but more importantly, they were the building blocks on which life here relied, feeding minnows, humpbacks, and everything in between. They formed the foundation from which all life above and below these waters flourished. We stared silently at nature's phosphorescent fireworks until the cold seeping through our long underwear coaxed us back to bed.

* * *

WE HAD GROWN accustomed to hearing "gale warning in effect" spoken by the familiar robotic voice in our VHF radio reciting the weather forecast, but most of the time we paddled in sheltered channels, far away from the impact of open ocean. However, we had one more crux move to make as we neared the British Columbia–Alaska border. The Dixon Entrance is another forty-mile-long section of coastline that is missing the protective outer islands. The international border runs right down the middle, and we were not sure when Mother Nature was going to allow us to pass.

Before leaving Prince Rupert, British Columbia, we called US Customs to let them know we would be crossing the border and to ask where and how we should check in. The distance from the border to Ketchikan, the first town we would come to in Alaska, was sixty-five miles—way too far for us to paddle in one day. The first customs officer we talked to was completely taken aback by our travel plans and said that it was impossible to cross the border by kayak. According to him, the only legal way for us to cross the border would be to procure a car, load our kayaks onto it, and drive across the border, clear customs, and then start kayaking again. Since we wanted to continue our travels by kayak, and there simply are no roads that lead into or out of Ketchikan, we decided to try a different number, hoping for a second opinion. Luckily the customs officer in Ketchikan was very friendly and instructed us to camp for as many nights as we needed to and then check in at the customs dock as soon as we arrived in Ketchikan. He wished us luck and added, "It might take you a while with that gale on its way." We hung up the phone and left Prince Rupert, paddling hard for the Dixon Entrance ahead of the storm.

Over the course of several days we hopped from one tiny, exposed island to the next. At dawn on our final day of crossing the Dixon Entrance, the seas were calm, but the winds were expected to reach forty-five knots (fifty-two miles per hour), churning up twenty-two-foot waves by evening. We hurried north, hoping to reach the relative protection of Foggy Bay, fifteen miles to the north, before the gale closed in. As we bobbed in the swell, Clayton said, "I can't believe we haven't seen any orcas yet. I figured we would have seen our first pod back in Puget Sound where we started. I really hope we see some before we get to Skagway." Within minutes the characteristic long black dorsal fin of an orca broke the surface a hundred yards offshore. Three orcas swam past, giving us an official welcome to Alaska.

We pulled into Foggy Bay at eleven o'clock in the morning and contemplated continuing on since it was so early, but the winds were showing signs of picking up. The thought of the coming storm prompted us to seek shelter on a small island ringed with white-sand beaches in the cluster of De Long Islands, about forty miles south of Ketchikan. A couple hours later the gale arrived, bringing rain and wind that pinned us down for twenty-four hours. Our supply of fresh water was running low, and the size of our island meant that it most likely would not contain any lakes or streams. It still felt strange to have to stock up on fresh water in towns and streams and then carefully meter it out, keenly aware of our need to find the next source. This was giving us an appreciation for the abundance of clean fresh water we had back home.

In the afternoon, we walked over to the exposed side of the island. Piles of gray driftwood, an old tire, and a shrimp trap had all washed ashore in previous storms. The wind was so strong that we had to hold on to our hats and lean into the wind to avoid being knocked off-balance. Frothing waves pounded the shoreline. Then, out on the water, we caught sight of a large sailboat practically flying in from the open ocean. Once in the relative calm behind our island, it dropped its sails and motored out of sight, heading to some protected anchorage for the night. They had cut it close; we could only imagine what it had been like out there. There was something appealing about that boat—about its size and the speed with which it moved. It was propelled by the wind, not the effort of a human body. It was a mode of transportation and home all rolled into one. Whoever was on that sailboat would not have to set up camp for the night. Once they dropped anchor, they were free to cook dinner or relax or sleep—no setup required. This sailboat awakened a desire to someday use that significantly larger, more comfortable craft as a means to explore distant waterways.

Dark clouds signaled rain, so we retreated to our tent, tucked in a clump of cedars. Stiff arms and shoulders reminded us of how we had paddled harder and faster than we were accustomed to. We slept for a couple of hours and then awoke to the sound of the wind whistling outside our tranquil little forest of calm.

When we returned to our kitchen area, we found John and Clayton sitting under the tarp, smiling coyly and every dromedary and water bottle full to the brim. They happily announced that our water scarcity was no longer a concern. While hanging out there chatting and snacking, as the rain increased in intensity, they'd noticed the abundance of water running off the tarp. With a little tweaking, they made one corner lower than all the rest to allow the water to funnel down into all our various water vessels.

* * *

UPON REACHING ALASKA we made our way through watery passageways surrounded by the United States' largest national forest—Tongass National Forest. At approximately seventeen million acres, the forest encompasses most of Southeast Alaska and contains "one-third of the planet's virgin temperate rainforest—the largest remaining single expanse."

Clayton peeled off from our little group shortly after Ketchikan. It had become clear that he wanted to paddle faster and travel farther than we did, and so it made sense for him to continue on his own. There were no hard feelings; it was a good decision for all of us. He could paddle at a faster pace and not be stuck waiting for the rest of us, and we could take our time without feeling rushed. We arranged to meet up with Clayton in early July in Skagway or Haines so that he and John could travel together back to Minnesota. John could have gone with Clayton or even gone solo, but he decided to stick with us. So the three of us made our way up to Wrangell, Alaska. We put in some long days to get there. John's shoulder was almost back to normal, and we were all finally in peak paddling shape. The summer solstice was approaching, so the incredibly long daylight hours added to our motivation. Or perhaps our bodies were adapting to the extra-long days, with the sun rising at four o'clock and setting a little before ten.

Leaving Wrangell, we had to plan our next move carefully with the weather forecast and the tides so we could make it through Dry Strait with enough water to float our kayaks. We spent June 20 exploring the rustic fishing town of Wrangell and then launched at four o'clock in the afternoon, with our headlamps close at hand. Dry Strait is so named because the delta of the sediment-rich Stikine River has silted the strait so much that even kayaks have to traverse the giant delta mudflats on a high tide.

A slight headwind ruffled the water surface for the first several hours after our departure. As we paddled into the shallowest section of the river delta, the tide was cresting and the sun cast a golden glow on the snowy peaks surrounding the LeConte Glacier. The wind vanished as the sun hovered near the horizon, and a remarkably smooth swell was the only reminder of the steady headwind. The hulls of our kayaks and the rare splash of a jumping fish were the only things disturbing the glassy surface.

As we chatted about how the Dry Strait didn't seem all that shallow, the bottom suddenly seemed to surge upward, and we were left gingerly dipping our paddle blades in six inches of water. If we didn't carefully gauge the water depth in front of our bows, we would run aground in thick mud, which happened to each of us at least once. For hundreds of yards we silently paddled with the mud inches below our hulls. It was a relief to know that the tide was still rising, because a buggy night stuck in the middle of a river delta was not our idea of a solstice celebration.

We cheered as we passed Dry Island and left the mudflats behind. It was almost ten o'clock at night, but there was still plenty of light. The sun's final rays highlighted icebergs on the eastern shore of Frederick Sound, from the LeConte Glacier, North America's southernmost tidewater glacier.

In honor of the solstice we were determined to paddle until midnight. Our kayaks were Current Designs Solstices, so we continually chuckled about paddling our Solstices on the solstice. We finally found a spot to camp around one o'clock in the morning and made quick work of setting up our tents and cooking macaroni and cheese while fending off mosquitoes. The sun had set long ago, but there was still just barely enough light for us to perform these tasks without our headlamps, which was a good thing because our headlamps would have attracted even more bugs to the swarms that already buzzed around as we ate.

\* \* \*

THE WEATHER WAS perfect as we entered Stephen's Passage—a light southwest tailwind, overcast and cool. We admired the pellucid, island-studded expanse from the beach on Cape Fanshaw as we ate lunch and watched the spouts from several humpback whales in the distance. That night, camped on an unnamed island between Cape Fanshaw and Hobart Bay, the eerie sounds of humpbacks singing broke the silent still darkness, their *OOOOOOO* . . . *UUUUUUUU* . . . *OOOOOOO* like the muffled sound of a massive bull moose calling underwater. What were they saying? Why were they calling? What a magical way to fall asleep.

The next day, as we approached Hobart Bay, we saw what was becoming a familiar scene—several whales surfacing about a quarter mile away. As we paddled closer, we observed how they would surface to take a few breaths and then a deep dive, their tails popping out of the water. A couple of miles offshore, we paused to pull out our cameras. The whales still appeared to be wrapped up in the act of feeding on krill three hundred yards ahead of us.

Suddenly we spotted two whales coming closer . . . and closer! Seeing these thirty-ton creatures surface twenty feet in front of our bows rendered us speechless. Soon we were floating next to them, dwarfed by their massive backs, listening to them breathe. A fishy miasma hung in the air above their blowholes. What were they thinking? Had they ever seen kayakers before? Did they think we were some sort of strange creatures moving around on the water surface with odd, rhythmic fin strokes? With one tail flick they could have ended our lives like a human swats a mosquito. But they seemed so sensitive to our presence that our twinges of fear were replaced with sheer wonder. One whale stayed near the surface. John, who was observing and filming from a few yards away, watched the whale slowly turn its dinner plate–sized eye to thoroughly check us out. The second whale sunk below the surface, gracefully gliding just below our kayaks.

The moment we spent floating next to these leviathans seemed to last an eternity, but in reality it lasted no more than a minute. After one last pungent breath, one tail rose into the air, followed by the next as they disappeared into the cold, deep, krill-rich waters below.

To think that an animal so massive would be curious about us tiny creatures, and could be gentle and cautious, is equally amazing. Up until this point our whale sightings were limited to glimpsing tails and spouts hundreds of yards off. We never imagined an encounter this close. It was life-changing to be in their presence, watching their shiny skin dotted with delicate wrinkles and clusters of barnacles undulate with every breath. Each pectoral fin was the size of a kayak; up close their dimensions were simply astounding. Like us, these humpbacks are restless souls, always on the move. They spend their summers in Alaska gorging on krill and their winters off the coast of Mexico, Central America, or Hawaii, one of the longest annual migrations in the world.

Humpbacks have made a dramatic recovery since the whaling

heyday, spurred largely by a global ban on commercial whaling that began in 1985. Their worldwide population was estimated to be more than eighty thousand in 2017. In many ways humpbacks are a success story, whose population has dramatically increased because of global cooperation to stop commercial whaling, but plastic pollution, climate change, overfishing, and other human disturbances are creating new stressors for whale populations around the globe.

* * *

AS WE PADDLED on toward Juneau, Alaska, the temperature suddenly dropped ten degrees, as if we were paddling into a refrigerator. A quarter mile farther and bowling-ball-sized chunks of ice appeared in the water around us. "Is that an iceberg?" John excitedly called out. Sure enough, minutes later bus-sized sculptures of ice radiating the most magnificent shades of blue floated past. Cold air and bergy bits were flowing down the Tracy Arm. We were twenty miles from the calving faces of the Sawyer Glaciers, but their presence was hard to ignore. We had heard it a million times, but now we were living it: everything in Alaska is bigger.

Paddling close to shore, looking for a place to stop for lunch, we spotted several long, black dorsal fins breaking the surface one hundred yards from shore. John happened to be paddling between us and the orcas. In thirty seconds a perfect shot appeared, with John floating in his kayak watching the orcas swim by. But then, as if out of nowhere, a fast-moving sixty-foot motorboat roared into view and started trailing the pod. The boat had come from Juneau, filled with a hundred passengers keen to see the nearby glaciers. The muffled sound of a tour guide on the loudspeaker wafted across the water along with the acrid smell of diesel. "Look off the bow to the left, there is a pod of six orcas. Get your cameras ready!" Despite our best efforts, it was impossible to get a photo of John and the whales without the damn boat in the frame. The three of us laughed at the absurdity of the situation but were sorely disappointed. We had been paddling for two months, hoping to see a pod of orcas up close; it just didn't seem fair that a hundred other people sat on a massive motorboat for thirty minutes to share this experience with us.

The highlight of our time in Juneau was a visit to the Mendenhall Glacier, which flows from the Juneau Icefield to Mendenhall Lake. The visitor center provided the frame of reference we needed to put this glacier's retreat into perspective. When it opened in 1962, the visitor center was a quarter of a mile away from the terminus of the glacier. As this glacier retreated, a lake emerged, and we used binoculars to view the glacier's terminus, now one and a half miles away from the visitor center. As we hiked over rock once covered by the glacier to get a closer view, the park ranger's message really sank in: by the end of the century the glacier will no longer be visible from the visitor center.

A cool breeze wafted off the mass of ice and snow. Icebergs drifted lazily in the cerulean lake. Occasionally we heard a rumble as chunks of ice fell from the face of the glacier, revealing a newly exposed cliff face of translucent deep blue. Freshly calved icebergs had that same blue glow. Our eyes traced the glacier from its ever-changing face up and back into the mountain from which it flowed. This was a frozen river. Stripes of sediment looked like permanent ripples on the surface. Although its movement is imperceptible (except for the calving), it was indeed moving incredibly slowly, shaping the land-scape with its flow. As we took in the scale of the glacier, a nagging idea crept into our thoughts. Our strong desire to see this glacier had stemmed from the knowledge that it, and most others, are retreating. Here, before us, was a physical manifestation of climate change, the canary in the coal mine; this ice was melting before our very eyes.

Glacier ice is actually Earth's largest freshwater reservoir, containing approximately 75 percent of the world's supply. The climate and topography of Alaska have been favorable for the formation of glaciers for the last 12.5 million years due to the combination of a maritime climate and coastal mountains. Moist air from the Pacific Ocean flows toward the mountains, where it rises, cools, and releases snow and rain. Historically, mild temperatures in the summer meant that the winter snow accumulation was greater than the summer snowmelt at higher elevations. This snow has accumulated year after year. Newer layers of snow weigh down on older layers, which slowly compact into solid ice.

Virtually all the glaciers that have been studied in Alaska are retreating. The meltwater of Alaskan glaciers comprises about half of the water that comes from melting glaciers around the globe. In general, glaciers have been retreating since about 1850. However, thanks to climate change, glaciers are retreating at faster and faster rates. Alaskan glaciers have been melting almost twice as fast in the past decade as they had previously. According to the Intergovernmental Panel on Climate Change, Earth is projected to warm by 2.2 to 3.5 degrees Celsius by the end of the twenty-first century; even if the warming is limited to 1.5 degrees Celsius, roughly half of Earth's glaciers will melt.

We walked to the library to write the weekly *Notes from the Trail*, an educational blog geared toward the kids that were following our journey. Once published on the Wilderness Classroom website, it and the photos of the glacier would be seen by thousands of kids scattered across the United States. We also wrote an article for adults to be posted on Paddling.com. These brief articles and handful of pictures wouldn't have the far-reaching immediate results we desired, but we began to feel as if our role was a little less ambiguous. We were in Southeast Alaska bearing witness to receding glaciers and hoped to one day figure out how to get people to care. We could tell kids to turn off the lights when they leave the room and ride their bikes to school for the time being, but our reach would have to expand exponentially, and our message would have to be much stronger. Big changes need to occur on a societal level if we're going to stand a chance of avoiding a climactic train wreck. While writing these articles we felt the first inkling of how we could give voice to the environmental threats we were witnessing. At the time, we had no idea where this would lead us, but like the elder in Bella Bella who explained that protecting the land and water is as essential as drawing a breath, we were slowly realizing we had no choice.

Looking back on this time, with a much larger body of climate change research, we now understand our situation is much more dire than we knew then. Through their cracks, rumbles, continuous flow to the ocean, the glaciers near Juneau would grind away in our consciousnesses, shaping our perceptions of the environment just as they shaped the valleys through which they flowed, long after we left the briny smell of ocean behind.

* * *

THE REMAINDER OF our journey up the Inside Passage occurred quickly, in part because our minds had already jumped ahead, planning for the next stage, but mostly because a fierce tailwind blew us northward once we entered the Lynn Canal, the deepest fjord in North America. Twenty-to-thirty-knot tailwinds churned up whitecaps that could easily capsize our kayaks if we weren't careful. Speeding along over the water's undulating surface, surfing on the white foam was like balancing on a razor's edge between control and chaos. Our daily toil of the past several months was suddenly made significantly easier; it was hard to resist that wild ride.

Paddling into Haines, we chose to paddle in the Chilkat Inlet. The grandeur of the topography left us wishing our time paddling up the Inside Passage was not coming to an end. The Chilkat Range to our left rose up from the water, dark at the base and mottled with gleaming white toward the line of jagged peaks at the top. Just beyond those mountains was Glacier Bay National Park and Preserve. Our route up the inlet took us past a couple more glaciers—the Davidson and Rainbow Glaciers. The Davidson Glacier, a cool white ribbon streaked with gray and accented with turquoise, was in a state of ablation. Its huge moraine made of speckled gray scree formed Glacier Point, which jutted way out into the inlet. The Rainbow Glacier was a pale mass of ice and snow hanging above a dark cliff face, interrupted by the white streak of a forceful waterfall of impossibly cold meltwater.

Haines was our kind of town, reminding us in many ways of Grand Marais, Minnesota, where we met. Haines felt like a slightly bigger version, plus mountains and ocean access. We had arrived just in time for the Fourth of July parade and picnic, during which we ate our fill of fry bread and pie. The fireworks under a dusky sky at ten o'clock served as a reminder of how far north we had come and the fact that the summer solstice had happened not long ago.

We reunited with Clayton in Haines, and the next day John and Clayton boarded the ferry bound for Seattle, beginning their journey home to Minnesota. We spent three more days in Haines waiting for the wind to diminish so we could continue to Skagway. For the first time since our "honeymoon" began more than two months before, we were alone.

When the wind finally subsided, we were up at four o'clock in the morning to launch our kayaks in the slack of low tide, ready to ride the current as the flood tide raced up the Chilkoot Inlet. The sun's early golden rays illuminated the glorious mountain peaks rising high above the swift channel of deep blue that carried us north to the culmination of our multimonth kayak journey in Skagway, Alaska. From here our mode of transportation would change and we would make our way through the Yukon and Northwest Territories. One thousand, four hundred miles done; 10,300 to Key West.

# 2

# Hiking and Paddling to the Arctic

## *Skagway, Alaska, to*
## *Norman Wells, Northwest Territories*

### 1,750 MILES

IN 1897, JOHN Muir described his motley crowd of companions traveling aboard *The Queen* to Skagway, Alaska, as "a nest of ants taken into a strange country and stirred up by a stick." A hundred years later this observation remained true, except the ants were cruise ship passengers rather than prospectors. After a couple of days spent resting and reprovisioning in Skagway, we made arrangements to transport our kayaks on a train and packed backpacks to hike the thirty-three-mile Chilkoot Trail in the footsteps of the Klondike Gold Rush.

The Chilkoot Trail existed long before the gold rush, created by the Łingít (Tlingit) people as one of several trade routes into the interior of Canada for exchanging their coastal goods like fish, seal oil, and seaweed for moose, caribou hides, and other goods from the interior. The Łingít and Tagish people managed to benefit from the early waves of prospectors during the gold rush as they were the primary packers hired to transport goods over the Chilkoot Trail.

In 1897 and 1898, some twenty to thirty thousand people crossed the Chilkoot Pass on their way to the Klondike. The Canadian government required each person to carry with them a year's worth of food and supplies—which weighed about one ton—to prevent starvation and make sure that those heading to the Klondike were prepared to be self-sufficient. Reaching the top of the Chilkoot Pass, they crossed into British Columbia, where officials collected customs duties and checked that each prospector had all the required supplies.

As we took our first few steps on the forested trail, we tried to imagine the effort it would have taken to shuttle those supplies. For the first ten miles we wound our way though the damp, dense temperate rainforest. The trail's well-worn, rock-strewn, muddy surface traced a ribbon of brown through a carpet of thick green moss and ferns. In contrast to the stampeders, our packs were featherlight and our pace brisk. We were tourists leisurely hiking on a National Park Service–maintained trail, carrying modern packs with suspension systems and meager thirty-five-to-forty-pound loads. We scanned the underbrush for decaying remnants of items discarded by the stampeders along the trail: the sole of a shoe here, a rusted saw blade or woodstove there, a shovel, parts from the tramway, tin cans nearly disintegrated by rust, a horse bone or two. One park ranger described it to us as hiking through the longest museum in the world.

The stampeders devised various means for getting their supplies from Skagway to Bennett Lake, where they would continue by boat. Some people hired packers or used horses. Later on, several tramways were built, allowing those who could afford it to have their gear hauled to Crater Lake for about seven and a half cents per pound. Perhaps the easiest way to transport supplies over the pass was in the winter using dog teams, despite the brutal cold, deep snow, and potential blizzards and avalanches. We struggled to fathom the sheer number of people who came through in the late 1800s, but we mentally transposed historic photos with the wild landscape around us, imagining the tent cities at Sheep Camp and Lindeman City, and the continuous line of men trudging like ants up the "Golden Stairs" at the crux of the Chilkoot Pass.

When we reached the Golden Stairs on our second day, we fell into a procession of hikers, scrambling up talus and over boulders and, eventually, snow. As we steadily climbed higher the dense coastal forest petered away. Snow and jagged rock stretched above us in all directions, disappearing into thick, dark clouds concealing the peaks that lay several thousand feet above. It was July 13 and snow and ice covered the top of the pass. We remained in that inhospitable place only long enough to snap a couple photos with numb fingers before continuing down the Canadian side of the pass.

The mood was light as we set up our tent on a designated wooden platform and gathered in the shelter with two dozen other people to cook dinner out of the elements. Everyone else boiled water to pour into pouches of diminutive commercial freeze-dried camping meals while we cooked an entire pound of pasta with a scoop of powdered pasta sauce and a handful of vegetables Dave's mom had dehydrated. By the time we were digging into second and third servings of pasta topped with Parmesan cheese sprinkled from its original full-size container, the other hikers—Boy Scouts, couples, families—were staring at us as if we were martians.

We hiked past the turquoise water of Crater and Lindeman Lakes, admiring the view of these rewilded bodies of water. High above the tree line, graced with a bluebird day, snowcapped peaks stretched to the horizon. The rocky, partially snow-covered trail required our undivided attention as we slowly descended toward the treed valley below.

At Bennett Lake the stampeders harvested lumber from the surrounding forest to build boats or rafts, readying themselves for the Yukon River. Just thirty-three miles into a six-hundred-mile journey, they probably thought the hardest part was behind them. They also used the lumber for shelter, cooking fires, and heat. Although the forest is recovering, the trees are still small and sparse, and the forest has not returned to its pre–gold rush state.

Staring across Bennett Lake we talked about how humans were impacting the earth then versus now. The trees from the surrounding valleys had been cut by men using crosscut handsaws. What one hundred men could clear in a day is now done by one or two people using massive machines powered by fossil fuels, controlled by a handful of buttons and joysticks. A century ago prospectors dug for gold with shovels and pickaxes; now modern mines utilize massive equipment that can be controlled by an operator in an air-conditioned office thousands of miles away. With the remnants of the Klondike Gold Rush so visible we had to wonder what humans a hundred years from now will see in the ripples of consumption our generation leaves behind.

* * *

INSTEAD OF BUILDING boats, we waited for the train, which was making its way over White Pass, to deliver our kayaks. Once the train arrived we hauled our kayaks and gear from the depot to the gravel beach. Wind rushed down from the Chilkoot Pass dotting Bennett Lake's turquoise water with whitecaps that raced across the valley toward the distant horizon. As we unloaded the contents of our backpacks into our kayaks, we thought about the stampeders loading their two thousand pounds onto their newly made boats. How seaworthy were they? Whether leaky or tippy or overloaded, from here they had to navigate windswept lakes, swift currents, tight bends, and several sets of rapids.

After carrying everything on our backs for several days it was extremely freeing to travel by boat again. With the wind at our backs paddling felt effortless. The water lacked the swell of the ocean, and a strong tailwind ruffled our hair and kicked up whitecaps, but the waves never got very big due to the lack of fetch. We excitedly realized that we were once again surrounded by fresh water, able to gather drinking water right from our kayaks, giving us a new sense of appreciation and security. But still, in the next several weeks we would catch ourselves scanning the shoreline for the level of the tide and pulling our boats up higher than necessary, expecting a rising tide that would never occur in these inland waterways.

After a few hours we landed on a sliver of beach on a small island the train conductor described as a calm cove, never touched by the strong and constant southwest wind. He was right; it was a beautiful spot to stop, and after being among a steady stream of hikers for several days, the quiet solitude of this island oasis was too perfect to pass up. Bennett Lake fills a deep, wide valley lined with forested hillsides that ascend sharply to barren ridgetops where patches of snow still lingered in the shadows. Gnarled, stunted pines, which provided little comfort from the wind, dominated the island's sparse vegetation.

After setting up our tent we hiked across the island to stretch our legs and stumbled upon two wooden graves. They sat on the highest, most windswept part of the island, gray and weathered, devoid of any markings that may have indicated who lay buried there. We wondered why these people had left everything they knew to head north. Of the one hundred thousand stampeders who struck out for Dawson, following various routes, only about thirty thousand made it to the goldfields, and far fewer struck it rich. Standing on this exposed ridge made the harsh reality of the risks, rewards, and broken dreams awaiting those who came before us very real. Were these people here solely to seek their fortunes, or might they have been drawn to this wild land like we were—imaginations coaxed into action by stories of mountains, wild vistas, and blank spots on a tattered map?

The next day a steady tailwind pushed us down the lake and into the Yukon River (Gwich'in in origin, meaning "white water river"). The days drifted by in relative comfort. Camping and paddling were easy and there was no reason to hurry. It took us only a couple of days to reach Whitehorse, Yukon. The pace of the river increased as we entered Miles Canyon and gazed up at its dark, steep rock walls, but it was just fast-flowing water; the Whitehorse Rapids that had wrecked hundreds of boats and even taken a few lives during the gold rush were a distant memory. Our only challenge was to portage around the Whitehorse Dam.

After depositing our kayaks and gear at the bottom of the dam we trekked back up the trail to check out the world's longest wooden fish ladder. The construction of the dam in the late 1950s had a detrimental effect on the migration of chinook salmon, so to help the salmon complete their migration from the sea to the head-waters of the Yukon, humans built a 366-meter-long water-filled series of steps along the side of the dam. Back at the dam's base we peered through underwater windows at salmon swimming in the current and wondered whether they would find the ladder and complete the final stretch of their journey to spawn where they had been born.

A mile downstream we turned into a small eddy and hauled our kayaks up a short gravel bank. The Robert Service Campground on the edge of Whitehorse would be our home for the next week. It was the height of summer, and the sprawling campground was bustling with campers. Cars, motorcycles, and the occasional bicycle had whisked people into this pine-dotted oasis along the river, which was just a short walk from the relative hubbub of the Yukon's capital and largest city.

Our muscles received plenty of rest during our sojourn in the city, but our minds and spirits were quickly frazzled. Budget, grants, tax reports, logistics, and a seemingly endless stream of correspondence left us sleep-deprived and constantly glued to the gentle glow of our laptop. We would have been happy to press on after a day or two in town, but periodic stops in places with ample power and internet were necessary to upload photos and video clips to the Wilderness Classroom website and share our journey with tens of thousands of schoolchildren. We both tossed and turned at night, finding it diffi-cult to sleep. The distant hum of cars and trucks, streams of infor-mation left undigested during the day's digital onslaught, and a lack of exercise left us staring at the thin nylon shell overhead. Unable to sleep, we talked about whales and seals, the smell of the duff in the temperate rainforest, and the wide-open vistas and delicate alpine plants of the Chilkoot.

* * *

To reach Dawson City, we had five hundred miles left of the Yukon River's history-drenched shores and cool, swift waters. We traded our sea kayaks for our white-water canoe, a Wenonah Cascade, kitted out with foam pads and a spray cover. Rounding a gentle bend in the river, Whitehorse disappeared in our wake. It had been nearly a year since we had been in a canoe, and we savored its familiar feel and marveled at how easy it was to shift our weight and stretch our legs after spending many months in the firm embrace of a sea kayak's sleek interior. Soon the sounds of birds, wind, and river replaced the last fleeting reminders of Whitehorse's urban landscape.

The sets of rapids were straightforward and easy to negotiate. The famed Five Finger Rapids was actually a bit of a letdown considering what we had read about it. The Northern Tutchone name for Five Finger Rapids is Tthi Cho Nédézhe, which means "rocks standing up across the river," and according to their folklore, it is where Raven (the creator and trickster) built a fish trap. After the town of Minto the river grew larger and muddier as we sped northward. Paddling seemed optional at this point, and we mostly paddled to keep the canoe in the strongest current and avoid logs, cutbanks, and the occasional obstacle. We spent many hours chatting while scanning the steep hills and rock outcrops for white specks of Dall sheep and other large mammals.

We couldn't help but notice the expansive dredge fields south of Dawson—a scar on the land left by gold miners that looked like giant worm castings from above. This sight, although a remnant from the past, served as a glimpse into the future—an example of what a landscape looks like after mines are abandoned. The gold rush significantly damaged the ecosystem in many ways: "The number of stampeders overwhelmed the available resources." Overharvest of wood for building and fuel resulted in large-scale erosion, which produced landslides and harmed aquatic life as streams and rivers filled with sediment.

The overharvest of game, especially moose and caribou, interrupted Native Alaskan and First Nations' hunting and foraging practices. Steam-powered dredges were eventually employed, consuming even more timber with a voracious appetite. Looking at the bare tailings piles, we tried to envision the machinery that had been used to produce them—a chain of huge buckets scooping up earth and dumping it onto conveyor belts. How much water had been used to flush gold from the soil? Although out of sight from the river, gold mining is still going on outside of Dawson. In addition to large-scale earth moving, chemicals like cyanide are used to separate gold from other minerals. These chemicals, of course, can filter into the water and soil, contaminating drinking water, harming plants and animals, and degrading the ecosystem.

As we landed our canoe in Dawson, we felt a fraction of the excitement that prospectors must have felt during the gold rush. The novelty of sleeping in a bed for a few nights and eating out at a restaurant was soon overpowered by a sense of loss and regret. We were leaving the Yukon River long before it ended. We stored our canoe at a local outfitter in town and prepared to hike through Tombstone Territorial Park to access the Mackenzie River watershed, which flows north toward the Arctic Ocean. The outfitter would deliver our canoe to us where the Dempster Highway, a desolate 458-mile-long gravel road, crosses the West Blackstone River. During our brief stay in Dawson we posted our latest update to the Wilderness Classroom and packed two weeks' worth of food. Before long we slung our backpacks over our shoulders.

Entering Tombstone Territorial Park, a roughly 850-square-mile area comprised of the "most important cultural and hunting sites in the Traditional Territory of the Tr'ondëk Hwëch'in" (Gwich'in), we walked on a rutted gravel road, munching highbush cranberries and admiring the view of Tombstone Mountain rising up to meet the sky in the distance. The Hän name for this area is Ddhäl Ch'èl Cha Nän, which means "ragged mountain land" in the language of the Tr'ondëk Hwëch'in, and it is certainly a fitting description. The mountainous peaks were dark and pointed, jagged teeth whose height made them appear impossibly steep. Eventually we turned onto an overgrown trail that was probably only traversed by the trapper who had left rusty pine marten traps here and there. The trail became increasingly difficult to follow, and the weight of our packs produced a nagging, dull soreness in our shoulders and hips. The Chilkoot Trail had been our warm-up for this venture. However, weeks of canoeing had made our bodies forget the encumbrance of loaded backpacks. We nabbed raspberries whenever we spotted a particularly full bush. Animal tracks and scat kept the hike interesting—wolf, caribou, moose, and even a small black bear.

The purpose for this abandoned road's existence had been to maintain a flume that was used by a gold mine one hundred years ago. It must have been quite an undertaking—a feat of engineering to harness several rivers over the many miles to Dawson. We camped near the site of an old sawmill used to process firewood, which powered the steam shovels that dug the trench. A rusted boiler protruded from the muskeg. Game trails crisscrossed all over. We stopped to set up camp at eight o'clock at night. Not that the time mattered, since the sun was still out until eleven, when it would dip slightly below the horizon, creating a dusk that lasted until sunrise.

We had been advised to make a lot of noise as we hiked, so as not to surprise a bear, and therefore deliberately carried on a conversation loudly and continuously. Alders choked the trail. We reached a low-lying bog where we dodged wet spots and savored the scent of black spruces. In a small pond up ahead a large bull moose was picturesquely standing in the middle, up to his shoulders, chowing down on aquatic plants. Our conversation instantly ceased. "Shh! There's a moose up ahead. Get the camera!" Then something rustled the small spruces just to our left.

A streak of brown moved behind the trees and our brains registered another moose very close to us. We were about twenty feet away, which felt uncomfortably close to such a large, wild mammal. Then the owner of the brown fur stuck its head through a gap in the trees to get a better look at us. It wasn't a moose—it was a grizzly bear! A startled grizzly bear standing very close to us. One minute it had been happily eating blueberries, the next it was accosted by these strange creatures that walked on two legs. For a couple of seconds all three of us—humans and bear—were gripped with fear and frozen in place. Within that time our minds raced through all the possible endings to this encounter as well as all the articles we had read about grizzlies and the advice we had heard. The bear huffed and took a couple of steps toward us. We both swallowed our fear, suppressing an overwhelming urge to run, and talked to it—with voices as mellow as we could muster.

"Hey, bear."

"We're just passing through."

"It's okay, bear."

We were letting the bear know we were humans, not prey to be chased, but also not something threatening to be challenged. The camera was forgotten at our feet and our fingers wrapped around bear spray canisters.

The grizzly huffed again and, to our great relief, turned and rustled deeper into the spruce trees. That was our cue to move slowly away—toward the gigantic bull moose that hadn't taken his eyes off us during the entire bear encounter. We nervously shot some video and took photos of the moose, all the while glancing over our shoulders in case the bear decided to return. The trail led right to the moose's mini pond. As we approached, he began to snort at us, clearly threatened. It didn't settle in until much later that this moose actually posed more of a threat to us than the bear. We bushwhacked well around the pond's perimeter to give him a wide berth. The moose, with dark gobs of aquatic plants dangling down between the points of his massive rack, slowly spun in a circle, always keeping a dark beady eye on us and giving the occasional snort, lest we forget he was there.

We trudged through the muskeg, relieved that in the past five minutes we had avoided both being mauled by a grizzly and trampled by the largest bull moose either of us had ever seen. As we continued, we raised our voices from a conversational tone to yelling—loudly—to imaginary bears. We told these bears that we didn't want to startle them and that there were plenty of blueberries in the woods, so they should—please—move away from the trail to let us pass. Once the adrenaline drained from our systems, we began excitedly discussing the post we would write for all the kids who were following our progress online. Students would often ask us to find a particular animal for them. Dozens had asked us to find a moose and hundreds wanted us to find a grizzly bear. We imagined them all going nuts when they saw our update on Monday morning.

* * *

AFTER A GLORIOUS campsite up on a ridge overlooking the forested Little Twelve Mile River Valley, we descended. With no trail to follow anymore, we were entering a new chapter in our journey. Since leaving Bellingham we had experienced challenges and wonders, wildness and solitude, but now we were on the precipice of wilderness on a much grander scale. For the majority of the next six thousand miles between the Tombstone Mountains and Lake Superior, distances between roads and towns would be measured in hundreds of miles and weeks of travel rather than tens of miles and days. It was scary and exciting to trek into the unknown, and in moments when our nerves began to overwhelm our sense of enjoyment, we tried to remind each other that this vastness was what we had been seeking—hardships and all.

As we dropped into the valley, the terrain quickly got brushy. When we weren't dealing with willows and alders, we were walking on top of two-foot-thick moss—which felt like walking on a sponge. We attempted heading down to the river to see if we could walk along it, but the banks were too steep and vegetation grew right up to the water's edge. The tangles of branches caused an overwhelming sense of claustrophobia. We also felt an underlying uneasiness about getting farther from civilization. We had left the comfort and convenience of towns behind us, and the prospect of bushwhacking into the unknown was frightening. Being on foot made us feel more vulnerable than we ever had in a canoe or kayak. What were we doing? Was it worth it? Were we out of our league? Our agonizingly slow progress involved regularly getting tangled in the alders and then cursing and pushing through until being halted by the next tangle. This went on for a while until we reached the spot where the valley widened. This tough day of hiking was one more challenge that we could overcome if we just worked hard enough.

We eventually found a less-intimidating spot to cross the river, having made enough upstream progress that the river was smaller and the depth of the icy water was just over our knees. We aimed for a ridgeline that would lead us to the pass between Chert and Sheep Mountains. Then we spent the afternoon battling vegetation as we climbed up the steep slope, taking frequent breaks to boost morale. It helped when we had climbed high enough out of the valley to peer down and see our progress.

When we finally climbed above the tree line, we were ecstatic and exhausted. After finding a place to pitch camp, we looked across the valley and realized that we could see the spot we had camped the night before. Our daylong hike had been a hard-won six miles, but as a crow flies we were probably just three miles away from our last camp. We had a good hard laugh at this over our dinner of trail mix.

The next day's progress was similar as we crossed the Tombstone River and slogged upward toward Syenite Pass under a blazing sub-Arctic summer sun. But our moods were lighter, perhaps because we had fallen into a routine, becoming more attuned to the slower rhythm of hiking. Or maybe our bodies were getting used to the weight of the packs on our backs and the motion in our legs. There was also deep satisfaction found in standing on top of a ridge, looking around at the forest and bogs below and realizing that we could not see a single man-made object. We were the only people in this vast landscape and instead of finding this thought frightening, we were empowered by it, elated actually. *This, we thought, is how the world looked before buildings, roads, dams, and power lines—undeveloped, untamed.*

We stopped to camp just below Syenite Pass, in a beautiful alpine valley dotted with house-sized boulders and a cold, clear stream running past. The only creature aware of our presence was a ptarmigan we disturbed while locating a suitable tent site. Ragged spires of granite and syenite rose up to the north, west, and east, giving us a new understanding for the name of the mountain range and park. To the south, where we had come from, we could see for miles down the valley to a small lake formed by our little stream.

That night we witnessed total darkness for the first time in months. Peering out of the tent in the middle of the night, there was no longer the dim twilight of the sun hovering just below the horizon that we had grown so accustomed to. True darkness finally allowed us to see the stars. The Big Dipper was coming up over one of the mountains, and the North Star was almost directly overhead.

The following day we scrambled up and over the pass to be rewarded with a new view of more exceedingly steep mountains framing a green-and-golden valley reflected in two deep alpine lakes below. We spotted a few white dots high up on an impossibly steep slope to our right—Dall sheep. These lakes would feed a stream that would become a river—the West Blackstone, which we could follow until the Dempster Highway crossed it, and we would switch back to canoeing.

After carefully negotiating a boulder field, we skirted the edge of the first lake, stopping for lunch and a swim. We spent the rest of the day piecing together game trails in the tundra-like terrain. There were no trees here, and permafrost lay under a layer of spongy moss and uneven muskeg. Sun-bleached caribou antlers lay scattered throughout the landscape, chewed at the tips by mice and pikas, reminding us of the ungulates that created the meandering trails we attempted to follow.

Clouds of black flies hovered around our heads, constantly flying into our noses, eyes, and mouths. They must have recently hatched, their mouthparts still undeveloped, because the small insects didn't bite us. Despite the heat we donned our bug shirts to lessen the annoyance. We followed the caribou trails through the spongy, brushy, and (at times) mucky tundra. The problem with game trails is that a trail may seem to go where you want for a few feet, but it inexplicably veers away from where you really want to go, or worse—it just ends abruptly.

We walked along one side of the steadily growing river and eventually realized that the trail we were following had widened and no longer meandered. Looking down revealed something different from the distinctive cloven hoofprints of caribou we had become accustomed to over the past week; a U-shaped print in the mud confirmed that we had found a horse-packing trail. We were excited about this at first, because it meant that our hike would be easier. It was inevitable that a few yards down the trail we would see the smooth, elongated shape of a boot—a human footprint. We continued walking in silence, letting that footprint settle into our minds along with all its significance. Even though its owner could have left that track a week ago, we no longer felt as if we were alone. It would take us two more days spent hiking in a steady rain to reach the ribbon of gravel running from Dawson to Inuvik, Northwest Territories—the Dempster Highway—and our next transition, from travel by foot to canoe.

A rusty minivan with our green Wenonah Cascade canoe strapped on top rolled to a halt in a cloud of dust on the side of the Dempster Highway. Colm, the outfitter tasked with delivering our canoe and gear, emerged with a smile. He was a sturdy Yukon character with dark, wavy hair, in a hoody and worn Carhartt pants. During our brief conversation he enraptured us with tales about paddling various nearby rivers. As soon as our last pack was extracted from the van, Colm waved goodbye and headed the hundred miles home to Dawson, leaving us alone with our thoughts and the river. Our stomachs were filled with nervous anticipation as we watch the Blackstone's cold, dark water roiling by. The Gwich'in call this river the Tth'oh Zraii Njik, meaning "boulder black river." We laced the sturdy blue North Water spray deck on the canoe and loaded it up with our Granite Gear Immersion packs. Luckily, we didn't have much time to ruminate on the fear churning in our stomachs. A cold drizzle sent us scrambling to don dry suits and load the canoe before everything was soaked.

After a quick hug and kiss, we hopped in the canoe and began to fly. The recent rain had caused the water level of the Blackstone to rise four or five feet, four times the average for this time of year—actually higher than a typical spring snowmelt. Having grown accustomed to working for every footstep as we trudged across tundra, over mountain passes, and through alder thickets, we whooped and hollered as the wild, bouncing water swept us onward. Tight, winding channels were constantly merging and diverging, making it difficult to choose our course. All the water led to the Peel River, but some channels rushed into undercut banks or tangled masses of trees. These were our most dangerous obstacles on the Blackstone. If we misjudged our timing or picked the wrong channel and were swept into any of the hundreds of trees that had fallen into the river, our canoe could have easily been overturned, leaving us pinned by thousands of pounds of water rushing through the trunks and branches like rinsing noodles in a strainer. The water was pulsing downriver at five to seven miles an hour. After we rounded a bend the Dempster Highway disappeared, and we were alone once again. There was no turning back—we could not paddle upstream against the current, even if we wanted to.

Mile after mile, the river rolled along with continuous Class I and Class II rapids descending through the Blackstone Valley. After an hour our grips began to loosen on our paddles, and in the stretches with smaller waves, we took in our surroundings. Ashen-gray gravel mountains rose several thousand feet from the thin band of black spruce covering the river valley. Striated pillars of rock dotted the landscape. We had entered Beringia, an ancient oasis that had not been covered by glaciers during the last ice age. This meant these mountains were shaped by long periods of weathering instead of getting mowed down and scoured out by glaciers. They possessed a rugged, wild beauty that set them apart. Rocketing down the river, we tried to grasp how this region had been cut off from the rest of North America by the ice sheet but connected to Siberia through the land bridge that had been revealed by a roughly three-hundred-foot drop in ocean levels. We imagined the trees away and in their place a dry grassland where woolly mammoths, steppe bison, Yukon horses, scimitar cats, and giant short-faced bears roamed. The lack of glaciation combined with permafrost created the perfect environment for preserving the bones and even mummified remains of these extinct creatures. Tales of woolly mammoth tusks jutting from banks kept us constantly studying the shoreline and slopes that plummeted to the river's edge from peaks towering overhead.

Our adrenaline was pumping, but with each curve of the river, each standing wave and little drop, we grew more confident. In white water canoeing you have to work together. The bow paddler's job is to make fine adjustments in the canoe's course through the rapids, initiating every move. The stern paddler responds by adjusting the stern to keep the canoe pointed straight downstream. You can't fight the river; you have to work with it—and we could only do that when our timing and balance were in sync.

We stopped for the night on a gravel bar thirty miles from where we put in. In four hours we had covered what normally would be a very full day's paddle. We had been giddy all afternoon, watching our speed on the GPS: eight to ten miles per hour. We pitched our tent on the ancient gravel a few feet from the river's edge and then ate dinner in silence, listening to the water rush by.

The next day we continued to fly down the river, winding through the mountains. It was like riding an escalator; we could see the river dropping before us and disappearing around each twist in the valley. Eventually, the mountains pulled away and the river meandered at a slightly slower pace through the spruces, cutbanks, gravel bars, and piles of roots and trees washed into giant tangles by the floodwaters.

We picked our way through the channels, trying to take the one with the most water in it. The river split several times, snaking around little gravel islands.

Suddenly, a massive black spruce tree loomed ahead of us. It lay across the river, bobbing and surging in the current. As we drifted closer, it was apparent that it blocked the entire channel. Instinct took over and we frantically ferried to the side and grabbed on to tree roots protruding from the bank to keep from being swept downstream into the strainer. A few seconds of indecision could have been disastrous. The place we managed to pull over was not more than a hundred feet from a torrent of water flowing into, around, and over a tangle of branches protruding from the tree's two-foot-thick horizontal trunk. If we had been swept into it, drowning would have been a real possibility, not to mention the loss of our food and equipment, especially the canoe, which could have been bent in half by the force of the water pinning it against the trunk. With a firm grasp on several large roots, we tied up our canoe and took a moment to collect ourselves on the muddy bank. Then, working against the powerful current, we slowly lined the canoe upstream to try our luck with a different channel.

Every paddle stroke drew us deeper into the wilderness, and the next signs of civilization lay more than three hundred miles and many rapids downstream, where the Peel flows into the Mackenzie River delta. We had never experienced remoteness on such a vast scale. The Peel watershed stretches across twenty-six-thousand square miles of the Yukon and Northwest Territories. It is the largest undeveloped watershed in Canada, covering an area roughly the size of Scotland. We would spend the next three weeks carving our way through the heart of this vast wild land, and there was no room for error. Far from roads and cell service, evacuation would only be possible by helicopter or floatplane. We carried a satellite phone with us, which we used to transmit our website updates and hoped we would never have to use for an emergency. Calling for help on a satellite phone is not like dialing 911 in a city; considering the hours or possibly days it would take a search and rescue team to reach us, our actions or inactions held an added weight. We were utterly alone and could rely on no one else.

A golden hue blanketed the rolling hills to the south. We rounded a bend, and a large, silty tributary—the Ogilvie River—merged with the Blackstone, forming the Peel River. The Gwich'in name for the Peel River is Teetł'it Gwinjik, meaning "head of the waters—along the course of." After paddling sixty miles in one day, it seemed like the perfect place to stop for the night. As we unloaded the canoe on a gravel bar between the two rivers, we watched several large trees float down the Ogilvie, swirling in the forceful current. Downstream on the Peel we would enter a new chapter with stretches of slower current punctuated by Class III and Class IV rapids, larger and more technical than those of the Blackstone. Our knowledge base of the various rapids consisted of conversations with several people who had paddled these rivers before and one guidebook. The easier rapids, we ran with no more than a brief discussion of strategy as we approached. For the bigger rapids, we would pull over to scout, which involved a scramble along the rocky bank to see the entire rapid and a conversation to determine our plan to paddle, line, or portage around.

As we paddled within earshot of the dull roar of our first major rapids on the Peel, our fear took hold and grew until we could see the tumbling water and mentally plot our course through. The drops and standing waves were indeed bigger, but not any more daunting than what we had trained in. Taking a breath, we plunged in and let instinct take over. We were carefully picking our way through the rapids when a small rock island appeared in the middle of the river. A moose stood on the rock, nonchalantly grazing on a knee-high bush. She exuded calmness as she watched us plunge over the first drop and then dodge rocks and a sizable wave train. It wasn't until we were drifting below the rapids, breathing deeply and letting the adrenaline dissipate, that we wondered how she had gotten out to that little island.

The river grew larger with each tributary that cascaded down from the mountains and the valley grew broader, the sides less steep, and the trees denser. With the river in flood some of the rapids we typically would have run were boiling masses of white formed by long rock ledges, which would surely swamp our canoe. Luckily for us it was relatively easy to make short portages over the smooth ledges along the river's edge. Still, we were hauling nearly three weeks' worth of food, plus all of our gear, and a sixty-five-pound canoe, so even the short portages over slippery, uneven terrain amplified the sense of relief when the sun dipped low and it was time to set up camp.

We were approaching Aberdeen Canyon, possibly the most dangerous part of our route yet. This canyon is named Nan Zhak Nadhàdlaii in Gwich'in, meaning "ground—underneath—water flowing," implying that the river used to flow underground here. The wilderness instructors at the National Outdoor Leadership School (NOLS) base in Whitehorse had told us that there is a one-and-a-half-mile-long series of rapids and ledges that get more difficult as you approach a treacherous Class VI un-runnable waterfall at the entrance of the canyon. We had to find the portage, which we had been told started mere feet from the top of the waterfall, at the canyon's edge on the right-hand side of the river.

Tingling with anxiety, we scanned the top of the rapids. Fifty-foot cliffs blocked the right side of the river so we could only see the first half mile of moderate white water leading toward the canyon. We decided to break up the rapids into manageable steps, setting a goal to run the top two small ledges and work our way over to the gravel bar below the cliffs. The rapids that we could see were one-to-two-foot ledges of rock forming two-to-three-foot waves. It was well within our skill level, but being days from help and with all the water rushing toward a waterfall, it took everything we had to control our breathing and keep calm.

Paddle, draw, pry, brace, water, light, noise, calm. Floating in the still water below the gravel bar, our sense of relief was palpable. Over the next hour we scouted, ran, and lined a series of ledges as the deafening thunder of Aberdeen Canyon grew louder. A half mile from the lip of the waterfall we pulled over to scout the churning rapids leading up to the falls. The right side of the river became a cliff rising fifty feet above our heads, limiting our options for pulling over. With normal water levels the long fingers of rock that form the ledges and rapids would be exposed close to shore, but now the water rushed over two ledges right up to the cliff face. This was the crux: one hundred yards below us, a sloping rocky shoreline along the right side of the river led to the edge of the canyon. We could portage the final one-third mile to where we assumed the normal portage trail began if we had to, but first we had to get past the cliff. For a long time we stood in silence at the water's edge, fifty yards upstream from the cliff, watching the water, and then we slowly rehearsed precisely how we would run the canoe over each ledge and reach the sloping, rocky shore beyond the cliff, uncomfortably close to the waterfall.

We held each other in an embrace that lasted longer than usual, neither of us wanting to be the first to let go. Deep breaths as we wiggled into the canoe, wedging our feet under the seats and our knees against the bottom. After a couple paddle strokes the bow crested the lip of the first ledge and plunged into the frothing foam below. Digging in with everything we had, we managed to maneuver the canoe through as aerated water filled our laps and drained off the spray cover. Draw right, draw right, we fought the river's pull toward the five-foot waves churning in the middle, aiming for a smooth patch of water just wider than our canoe. We had enough time for one breath before succumbing to the pull of the river rushing over the second ledge. Bigger than the first, the bow plunged into the frigid maelstrom as the wave broke on our chests and our arms locked in a high brace.

Seconds later we eddied out alongshore in a pool of calm water. Several inches of water sloshed in the bottom of the canoe, but we had made it. Our bodies shook with adrenaline as we stumbled out of the canoe and pulled it up on the rocks, safe from the grip of the river. For several minutes we just sat on the rocks staring out at the hazard we had avoided, mesmerized by its surging, powerful waves.

Soon a cool drizzle gave us the urge to keep moving, so we lined and paddled the final stretch to the edge of the canyon. The whole time we stayed within a canoe's length of shore, constantly aware of the river's pull toward the waterfall. As we inched closer the sound of the falls increased from a dull rumble to a deafening roar. A thin ribbon of pink flagging a few feet from the canyon's edge marked the beginning of the portage. We were excited to find that there was, in fact, a rough trail to follow, but it would have to wait until morning.

The rain strengthened, so we strung up our tarp along the rocky shore and spent a while reading and relaxing, hoping for a break in the weather to set up our tent. Time had become somewhat irrelevant. When we were hungry, we ate; thirsty, we drank; tired, we rested. It had taken us several months to stop constantly looking at our watches. Especially now, we had plenty of food and nowhere to be. The only thing driving us was the desire to see what lay around the next bend and the faint hint that fall was just around the corner. Each night grew a little longer and a little darker, but we didn't feel like it was time to migrate just yet. Once the rain finally let up, we pitched the tent on a rock ledge above the start of the un-runnable canyon. Big water surged below in a continual roar.

A rainbow formed over our camp, ending in the river. A comforting sight after an intense day. We made a huge pot of rice and lentils for dinner and ate with a view upriver, a chance to see all we had just been through. The water glimmered, backlit by the setting sun. We were totally alone and vulnerable but had never felt closer to the earth and to each other.

\* \* \*

THE THRILL OF the Peel's white water soon evaporated in the slow, steady grind of a difficult portage. The only guidebook about the river reported a five-to-six-mile portage. However, Jaret at NOLS

Yukon base had told us that it was shorter. Braced for six miles but hoping for fewer, we left the river and headed into the bush. We packed our gear so we could shuttle it in two trips. Our strategy was to hike until we needed a break, drop that load, and hike back for the second. Our food was split between the two loads in case a bear happened across one of our caches. As added insurance, we marked waypoints of each cache on the GPS.

Thankfully the terrain was relatively flat. We did, however, have to stay alert to tripping on rocks and roots, or sliding on mud underfoot. Although the path was easy to find, much of it was choked with willow and alder and often under several inches of water, which concealed pockets of boot-sucking mud. We had to choose our footing carefully, otherwise we'd end up knee-deep. Getting out of the mud was complicated by a sixty-pound pack or the canoe. Ramming the canoe through the alders was frustrating work.

Shuttling the gear was a slow process, and discouraging at times. We'd hike for about a quarter of a mile before turning around to get the next load. Back and forth through the tangles of trees and muck. During our lunch break we were shocked to learn that we hadn't quite gone a mile yet! On the move again, we tried to focus on each step, forcing to the backs of our minds the thought that we could have four more miles and therefore several more days of this ahead. We tried to focus on our surroundings—the delicate leaves of the bog laurel, the scent of spruce in the breeze, the rhythmic pounding of our hearts, and the breath flowing in and out of our lungs. The fresh, soapy scent of the Labrador tea that constantly brushed past our shins kept our focus on the present. Wild beauty was all around us, and we tried to take it in whenever a break in the tangles of branches afforded a glance of the river.

There was no room in our thoughts for our final destination, years from now, in Key West or even for thoughts of the following day. What we would accomplish in the next few seconds or minutes was all that mattered. We set minuscule goals for ourselves: "Let's keep moving for ten minutes before pausing to catch our breaths," and

"After three of these ten-minute trudges, we'll take a water break." Confronted with discomfort or danger, our fields of view narrow to the immediate. There is something so simple and gratifying when risk, effort, and reward are easily defined.

We were exhausted, and as the sun dipped low, we started looking for a campsite. The trail was getting closer to the river bluff and dropping in elevation. Just before the start of a steep downhill, we found an epic campsite. There was a small clearing in the trees a couple of feet from the edge of the sheer canyon, with a flat spot twice the size of our tent. We set up the tent with a commanding view of the canyon as it began glowing in the low-angle light of late evening before we went to get the rest of our gear for one final relay of the day.

Once we completed the final shuttle, we couldn't resist scouting the next day's trail. Down we went, and moments later, we were standing on a pebbly beach. Waves of relief and elation overtook us as we realized that this spot was the end of the portage. It was a half past nine o'clock by the time we were cooking dinner, but the lateness of the hour no longer mattered. We contentedly went to sleep perched on the canyon's lip.

In the morning we took our time, watching the light slowly change in the canyon below us. The magic of this place was palpable. It had already given us so much, and we still had two weeks of paddling ahead, following the Peel northward toward the Arctic Ocean. Oneness, confidence, happiness, perspective, hardships—this place was so full of life and left us both feeling small, yet like we could tackle anything. These seemed like priceless gifts, but as we watched the ribbon of water flow by hundreds of feet below us, we thought about how developers were trying to put a price on it.

The awareness of a threat to this extraordinary place welled up in the backs of our minds like a dark rain cloud looming overhead. When we had paddled through Whitehorse and Dawson, we read in the local papers about proposals to develop the Peel watershed. We queried several locals about this topic and learned that the Yukon government and the First Nations communities—who have treaty rights to hunt, fish, and gather throughout this vast landscape—were locked in a heated debate over the fate of the Peel watershed. While most of the First Nations communities in the region wanted the watershed to remain largely undeveloped, the Yukon government was pushing to open up large swaths of the region to oil, gas, and mineral development.

The Peel watershed covers about 14 percent of the Yukon territory. This watershed actually spans parts of Alaska, the Yukon, and the Northwest Territories. It is the apex of Canada's boreal forest, the northern end of the Rocky Mountain chain, not to mention Beringia. It is home to woodland and Barren Ground caribou, wolverines, grizzly bears, the threatened American peregrine falcon, unspoiled aquatic habitats, and many different kinds of boreal songbirds. It is the traditional territory of the Na-Cho Nyak Dun, Tr'ondek Hwëch'in, Vuntut Gwich'in, and Tetl'it Gwich'in First Nations. The threats to the area are many, including the extraction of oil, natural gas, coal, iron ore, copper, and other metals. The Canadian Parks and Wilderness Society (CPAWS) and many other Canadians are working to protect 80 percent of the 26,000-square-mile watershed.

It was hard to comprehend the thought of roads, mines, and oil fields slashing into the wildness that enveloped us. The Gwich'in have lived, hunted, and fished here for generations; the loss seemed unbearable even for outsiders like ourselves. Sure, most Canadians will never visit this place, but can't they see that places like this are finite and invaluable in their own right? Is there any end to our quest for resources and expansion? Do the tentacles of human progress have no limits? If this place isn't safe from development, then what is? Prior to this we had assumed places like the Peel were so remote that they would always remain wild and out of reach from civilization's constant din. As we journeyed ever deeper into this wild land, we came to understand the threats that it, and other places like it, constantly face—no matter how remote.

We packed up our tent, still wet with the morning's dew, and carried the last of our belongings down to the water. The final two hundred yards were steep and muddy, and we had to hold on to trees and roots to control our descent. We slid the canoe down the hill, belayed on a long rope.

Magnificent striped canyon walls stretched above the last of the un-runnable rapids as they came to a thundering finish just upstream from the pebble beach where we stood. How long had it taken for layer upon layer of rock to form, and what events caused their unique folding and bending, like the waves of the rapids frozen in rock? Our visit here was an insignificant blip on the radar of geologic time. Swift water grabbed our canoe and swept us onward. Squirrelly, swirling boils and small whirlpools tugged at the bow, but there were no technical rapids to draw our attention. So we gazed upward, trying to etch in our memories the beauty of the canyon, the perpetual drumming sound of the water, and the faint scent of spruce. Occasionally we spotted or heard peregrine falcons perched on high ledges. The recent rains caused thin ribbons of water to cascade down the canyon walls, sprinkling us with a fine mist when we paddled close.

All too soon we were out of the canyon, the river opened up, and the Wind River entered. Suddenly the Peel became a much larger river, but the current remained swift. After all the portaging we were content to take it easy and enjoy the gentle sensation of paddling, with the pull of the river doing most of the work. In honor of being done with the rapids, we decided to have a floating lunch. During our lazy lunch watching the landscape glide by we covered more miles than we had during the entire previous day of portaging.

We talked about what our near future would be like once we reached the Mackenzie River and turned south to paddle upstream. We looked forward to visiting the smattering of remote communities along its banks and returning with our sled dogs once winter had taken hold. Comfortable moments of wilderness travel allowed such indulgences. Thinking about far-off things, family, or friends was a luxury that was best saved for quiet moments when life was easier. This wandering flow of thoughts as the miles ticked by stood out in sharp contrast to the laser focus each of us experienced during the portage or running rapids.

As the days passed, the river character changed. The current swept us along through wide, braided channels lined with gravel bars, but the rapids became smaller and less numerous. While still wild, the landscape mellowed. The normal annoyances of cold, headwinds, and bugs still reared their heads, but travel was easy. Also, seasonal change was in the air. As August barreled toward September the willows were turning golden and the stars shone brightly for us whenever we woke up in the middle of the night. We were torn between lingering in this easy, wild land with vast gravel-bar campsites and the realization that we had hundreds of miles of upriver travel ahead of us on the Mackenzie. The days would only grow darker, colder, and windier as fall took hold.

We could spend a lifetime here, as the Gwich'in have done for countless generations, and never unlock all the land's secrets. Our time in the Peel watershed was fleeting, but the waters flowing through this rugged land seeped into our souls. There is intrinsic value in simply keeping truly wild places like this forever unmarred. How could we help others see this intrinsic value? Watching the waters swirl and pulse northward, the cracks in our thinking deepened and our previous idealistic assumptions began to crumble away. What was left was the realization that love of a place is the inspiration needed to give it voice. The concerted struggles of people speaking loudly for the wild places they care about allow these places to remain. Although this would be twelve years after we paddled the Peel, the watershed was finally protected in 2022 after a battle that went all the way to the Supreme Court of Canada when it became evident that the Yukon government was not consulting with and protecting the interests of First Nations peoples.

The current slowed where we crossed the Arctic Circle, our GPS reading 66.6 degrees north, and gravel bars were replaced by mud banks. Cold north wind rushing down from the Arctic Ocean forced us to dig our paddles in once more and work for each mile as we slowly plodded into unrelenting headwinds. The small town of Fort McPherson, our first taste of civilization since leaving the Dempster Highway, beckoned. The thought of buying a bag of chips, or perhaps a four-dollar slightly bruised apple, and the sounds of laughter from kids playing and dogs barking swirled through our minds. Maybe we could even take a shower. We never really missed these things when they were far out of reach, but after weeks of solitude we found our conversations shifted as we approached even the smallest outposts of humanity.

When we pulled up to the muddy landing by the ferry, we were greeted by a gray-haired Gwich'in man sitting in a black truck. "First question," he said as he pulled off aviator sunglasses to reveal warm eyes bordered by deep laugh lines, "where did you paddle from?" When we told him the Blackstone, the corners of his mouth turned up into a satisfied smile. "Hop in!" Before we buckled our seat belts, Robert had already begun telling us about his adventures on the land—in the Peel and Mackenzie River valleys and the surrounding mountains. He took us to a visitors' center at the Nitainlaii Territorial Park campground where he was working so he could show us photos and fill our heads with stories of hunting, trapping, and traveling throughout the great land we had just experienced. "I've been on long winter treks by snowshoe and dog team, and moose and caribou hunts deep in the river valleys. We live off the land, you know, netting whitefish and gathering berries in the fall."

The Gwich'in name for Fort McPherson is Teetł'it Zheh, which means "head of the waters-town," and it is the community home for the Teetł'it Gwich'in—"people of the headwaters" or "people in the middle." His stories flowed freely like the river and filled us with both joy and sadness when he shifted his attention to the pending development of his people's traditional lands and disconnected youth whose ties to the land were slipping away. "The kids these days—they don't care. They walk around with things in their ears (earbuds) and they drive their Ski-Doos; they have no connection to the land like my generation," he lamented. "And the government wants to develop it, you know. I'm doing what I can—I go to all the meetings and I speak up." The sadness in the Gwich'in elder's eyes as he described the prospect of carving up their land with roads, wells, and mines was now woven in our brains like the river's braided channels, along with the gifts this great land had given us. Learning of the final ruling to protect the Peel watershed more than a decade later, we could envision how he and other community members had spoken up for this land they loved and were a part of.

At the post office we picked up two massive boxes full of food, warm clothes, and our canvas tent and woodstove that we had mailed to ourselves in anticipation of the changing seasons. As we paddled away our canoe maneuvered like a log because of all the extra weight. The rapids were all behind us, and in another day or two we would reach the Mackenzie River, turn our canoe south, and begin what we assumed would be a long, slow journey upstream for several hundred miles.

* * *

ON THE LAST day in August we reached the confluence with the Mackenzie River, which is a thousand miles long, flowing north to the Arctic Ocean. The Gwich'in name for the Mackenzie River is Nagwichoonjik, meaning "river through a big country," and the Dene name is Dehcho, meaning "big river" or "river of great significance." We were a few days ahead of schedule, but the shrinking days and rapidly cooling weather created a sense of urgency that kept us moving as quickly as we were physically able. Our travels were affected by a new variable as soon as we made the turn—traveling upstream. This point was the farthest north we would get during the North American Odyssey, above the Arctic Circle, one long day's paddle from the Arctic Ocean. We adjusted our general course from north to south, headed eventually for Key West, the southernmost point in the United States. From here until the end of this stage we would be facing many unknowns, and our planning for this part of the trip had purposefully been open-ended. We didn't know what the current against us would be like, so we set the bar low for our daily progress at fifteen miles. When would the weather turn too cold or the days too short? Who would we encounter along the river? We were aware of the widely spaced towns of Tsiigehtchic (Arctic Red River), Fort Good Hope, and eventually Norman Wells, but we didn't even know which town we would choose for our end point.

We figured that we had about a month to travel as far south as we could before freezing temperatures and howling fall storms brought an end to the paddling season. Once we could paddle no farther, we planned to take a break and return to Minnesota to assemble our dog teams and visit dozens of the schools following our progress through the Wilderness Classroom. When we would resume the journey by dog team, temperatures of forty or even fifty degrees Fahrenheit below zero would not be uncommon. With this in mind we were anxious to make it as far south as we could. Every mile we made now would be one less we had to cover by dog team.

Tsiigehtchic (meaning "mouth of the iron river" in Gwichya Gwich'in) had been our initial goal for this leg of the journey, but that was only two days travel from the confluence with the Mackenzie. We decided to set our sights farther since we were ahead of schedule. Fort Good Hope, 250 miles upstream, would be our new goal. Norman Wells, 125 miles farther still, was a possibility if the stars aligned.

We had studied Alexander Mackenzie's journals from 1789 for clues about how his party managed to travel up the river that bears his name. Having reached the Arctic Ocean instead of finding the sought-after route to the Pacific, he and his party returned upstream using an even mix of three different methods of travel, fluidly switching whenever conditions changed. When the wind was in their favor, they paddled with a sail to assist them. When the current was light enough but winds were not in their favor, they paddled. When wind and current were against them, they lined.

Growing up in the United States we had learned about Lewis and Clark but hardly anything about Alexander Mackenzie, the Scottish fur trader and explorer who succeeded in crossing the North American continent twelve years prior to Lewis and Clark. Mackenzie was searching for a trade route between the Atlantic and Pacific Oceans when he became the first European to follow the Dehcho River to the Arctic Ocean in 1789. Some sources even say that Mackenzie called it the Disappointment River, but the river was later named after him. He did succeed in reaching the Pacific in 1793, and his journals prompted Thomas Jefferson to commission the Lewis and Clark Expedition.

Of the three methods we used to travel upstream, lining the canoe was the slowest and most labor-intensive. It required us each to walk alongshore handling a rope, one attached to the bow, the other to the stern. Despite the slow nature of lining, we enjoyed the break from sitting in the canoe. Our bodies warmed up quickly as we walked and pulled—the perfect antidote to the cool weather of September. The person in front had the tougher job of pulling the canoe, while the back person used their rope to control its angle. For the front we rigged up a harness of sorts by attaching the rope to a life jacket. We would switch every fifteen to twenty minutes to divide the hard labor evenly. We effectively wanted the canoe to travel in a straight line parallel to shore, but the shoreline was never straight. Navigating rocky protrusions, indentations, and shallow spots meant whoever handled the back rope had to constantly be on the lookout.

During our first couple of days on the Mackenzie, the wind was against us, so we lined and paddled. We could paddle wherever we found an eddy (with current actually propelling us upstream) on the inside of a bend or in places where the river was straight and wide, resulting in less current. When we did finally have a significant wind at our backs, it was a happy day. With a small sail attached to the center thwart of the canoe, we could both still paddle if the wind slackened or the current increased. When the wind blew really hard we could kick back and relax, just steering while the wind did all the work for a few glorious moments. In the end we found that we used each mode of travel about a third of the time—a breakdown just like Alexander Mackenzie's party more than two hundred years before us.

We slowly progressed upriver, making fifteen to twenty miles per day. While paddling we monitored our GPS to make sure our pace didn't drop below two miles per hour. If it did, we'd either dig in to paddle harder or we'd pull over to line. As fatigue inevitably set in, tensions would sometimes rise until we remembered that we were in this together and the only way back home was to propel ourselves and our canoe upstream. Observing our surroundings provided a distraction from the tedious grind against the largest river system in Canada. The river undulates northward like a thousand-mile-long, one-to-two-mile-wide snake through the boreal forest. Spring floods scour away at the land, leaving mud- and gravel-cut banks rising sharply from the outside of bends, while gravel bars and willow thickets dominate the inside edge. Day by day we could feel the rapid onset of winter, losing almost an hour of daylight each week. The willows and grass, which had been green and lush a few weeks before, were now a golden-brown carpet. Each morning we awoke to a canoe layered in frost. Headlamps that had remained buried in our packs for months quickly became a daily necessity.

The first time we spotted the elegant, white forms of two tundra swans we were enchanted. But soon these massive birds with their impossibly long necks became a familiar sight—and sound. Large flocks of Canada geese, tundra swans, and snow geese were heading south along with us, passing noisily overhead, day and night. Our migration seemed laughable in comparison to the tundra swans that were just at the beginning of their nearly four-thousand-mile journey to the Pacific Slope in California. We would fall asleep to the loud *honk, honk, honk* of geese and swans flying overhead.

The ground squirrels, moose, and bears were also preparing for winter, eating as much as they could. Evidence of their frenzied activity lay in tracks alongshore, along with those of caribou and wolf. Grizzly tracks in the mud occasionally gave us pause, but most often their owner was long gone. One morning, as we were lining the canoe, we scanned the shore in front of us and saw a large, brown lump. Having seen many things on the shore that look like animals from a distance, but turn out to be tree roots, rocks, or driftwood upon closer inspection, we assumed that it was the root ball of an over-turned tree. But then, it moved. We quietly hopped in the canoe to pass by this large male grizzly without disturbing it, pausing to watch it digging and eating roots, oblivious to us, completely engrossed in the task of bulking up for winter. Floating about a hundred feet away, we shot a few photos and some video. He was big, old, and had a damaged left ear. He eventually looked at us, but the roots he was eating were more important than the presence of two humans in a canoe.

As we neared Fort Good Hope (K'asho Got'ine) we realized that many of the local people were stocking up on food as well. While we were loading our canoe the morning after sighting the grizzly, a man in a small motorboat approached from upriver. He introduced him-self as Michael and said, "The water in the river is rising." We asked how he knew, and Michael pointed out numerous sticks floating past. "These sticks were lying onshore, and now they're getting picked up as the water level increases." It served as a warning to maybe set up camp a little higher next time. He told us we'd reach his fish camp later in the day and invited us in for tea.

Several hours later we were sitting inside the snug, warm cabin sipping hot black tea, chatting with Judy and Michael. This kind and welcoming Dene couple in their sixties lived in Fort Good Hope, but they clearly relished time spent at their simple cabin in the bush. Calloused hands, weathered skin, and sturdy, worn clothes made it easy to see they were at home out here. Their adult children and other interests drew them to town, but they had grown up on the land, hunting and fishing. "We hope to catch about four hundred fish over the next ten days. We're drying them over a smoky fire. Four hundred fish will last us all winter," Michael said. They were part of a dwindling group of people who still went out on the land to harvest food and use traditional means to preserve it. "There are others who net fish," Michael observed, "but they just freeze their fish instead of taking the time to dry them."

Getting a tour of their camp, we saw the fish cut in thin strips, hung over a small, smoldering fire inside a tarp tent, and met two young, lanky, blond Alaskan huskies standing near food bowls filled with whitefish eggs. "I'm trying to fatten them up; they look nothing like the sled dogs we had when I was a kid. No one has sled dogs anymore." Sled dogs had historically been the primary means of winter transportation for everyone in the region. However, they were replaced by a mode of travel that didn't have to be fed and cared for year-round—Ski-Doo snowmobiles. This story of the erosion of traditional ways and culture was one that we would hear over and over in Indigenous communities throughout northern Canada. Everyone, it seemed, now depended on motors to get around— snowmobiles in the winter and motorboats and ATVs in the summer. These sled dogs that Michael and Judy were trying to fatten up had come from a racing kennel of Alaskan huskies and would never look like the well-furred, sturdy-pawed sled dogs of Michael's childhood memories. Those dogs had been used as draft animals, running in single file, pulling heavy loads on narrow toboggans through deep snow and intense cold. The dogs of Michael's youth reminded us of the Canadian Inuit dogs we were familiar with through our years of working as dogsled guides at Wintergreen.

We could have easily stayed all day, learning from this fascinating couple, but we felt the need to push on. With a bag full of treats, we hopped into the canoe. This visit made us even more eager to reach the remote First Nations community and learn more about traditional Dene ways of life.

The next day we landed on the riverbank below Fort Good Hope in the late afternoon and headed straight for the grocery store. We didn't see anyone else on the street as we walked up, but a handful of people were hanging out near the Northern Store. It was small, with a limited but expensive selection of mostly nonperishable food. Unable to resist the temptation of eating anything other than the same old items we had in our food pack, we bought a can of peas and a box of crackers to supplement our dinner.

As we walked back down the hill toward our canoe we heard a shout from behind. "Hey, tourists!" In this town with no roads to it, only accessible by boat or airplane, everyone knew everybody, so we were indeed tourists. We turned around and smiled at a young, dark-haired man in a baggy flannel shirt, probably in his early twenties. With a big smile on his face, Charlie introduced himself and asked if we had ever tried dry meat. When we said no, he invited us over to his house.

There was an assortment of teens and twentysomethings inside, with several toddlers playing out in the yard. They queried us about our journey up to this point. We asked them about life in the region, and they told us about fishing and hunting. Several of them had been out in a boat on the river recently and shot a moose. They dressed it right there and hauled the meat home. One of the girls was upset about how her new white jacket, which she had ordered from the south, was now hopelessly stained with moose blood. Apparently, Colville Lake, an even more remote community out on the tundra, was a popular place to visit in the summer. They also described their family fish camps along the river. We were impressed to learn how much time these young people spent on the land.

Charlie proudly introduced us to dry meat, which is traditionally dried caribou or moose—this batch was caribou. We were surprised when his wife pulled out a tub of lard, scooped some up with her piece of dry meat, and sprinkled salt on it. We followed her example and savored the chewy, salty, richness. We were even given some to take with us, along with slices of banana bread and a bag of Halloween candy. As we exited the front door, a burst of cold registered on our faces. The air temperature had dropped to near freezing, and the sky was a dim twilight.

We ended up staying in Fort Good Hope for several more days, doing a presentation at the school and meeting a variety of people. Our social calendar included dinner with the principal and several teachers and a tour around town, including the local radio station. Most people laughed when we told them about how we were paddling upriver. Apparently no one had done such a thing for a really long time. We also learned about some of the latest concerns for the surrounding land and community. Oil companies were talking about putting a pipeline along the Mackenzie River to transport oil from near Inuvik in the north down south. This would mean an all-weather road running to Fort Good Hope and other communities farther south along the river. About half of the community was in favor of the pipeline and road, with the other half firmly against. Benefits would mean more jobs and money coming into the community. Concerns were about the environment and the effect on the local people. The road was a mixed bag—it would allow for easier visits to the surrounding communities, bringing Fort Good Hope out of isolation, but the road would also inevitably bring drugs, alcohol, and other vices to town. People were also worried about how the construction of the pipeline would affect the caribou migration, potentially negatively impacting an important source of food.

Students via the Wilderness Classroom had requested that we interview an elder when we got the chance. A local teacher offered to introduce us to Adeline and Frank, and we found ourselves climbing their wooden front steps on a Sunday morning. Sometimes we were introduced to elders who appeared to be as young as fifty, but Adeline and Frank were clearly from another generation. In their seventies or eighties, they had spent most of their lives in an era that hardly resembled our modern world. We opened the door of their porch to find a bounty of dried fish lining the floor. Mostly whitefish, they came from Frank and Adeline's annual trip to their cabin. We shook hands with a spritely Adeline, who was concerned about how stained her hands were—the consequence of tanning a moose hide the day before. Petite and wiry, she moved about the house and yard with more energy than most people half her age, a discernible twinkle in her brown eyes. Frank was almost as wiry, with wrinkled, weathered skin from a life spent out on the land.

"Come in, come in! Are you hungry?" Adeline asked without waiting to hear the answer. Soon we were sitting at their kitchen table eating dried fish with lard and salt. Frank plopped into a comfortable chair and sat calmly as Adeline bustled about the cabin. "I spent my whole life in the bush, you know, except for three years of residential school in Aklavik," she began. "Oh, we love living off the land. Even in our old age, the two of us stay busy with fishing, trapping, drying our food, and making mittens."

Frank, warmed up by our open-ended questions, chimed in, "I ran a dog team to check my traplines years ago. We had seven dogs, and they ran in single file, pulling my sled." He added, "No one has sled dogs in town anymore, just Ski-Doos."

Adeline interjected, "I never worried about Frank when he went out with the dog team. Sled dogs don't break down like a Ski-Doo can, leaving you stranded miles from town, in a blizzard out on the tundra. I knew the dogs would always bring him home."

Frank continued, "People are just lazy nowadays, you know? They spend less time out on the land—and more time around town." He shifted topics. "Things are so much more expensive now too." Rising from his chair, he ambled into the bedroom and returned with a thirty-year-old receipt from the Hudson's Bay Company store that included candles, flour, and lard.

They also helped us anticipate what lay upriver. "According to local legend, a giant shaped the land a long time ago. Look for an island, which is the giant's upside-down canoe. His footprints are several small lakes just off the river. The giant shot three beavers and hung their pelts high on a cliff. Then he cooked the beaver meat. There is a hill that still smokes from his fire. If the land is happy to see you, you will see smoke," Adeline said.

We parted company with tentative plans to return in the winter. Frank invited us to their winter cabin on Muskrat Lake and Adeline asked us to bring her an ulu from Inuvik. Adeline was in the middle of the involved and very physical process of traditionally tanning a moose hide, and we were excited to see the finished hide on our return. To our dismay, we would find out a week later, once we arrived in Norman Wells, that Adeline had passed away in her sleep.

Map of the North American Odyssey.
*Graphic by Patrick Nash.*

Dogsledding away after our wedding ceremony.
*Photo by Stephan Hoglund.*

Paddling north through Alaska's Inside Passage.
*Photo by Dave Freeman.*

Watching humpback whales surface around us near Juneau, Alaska.
*Photo by Amy Freeman.*

Happy to be above tree line in Tombstone Territorial Park, Yukon, Canada.
*Photo by Amy Freeman.*

At the top of Syenite Pass in the Tombstone Mountains during our hike from Dawson to the
Blackstone River, Yukon Territory. *Photo by Dave Freeman.*

Paddling up the Mackenzie River, Northwest Territories.
*Photo by Dave Freeman.*

Approaching Tulita, Northwest Territories.
*Photo by Ron Doctor.*

Dogsledding through the blizzard on Great Bear Lake, Northwest Territories.
*Photo by Ellen Root.*

A student modeling our dogsledding outerwear at one of many school assemblies.
*Photo by Amy Freeman.*

Pushing our way through the ice on Great Slave Lake.
*Photo by Amy Freeman.*

Wildfire along the Tazin River, Northwest Territories.
*Photo by Dave Freeman.*

Paddling across a glassy Wollaston Lake.
*Photo by Dave Freeman.*

Approaching Boston by sea kayak.
*Photo by Dave Freeman.*

Paddling past the Statue of Liberty.
*Photo by Dave Freeman.*

Standing at the southernmost point in the continental United States in Key West, Florida.
*Photo by Jim Voytilla.*

Stories of cliffs and roiling, deadly rapids upstream caused us to alter our plans. Fort Good Hope could have been where we stopped canoeing and began dogsledding, but two sets of rapids lay between here and the town of Norman Wells. The Ramparts and Sans Sault Rapids would be much easier to ascend now with our canoe rather than dodging open water, navigating thin ice, or detouring away from the river over miles of cliffy terrain with our dog teams. We continued upriver with our canoe and set our sights on Norman Wells.

* * *

ONCE WE WERE past the white water and the current slackened to its normal speed above the Ramparts, we set up camp on a gravel bar near an abandoned Ski-Doo. The next day, under gray clouds threatening snow, we passed a bloody moose hide and gut pile resting atop a carpet of spruce boughs, with fat ravens perched in tree branches overhead. We envisioned the teens and twentysomethings from Fort Good Hope motoring past, spotting the bull moose, one of them taking aim with their rifle, followed by a flurry of activity as they all participated in butchering the thousand-pound animal. We crossed the river to be on the inside of a slight bend as we approached the San Sault Rapids. Mountains that had once been distant were creeping closer as we progressed upstream.

The next morning we emerged from the tent to see a dusting of snow covering the ground, canoe, and surrounding hills. The mountains, now a gleaming white, seemed to have snuck even closer in the night. We had seen a snowshoe hare with white feet a couple of days ago and now felt a sense of relief for its sake. The hare's white feet had shifted from a liability to an asset overnight.

We mounted a sneak attack on the San Sault Rapids, taking a side channel to the west of the main river. At times we had to swing out from shore to avoid shallow spots, but that meant battling stronger currents. Once we admitted defeat to paddling against the current, we lined our way up the small channel, sometimes wading in the icy water, lifting the loaded canoe over the occasional ledge. Back in the main channel, we peeked across at the intimidating standing waves of the rapids on the east side of the river.

We came to enjoy paddling in the snow, watching it come and go in waves and judging the movement of flurries like oncoming rain showers. A white haze with a dark center would blow by, and suddenly we'd be in it, the promise of winter swirling in the air around us. Soon the water on which we paddled would become a frozen highway, tread by dog paws and Ski-Doo tracks. For now, though, the flakes disappeared upon contact with the dark water.

We were no longer alone on the river. As we got within a few days of Norman Wells, we grew accustomed to the occasional whine of a motorboat speeding past. Hunters were after moose and caribou, seemingly motivated by the same instinct as the squirrels stashing seeds to sustain life during the upcoming cold and dark months. A cluster of motorboats alongshore drew our attention, so we decided to stop and chat. A large man dressed entirely in camouflage named Brad, who was in search of caribou, explained that folks were stopping to visit a friend for lunch and invited us to join them.

Inside a small, green cabin we were introduced to W. He was the oldest man in the room and probably the most knowledgeable of the comings and goings of the animals in the region. Thin, wearing an oversize red-and-black plaid jacket, W. sat at the wooden table with his back to the woodstove while half a dozen people stripped off outer layers and hung gloves to dry. We basked in the warmth as we sipped steaming cups of tea and teased out W.'s story. "Long ago I decided to move from town and spend most of my time out here," W. began. He was content to occupy his time with observations of the natural happenings of the woods around him. "I don't really get lonely because so many visitors—like you guys—stop by." His intimate knowledge of the behaviors of his animal neighbors, paired with decades of handwritten weather records, made him an eyewitness to climate change.

Initially our interest lay simply in ascertaining when W. thought the river might freeze up, so we could gauge when to return with our sled dogs, but soon the conversation shifted to the trends of later freeze-ups, earlier ice-outs, and generally warmer temperatures. He went even deeper, explaining the consequences this warming trend had on the various inhabitants of the forest around him. "Bird and caribou migrations are now sometimes out of sync with the things they eat. I see snowshoe hares that turn white long before the first snow, or snow melted in the spring before they turn brown again, which makes it far easier for lynx and other predators to find them." In this little cabin along the Mackenzie River, here was a sage man effectively ground truthing climate change. As the teapot ran dry the hunters were bundling up in their warm layers and stepping out into the chilly afternoon. Although we were reluctant to climb back into our frosty canoe, we had a few more miles to go before we could camp.

We paddled about ten more miles and set up camp on an expansive gravel beach. This would position us within an easy day's paddle to Norman Wells and the end of this leg of the journey. As we drifted off to sleep, a strong south wind began to rustle the tent canvas. We were startled awake by a loud, violent flapping sound sometime in the middle of the night. The wind had caught a corner of our tent that we hadn't anchored well enough. Running outside in just our long underwear, we quickly had the tent shored up and climbed back into our sleeping bags with the knowledge that the next day would not be our last after all. Earlier in our journey we may have felt compelled to press on in weather like this, but within an easy day's travel of Norman Wells, we didn't see the point in fighting the elements.

Being windbound for one last day was actually a relief; we were not necessarily eager for the major shift in lifestyle that we were about to undergo. We were on the verge of extracting ourselves from five months spent living out of our tent, traveling under our own power, used to only the company of each other. Sure, there were aspects that we looked forward to—seeing family and friends, warm showers, ice cream—but we were anxious about returning to a world of cars, electricity, and schedules. We spent the day lazily reading and drinking tea as the wind raged on outside.

The warm, calm weather of the next day was a gift, and we knew to take full advantage of it. We packed up eagerly and efficiently. A light tailwind aided us under sunny skies. Clouds to the north loomed closer and darker as the day progressed. Bright white snow-dusted mountains lined both sides of the river. With just about eight miles to go, we ran into W. motoring upstream in his aluminum boat. He was on his way to visit his daughter in town and offered us a tow. We thanked him but continued on our own.

About a mile from town, several islands gradually came into view. The relatively large islands weren't forested. Instead they had dark, man-made structures on them that were slowly bobbing up and down. We eventually realized they were oil wells, perched on what we would later find out were man-made islands. Within half a mile of our destination, the surface of the water shimmered with the colorful, psychedelic swirls of an oily sheen. Paddling closer yet, our nostrils were assaulted with the noxious smell of the oil too.

How ironic that this leg of our wilderness adventure would end in Norman Wells—a town that was created not for hunting routes or fishing grounds, but the discovery of oil. The rhythmic march of the oil wells served as a stark reminder that soon we would find ourselves back in a lifestyle dependent on fossil fuels.

An impending storm signaled by the darkening sky compelled us to get off the water just as we reached the edge of town. We paddled around a jetty and pulled over near a dock where a bunch of small motorboats were parked. Absolutely no one was around. It didn't really sink in that this would be our last landing for a while as we stepped out of the canoe onto the gravel. In a rather dazed state, we ambled up the hill into town, which consisted of the Northern Store, two restaurants, and two hotels.

We stopped in the Northern Store to buy something that could transform our ordinary dinner of spaghetti into a celebratory meal: a pound of ground beef and a package of cookies. The Northern Store was right next door to a little diner, so we decided to stop in and warm up over hot chocolate and poutine—quite the splurge.

As we walked back to our canoe a white truck with a large decal of a polar bear on it pulled up. A man wearing an ENR (Environment and Natural Resources) baseball cap pulled low over wire-rimmed glasses and a brown mustache subtly streaked with gray introduced himself. "You must be Dave and Amy. I'm Keith." We had been emailing with Keith for a while about storing supplies in preparation for winter. It was great to finally meet this welcoming and generous man. We emptied our canoe and loaded our stuff in the truck, pausing to watch a curious cross fox run by. Keith drove us to a campsite south of town. We set up our tent so it would be sheltered by trees to the northwest in anticipation of incoming high winds.

The next day was Dave's thirty-fourth birthday and a whirlwind of activity. After a breakfast of leftover spaghetti at our campsite, Keith invited us over for coffee, showers, and laundry. Then he took us to the school to give a presentation to grades K–6. We were invited to dinner with a couple of teachers, one of whom offered for us to stay at his place. Tall and thin, Erik was close in age to us and had a light reddish goatee that highlighted his warm smile. We were impressed that this man we had known for just a few hours was opening his house to us. Erik drove us back to the school to pick up his girlfriend, Julie—who was the school librarian. With long brown hair and deep brown eyes, she introduced herself with a glowing smile. Together they drove us to our campsite to pack up. It was dark by the time we inflated our air mattresses and spread out sleeping bags, effectively setting up "camp" once again in their warm, dry spare room.

During the next several days we got to know Erik and Julie, and they happily offered for us to use their place as a base for launching the dogsled leg of our trip when we returned in January. We sorted our gear and worked on finalizing travel arrangements to get home, making the mistake of booking a flight to Inuvik on the smaller of the two airlines that serviced Norman Wells. On the day of our flight, a dense fog emanated from the river valley. The smaller planes were grounded because they made a stop in Fort Good Hope where there was no proper instrumentation to land in limited visibility. After our second day of showing up for a flight that was canceled due to fog, a cheery woman explained that the Mackenzie River is always foggy for the entire month of October. If only we had this information when we booked our original flight for October 1!

All was not lost by spending a few extra days in town. Keith suggested we go get a free meal at a community meeting for a new fracking operation. Put on by the oil company, the free food came after a slick presentation by a spokesperson who painted a rosy picture of what a new fracking operation would mean for the community. We found the spokesperson's claims that the polymer used in fracking liquid was completely benign and "actually a common ingredient in salad dressing" questionable. For the most part we tried to contain our incredulity—we were not members of this community after all.

We made the mistake of asking one too many questions before the presentation concluded. Although we genuinely wanted to understand the process, a loud woman in the audience angrily halted our second question (about how much water was required to be pumped underground into the wells) by accusing us of being some kind of "environmentalist agitators from Minnesota" just here to "stir up trouble." She was either a proponent of the new operation and the jobs it would create for the community, or she wanted to move the evening along to the free food. We were left with the realization that whenever meetings of a similar nature happened back home, we wanted to be engaged citizens.

On our third day of attempting to leave we managed to cancel our tickets with the airline of perpetually grounded flights and hop on a larger plane. As the plane took off over the gray, snow-covered river valley, we could hardly believe that after 166 days and 3,000 miles we were finally on our way home.

# 3

# Dogsledding to Great Slave Lake

*Norman Wells, Northwest Territories,*

*to Fort Resolution, Northwest Territories*

## 900 MILES

WE SPENT SEVERAL months at home waiting for ice to form, snow to fall, and daylight to increase. Our time was put to good use as we set a frantic pace of delivering presentations at schools, writing grants, and planning for the next phase of the journey. The dogsledding stage was, perhaps, the most logistically challenging of the entire North American Odyssey. We no longer had just our own needs and well-being to look after, but those of two more people and a dozen sled dogs. The remoteness of the terrain we would be traveling through added to the complications. We had many decisions to make, but fortunately, our two new traveling companions, Ellen and Van, were putting in a tremendous amount of work to get ready for our launch in early February.

We had worked with Ellen for several seasons, guiding dogsledding trips at Wintergreen, and she had proven herself more than up to the task of dogsledding in the Northwest Territories. Around Wintergreen it was a running joke that Ellen and Amy were interchangeable because their similar appearance and demeanor caused guests to often get them confused. With short brown hair, similar height, and glasses, it is no wonder guests got them confused or thought they were sisters. Ellen's studiousness, thoughtfulness, attention to detail, and perpetual good attitude made her a great expedition partner.

Van had cut his teeth in a similar fashion, leading weeklong to monthlong dogsledding courses with the nearby Voyageur Outward Bound School (VOBS). With wild sandy-brown hair and a mischievous grin, Van liked to kid around. If you happened to be unsure whether he was joking, his one raised eyebrow would be the tip-off. Van's wilderness skills as well as his ability to fix and build things were a real asset. He seemed happiest when he was working with his hands, and the dogsled he built for the journey was the best we have ever handled. Even while we were still paddling, Ellen and Van were planning our menu, securing sponsorships, and gleaning knowledge from their Ely neighbors who had previously conducted successful Arctic expeditions.

The last two hundred miles of our three-thousand-mile drive from Ely, Minnesota, to Norman Wells, Northwest Territories, would be over winter roads. These are not just snow-covered roads but roads that exist only in the winter, as they are made across frozen lakes, rivers, and bogs. We watched episodes of *Ice Road Truckers* to see what sort of driving conditions to expect, leaving us with an overdramatized impression of harsh road conditions in which trucks regularly slid off and broke through the thin ice. While we knew it was made for TV, we were still anxious about the journey.

The four of us had been debating for months about how many dogs we needed. We've generally observed that the more dogs one has, the more potential for chaos. Also, you reach a point of diminishing returns, because for every dog you add, you must factor in the added weight of that dog's food. In many ways, traveling with pulk sleds and one dog per person has its appeal. Pulks are smaller, individual sleds that are designed to be pulled by a person on skis or snowshoes. One dog per person, hooked up with a skijoring harness would allow for added power and speed. However, we wanted to be able to offer dogsled rides to all the kids in the remote communities we would travel through, and four dogs pulling small pulk sleds wasn't quite the image we were going for. We elicited opinions from our various mentors and fellow guides but received a wide variety of answers. In the end, we decided that two dogsleds pulled by six dogs each would be the most versatile and fit the loads of food and gear we were anticipating. This would also allow for two people mushing and two people skiing or snowshoeing to break trail.

As for trail conditions, we had no idea what to expect. Along the Mackenzie River and large lakes we anticipated firm, wind-packed snow, but in between was anybody's guess. Ellen had made several attempts to contact people in various communities along our route to determine whether any portion was regularly traveled by snow-mobile, and the answer she got was "It depends on the caribou." Apparently, if the caribou had chosen to travel through an area, then people would be out on their snowmobiles hunting them and we would likely find a well-packed trail. If the caribou were not in the area, we would most likely be breaking trail through waist-deep snow in the forested sections of our route. Trees block the wind, al-lowing snow to accumulate in deep, fluffy pockets. On wide-open lakes the wind packs the snow, creating a firm surface, meaning sled runners, skis, and paws don't sink in as far. On a wind-packed lake the dogs and skiers could travel as fast as five miles per hour, while six inches of fresh snow would slow our progress to one to two miles per hour. A foot or more would bring our progress to a crawl and greatly increase the physical toll on people and dogs, with two peo-ple packing a trail on snowshoes and the other two pushing sleds to help the dogs.

Our goal was to piece together two teams of hearty, well-furred sled dogs from a variety of sources. Our friend and fellow dogsled guide, Chris, loaned us six young dogs that were a mix of Canadian Inuit and polar husky—Tally, Porky, Domino, Jasper, Spyder, and Sage. Four malamutes came from a young musher in Ashland, Wisconsin, who raced with a team of Siberian huskies. Since she was increasing her racing schedule that winter, she worried that the malamutes would not get the attention and running time they deserved. Our nine-hundred-mile journey sounded like the perfect adventure for the malamutes, too, so Maddalen Malibu, Jim Beam, Nikai, and Iceberg joined our crew. Van had arranged to adopt a feisty purebred Canadian Inuit dog who was nearing retirement age from Outward Bound—Cirrus. She was a veteran lead dog, but we would have to keep her well away from any other female. That left one vacant spot.

As skim ice was forming on the lakes around Ely, we convened at Ellen and Van's place to work intensively, preparing gear, making things, and hatching plans. Stake out lines, ganglines, tug lines, a snow hook, and even a dogsled had to be made. Van was wrapping up construction on the light yet durable high-capacity dogsled. Now we just needed to figure out how to run the mishmash of dogs that we hoped would form two cohesive dog teams without too much fuss.

After a couple of weeks at Ellen and Van's, we had finished making and acquiring most of the dogsledding equipment that we would need, so we trucked our equipment and dogs east to our place. We had twelve acres, a sixteen-by-twenty-foot wall tent to live in, and a fenced-in patch of forest in which to contain the dogs. It was an ideal spot for training the dog teams, along a little-used gravel road just south of the Boundary Waters Canoe Area Wilderness. Here we could run the dogs pulling a four-wheeler until the snow and ice were thick enough to use dogsleds. We made steady progress with our training, building two teams that didn't tear each other apart. Dogs are creatures of habit, and as we consistently fed and ran them, we gradually built the dogs' trust in us.

Before long snow blanketed the ground and we were able to use our dogsleds. Each day we made it farther and farther down the Brule Lake access road until it became commonplace to reach the end of the road four miles from our tent. Once the lake ice grew thick enough and we had most of the equipment we needed, we decided to go for a two-night training trip.

Ellen and Van had gone to Ely to wrap up loose ends, and while they were there, they heard that our retired sled dog, Fennel, was fit and energetic. Shortly after our wedding, we had brought Fennel back to his original owners, figuring we had no way to care for him while we were gone. Fennel was ten years old, so we assumed that it was time for him to retire and live out his final days as a house pet. Hearing that Fennel was full of pep was enough of an endorsement to at least see how he did on this training trip, so Ellen and Van stopped to pick up Fennel on their way back to our place.

Fennel was half black lab, half polar husky. He had been quite a surprise when he was born considering that all of his littermates were entirely polar husky. His owners, Bert and Johnnie, recalled a black lab visitor at the neighbor's and realized how Fennel came to be. Fennel grew up to become a sled dog despite his black lab appearance. He had floppy ears and the black sheen of a lab with the warm, downy undercoat of a sled dog, plus a white belly and white markings on his front paws that looked like socks, weighing in at a little over a hundred pounds. Over the years of running on Bert and Johnnie's team and then on ours, he became a stalwart lead dog. Perhaps the black lab in Fennel made him such a good lead dog, as he was especially eager to please humans. His only vice was that anytime the dog team was not moving forward, he would bark—continuously.

It was dark and snow began to fall by the time Ellen, Van, and Fennel arrived. Slightly overweight, but very enthusiastic, Fennel burst out of the car door as soon as it came to a stop. This was a homecoming for him, having spent many summers on this land. He was rather surprised to find his dog yard full of dogs he had never met before. Hearing him root around the perimeter, the eleven occupants erupted in a howl to greet him.

In the morning we loaded up our sleds and harnessed all twelve dogs. The dogs picked up their pace when we told them to keep going beyond our usual turnaround point. We gracefully glided onto the snow-covered ice and across Brule Lake. Fennel fit right in, taking over as the experienced male lead dog that we needed.

After just two days of dogsled camping in subzero weather, we assessed what changes we needed to make to our gear and, more importantly, how we got along as a team. All went well as we completed our loop over frozen, trackless Boundary Waters lakes. Just two nights of sleeping in such close proximity in our Snowtrekker canvas tent led to the addition of one critical piece of gear—earplugs to mitigate the intermittent snoring of both male members of our party.

The final couple of weeks were spent at Van's parents' lake home, running dogs and working in their heated garage to construct our dog trailer and put the finishing touches on Van's dogsled. Dave made a final trip to Chicago to conduct several school assemblies. He returned with a Chevy Suburban, which we would use to haul ourselves, the dogs, and all our supplies north.

We packed massive quantities of human and dog food. Each one of us would consume two pounds of food per day, roughly the caloric equivalent to eating three Thanksgiving dinners every day. The dogs had a high-powered kibble that we ordered by the pallet-full, plus lard that came in fifty-pound blocks. Contemplating how difficult it would be to chop up equal portions for the dogs each night in temperatures of negative 40 degrees Fahrenheit or colder, we opted to precut all of the lard. The human food equivalent to the lard were hundreds of chocolate truffles that Ellen and Van made. Our daily truffle ration would be four per person.

Our time at home had been important and productive, but stressful. As our date of departure neared, we were all anxious to leave, craving a return to the rhythm and simplicity of life on the trail. Preparing gear, packing food, living together, and running dogs provided us with a chance to bond. Of course, we had the occasional disagreement—which was eventually resolved by polite discussion and a vote. All of this interaction would be critical once we began dogsledding because we would have a better understanding of each person's demeanor, communication style, and limits. In other words, we could trust one another as if our lives depended on it, because they did.

A cold snap hit Ely as we departed in the afternoon on January 18, 2011, bracing ourselves for the three-thousand-mile drive. The Suburban and trailer were filled with four people, twelve sled dogs, thirty-five hundred pounds of food, two dogsleds, and a canoe. (Always thinking ahead, we would store our lightweight Wenonah Itasca canoe in Fort Resolution to be ready for resuming our travels in the spring.) The negative 28 degrees Fahrenheit reading on the bank's digital display was warm, we joked, in comparison to the cold and darkness we would be experiencing soon. It would take us ten days to reach Norman Wells.

After Yellowknife, Northwest Territories, carefully portioned-out human food and bags of dog food were squirreled away in storage sheds and garages along our route. From Norman Wells we planned to dogsled down the Mackenzie River, over to Great Bear Lake, past six First Nations communities plus Yellowknife, and then across Great Slave Lake to end in Fort Resolution. Our maximum load would be three weeks' worth of food; at a rate of two pounds of food per dog and human per day, a maximum of 672 pounds of food would have to fit in our sleds, plus all our camping gear.

Our round-the-clock driving schedule and the diminishing daylight as we drove north left us regularly viewing a night sky filled with dancing green aurora. The landscape grew hillier, and the winter road began at Wrigley as we braced ourselves for a harrowing *Ice Road Truckers*–like experience that never materialized. Blowing snow and the occasional slippery spot were all the drama we encountered.

\* \* \*

WE ARRIVED AT Erik and Julie's in Norman Wells on January 28 after ten days and nights on the road. Despite the onset of twilight and negative-40-degrees air, Erik, Julie, and their gangly boxer, Tuku, ran out of a steaming doorway at twilight to hug us and greet the dogs.

The dogs stretched and sniffed the dry, cold air as we lifted them from their dog boxes and onto the squeaky snow. They were glad to be out, and their excitement seemed to be cued by our own. Porky especially had a new glimmer in his eyes, indicating his keen awareness that we were about to embark on a new adventure. Immediately it was clear that these dogs were all well suited to this climate as most happily rolled in the deep snow. We, on the other hand, were freezing. The time spent in the climate-controlled vehicle had made us soft. The subzero air stung our noses and throats as we inhaled; our fingers in insulated leather work gloves soon began tingling—a sign that numbness was not far behind. Once the dogs were fed and bedded down for the night, we were all relieved to retreat inside to the heated workshop and spare room in the cabin.

It wouldn't take long for us to settle into some semblance of a routine that involved waking up several hours before sunrise and going to bed four or five hours after sunset. On the day we arrived the daylight lasted for about six hours, with the sun rising around 10:30 a.m. and setting shortly after 4:30 p.m. Although we had known to expect such short days, actually living them took some getting used to. We had, however, planned our launch after the solstice, so we knew that the days would quickly increase in length. In fact, an hour and ten minutes of daylight would be gained by the time we departed on February 7, and every day we would gain about seven minutes more. This knowledge helped us endure the cold and darkness at the outset.

We harnessed up the dogs and went for a training run every other day to get acclimated. After a couple of blocks of residential streets and a thicket of willows we entered a narrow tunnel of snow-plastered, stunted black spruce trees, reminiscent of *Doctor Zhivago*. The snow that coated the spruce branches in bread loaf–sized lobes weighted the branches so much that they angled down severely, like a forest of closing umbrellas. How could their branches support such an absurd load of snow? The scraggly trees were not much taller than the tops of our heads, but they were probably quite old—belying the harsh climate in which they grew. Most days were clear and oppressively cold despite the dazzling sun glinting off each of the billions and billions of snow crystals that coated the spruces and piled in waist-deep undulating waves on top of the frozen bog. We squinted into the glare to keep an eye on the dogs as they happily trotted along. The heat of their bodies and vapor from their breaths rose around us like a jet contrail.

The snow-covered spruce branches surrounding us muffled sound. All we could hear was close and self-created: the rhythmic panting of the dogs, the faint jingling of the tags on their collars, the continuous swish of sled runners across the snow. We each became more aware of the rhythmic pulse of our own heartbeat and breath, which increased in cadence and volume when running behind the sled to warm up.

As enchanting as the frozen landscape was, the cold that seeped into mukluks from below and stung our lungs if inhaled too quickly served as a reminder that it was a harsh place. Any little mistake could rapidly cascade into a serious emergency in an unforgiving climate like this. Our training runs lasted only a couple of hours before the dogs returned to their straw beds and we returned to Erik and Julie's warm cabin.

An ecstatic Julie, in her black down parka and oversize rabbit-fur mittens, joined us for one run as we made our way through their neighborhood and out to the river for the first time. At some point she hit a bump and the sled tipped over, but like a true musher, she held on and was dragged until Ellen came to her aid and stopped the dogs. Julie kept smiling despite a rapidly swelling black eye. Too bad she had to go to work at the library immediately after. This incident, plus an accidental detour through the neighbor's yard to investigate their two stunned and frantically barking pet dogs, resulted in several people in town telling Erik, "These people don't know what they're getting into. They'll die out there." To the four of us who were about to head out on the land, this expression of concern was more humorous than startling.

Although it didn't look like it at times, we did know what we were doing. We just had to iron out the kinks, and we were glad to be doing it near town.

The highlight of our time in Norman Wells was a visit to the school. We selected the fluffiest and calmest dog to join us—Iceberg. After several assemblies and classroom visits, the four of us plus Iceberg had met every student. The students' favorite activity seemed to be calculating the weight of our dogsled and then determining how many students equaled that weight. We then loaded up the sled with six to ten students and had another group pull the sled across the room along with Iceberg in the lead.

By the end of our stay in town we no longer cringed every time we stepped out the door. The dogs were happy, strong, and fat. We left Norman Wells on Monday, February 7, 2011. Before heading to work, Erik gave us tobacco in a handwoven pouch to make offerings during our journey. We harnessed up the dogs and were off by sunrise as Julie stood in the driveway waving.

* * *

WE BREATHED A sigh of relief after successfully navigating the snow-covered streets leading to the river. The weight of the sleds and our more serious demeanor cued the dogs into the fact that this was not just another training run. Shortly after getting down the steep riverbank we stopped the dogs to place an offering of tobacco on a piece of driftwood, asking the Mackenzie River to grant us safe passage amid the frenetic energy of barking and lunging dogs. As soon as we released our snow hooks the dogs fell silent and focused all their energy into moving forward.

The snow on the river was perfectly wind packed, just as we had hoped. The dogs soon learned the best route was a little lane of firm snow over smooth ice that lay between the steep shoreline and a jagged ridge of ice a few yards out on the river. That ridge consisted of jumbled pans of ice that had been kicked up by the current as the river froze. After a couple of hours of easy travel, we spotted several dark figures moving along the shore in front of us.

As we got a little closer, we could make out the silhouettes of five wolves. They were cruising ahead, close to shore. For the next hour they stayed one hundred to two hundred yards in front of us, meandering and frolicking at times. The scent of their canine relatives kept the dogs interested and moving at a fast pace. Even when we stopped for lunch on the ice the wolves seemed to wait for us. Eventually they crossed the river, picking their way through the jumbles of ice. Even after the wolves had vanished somewhere along that distant shore, we could hear them howling from time to time.

We came to think of the flat lane of ice as our own personal dog-sled highway. We were grateful to have easy travel conditions for our first day. Occasionally we would have to swing wide around the mouth of a creek to avoid overflow, where water from the creek had poured over the ice on the river before freezing. These spots could harbor dangerous pockets of slush, so we proceeded carefully, taking in the slopes of glare ice, cloudy blue green, with little crops of large white hoarfrost crystals coating the newest ice.

For our first campsite we tucked just inside a little frozen creek. We fell into a rough schedule of rotating chores that involved unloading what we needed for the night from the sleds, anchoring the stake out lines for each dog team, deharnessing the dogs, packing a spot for the tent with snowshoes and digging out a pit for the entrance and stove, gathering, cutting, and splitting firewood, building a fire to melt snow for the dogs' water, feeding the dogs, pitching the tent, hauling sleep systems and other items we would need for the night into the tent, and finally cooking dinner on the woodstove. Oftentimes we would drill a hole with a hand auger in the three-to-four-foot thick ice to gather water, but we would melt snow if we were camped too far from a good spot to gather water or if the snow and ice were too thick. While sawing logs for the stove, we admired the view from our perch on the riverbank—the terrain we had just covered that day, now glowing orange and pink in the setting sun, and the dogs curled into balls with their noses tucked in their tails in front of glistening, irregular blocks of river ice.

Eventually we lost our little highway as we rounded a bend in the river that collected deep snowdrifts. This spot had been immune to the wind, so the snow was loose and sugary. To make matters worse, the jumbles of ice butted right up to the shore. For much of the day our best option was to work our way along the slope of the shore. The slant we were traveling on meant not riding on the sleds but trudging behind, pushing and working to keep them upright. Van skied ahead to scout the route. Dave switched to snowshoes to help maneuver the sleds in tricky spots. The lead dogs swam through the sugary snow as the other dogs dutifully followed. The pushing and pulling and periodic uprighting of the sleds was strenuous work.

Later in the day Van, too, donned snowshoes and hooked up a rope to the first sled, to essentially become a seventh dog. All humans and dogs were thoroughly spent by the time we pulled up to a creek mouth for the evening. The dogs were asleep immediately after their harnesses came off. Luckily wood was easy to find and the temperature was mild. The sky clouded over, and it actually warmed up throughout the night. Although our day had been challenging we never thought of ourselves as battling the elements. We would instead pay attention to our surroundings and follow Mother Nature's lead.

People and dogs settled into a rhythm, and negative 20 degrees Fahrenheit began to feel warm. We grew accustomed to the rotation of camp chores as well as alternating skiing and dogsledding days. Our system of lashing the sleds with Ellen and Van's innovations allowed us to do so without removing mittens. Packing the sleds coincided with the coldest time of each day. With the sun's rays still hidden below the horizon, a sense of urgency loomed over us as the cold seeped through our thick down pants and parkas and layers of fleece or wool to chill us to the core. At negative 40 degrees the only way to stay warm is to move by running, skiing, hauling wood, or jumping jacks in a moment of delay. The twenty minutes it took to load and pack the sleds felt like an eternity. Fingers stung as extra skis and poles were lashed on top of the load.

By the time we were approaching the town of Tulita, where we would pick up our first resupply, we all felt as if we could continue this mode of winter travel indefinitely. Bear Rock rose up to the east, identifiable by its 400-meter (1,312-foot) height and three dark splotches. We heard the buzz of a snowmobile several minutes before we saw it; a man in a traditional style anorak and large fur hat appeared and paused to take photos of us. Before long we were shaking mittened hands with Ron. He wore large beaver-fur mitts embroidered with tiny colorful beads, which we would later learn his mother made for him. He appeared to be in his fifties, but his weathered face, partially hidden behind shiny aviator sunglasses, made it hard to know his actual age. "Did you see any moose?" were the first words he uttered to us. We had not seen the animals themselves, but we had seen moose tracks and depressions in the snow where several had bedded down recently. Apparently this time of year the moose made their way to the Mackenzie River. Ron explained that the local people were well aware of the habits of the moose because they are an important food source.

He then explained the meaning of Tulita—"where waters meet"— since this was where the Great Bear River enters the Mackenzie. The origin of the dark ovals on Bear Rock reminded us of Adeline's story of the smoking hillside. This Dene legend involved a family of beavers that were attacking people, so a giant named Yamoria tracked them along the river. He killed the three beavers and skinned them. He stretched their massive pelts on Bear Rock.

Ron led us into town. The dogs, excited at first by the snowmobile, grew accustomed to Ron zipping off ahead to show us the way and periodically pausing to shoot more photos. On the hard-packed winter road, with light sleds and a snowmobile to chase, the dogs increased their speed, outpacing the skiers, who hopped on top of the dogsleds. After climbing a hill and leading us through several residential blocks, Ron stopped his snowmobile outside a substantial tan building—the ENR office. This would be our home for the next several days. We got the dogs situated and pulled our personal bags out of the sleds before Ron gave us a tour inside and treated us to steaming cups of black tea and fascinating conversation.

Ron shared with us his landscape photography to "give us a feel for the land when it isn't covered in snow." He told us about the semi-annual caribou hunt, which was by snowmobile or boat depending on the season. People would travel to a lake along the caribou migration route, then hunt and harvest caribou for food and hides. The community and government would send a plane to the lake to pick up the meat and hides.

Ron arrived the next morning, started the coffee maker, and gave us homemade bannock and moose meat. He described the traditional Mountain Dene method of hunting moose in the mountains: trekking uphill on foot, hunting several animals, and then building boats out of moose hides to paddle the meat downriver to the village. Ron later took us to a community lunch, where we met several elders and learned "mahsi cho" is how to say "thank you" in Dene. A man at the lunch, Jonas, took an interest in us and guided us over to the school to show us a traditional moose-skin boat that had been made the previous summer.

Back at the ENR office we poured over more of Ron's images, and he shared part of his personal history with us. "When I was a young boy the Canadian government was forcing First Nations kids to go to residential schools." Ron described how he hid when people came to collect the youth in his community. But he was eventually caught and forced to leave his family to attend school in Inuvik, over three hundred miles away. Ron matter-of-factly told four almost strangers about this traumatic part of his life, but his expression changed as he said, "When I returned, years later, I couldn't speak to my father. They made us speak in English, and I had forgotten the Dene language." Prior to this conversation we knew of this dark chapter in Canadian and United States history, but Ron made the horror of it sink in.

In Canada, "First Nations, Inuit, and Métis Nation children were taken from their families and communities to attend schools which were often located far from their homes." Over a 150-year period more than 150,000 children attended Indian Residential Schools in Canada. The first such school opened in 1831 and the last closed in 1996. According to the National Centre for Truth and Reconciliation, "The explicit intent was to separate these children from their families and cultures." The Indian Act of 1920 was the beginning of forced attendance for Indigenous children ages seven to fifteen. The schools, often underfunded and overcrowded, lacked in the quality of education provided and harshly punished children for speaking their own languages. Thousands of students "suffered physical and sexual abuse at residential schools," and all suffered from "loneliness and a longing to be home with their families." The damage of this forced assimilation resulted in an erosion of the distinct cultures, traditions, languages, and knowledge systems of these peoples— and it is still felt today.

This dark chapter of history was not unique to Canada. The United States opened its first Native American boarding school in 1801, and Canada modeled their residential schools after the US boarding schools. Eventually, hundreds of these boarding schools were established or supported by federal agencies like the US Department of the Interior or the US Department of Defense. "Congress enacted laws to coerce Native American parents to send their children to the schools, including authorizing Interior Department officials to withhold treaty-guaranteed food rations to families who resisted." Assimilation was the goal, cutting students' hair, renaming them, and punishing them if they spoke their native language.

Progress has been made toward acknowledging the past wrongs in both countries. Between 2007 and 2015, Canada's Truth and Reconciliation Commission heard from more than 6,500 witnesses, hosted events throughout the country to engage and educate the public, and created a historical record of the residential schools system. The six-volume final report included ninety-four "calls to action" to further reconciliation between Canadians and First Nations peoples. The United States lags behind but is following suit with the Truth and Healing Commission on Indian Boarding School Policies Act, which was sent to the House or Senate for consideration on June 7, 2023, and ordered reported (meaning a committee has voted to issue a report to the full chamber recommending that the bill be considered further).

We left Tulita on a Saturday with warnings about traffic on the winter road related to an ice-fishing derby and volleyball tournament in next community, Deline, roughly seventy-five miles away. Several people gathered to see us off, including Ron, even though he was preparing to head out moose hunting. He pointed to our overfull sleds, newly packed with two weeks' worth of human and dog food, and wryly commented, "It looks like you have a lot of stuff." Barking dogs hindered any further conversation aside from a sincere "mahsi cho" from all four of us to Ron. We followed the Ski-Doo trail that paralleled the pipeline out of town and eventually popped out onto the winter road. Soon we realized that there was no need to be concerned about traffic; we saw a total of two cars—driving very slowly with their occupants excitedly waving and taking pictures of us.

* * *

THE DOGS WERE running fast despite the added weight to the sleds. Conditions were certainly faster than ever on the icy winter road, but that wasn't the sole reason for their pep. At negative 50 degrees Fahrenheit, the dogs, with their thick fur coats, were comfortable. We've observed the Canadian Inuit dogs run slower at temperatures above negative 20 degrees because they are too warm. It was difficult for the skiers to stay in front of the dogs, and they began shedding extra clothing despite the extreme cold.

Fortunately, we found a small trapper's cabin that we ducked into for lunch. With a fire going in the barrel stove, we were able to ward off a chill and even dry our sweaty base layers. It didn't take long for us to decide to just stay put for the night. There was an ideal sheltered spot for the dogs, and we anticipated the coldest night of our journey so far. We gathered more firewood and cleaned up the place, namely removing a few frozen pine marten carcasses before they thawed. The twelve-by-twelve-foot cabin was beyond rustic, but at negative 50 degrees it felt like a palace.

A cold morning greeted us outside the cabin door. Standing still was simply not an option. Fingers and toes would begin cooling as soon as our heart rates slowed, no matter how many thick layers we wore. We stomped our feet and took turns running in circles as we packed the sleds and prepared to leave. Steam rose from the dogs' mouths and bodies, collecting in a cloud above the teams, backlit by the rose-colored glow of sunrise. This was a cold none of us had experienced before.

At some point the next day Cirrus managed to attack her arch-nemesis, the young, spunky malamute Maddalen Malibu. And Maddalen handily won by biting Cirrus's ankle just above the paw, which didn't bleed but soon swelled to twice its normal size. We looked for a spot to camp ASAP, pulling off onto a frozen creek, and quickly set up camp before bringing Cirrus inside the tent to inspect and wrap her leg. We let the invalid sleep in the tent until she got too hot and was pawing at the door to go back out into the negative-54-degree night. The next morning we decided that Cirrus's injury warranted a day off. It also happened to be the coldest day of our trip thus far. So we stoked the fire in the woodstove and settled in for a cribbage tournament, with Cirrus contentedly napping in the coolest corner of the tent.

We chose the warmest part of the day (negative 40 degrees Fahrenheit) to venture outside and gather more firewood. We strapped on snowshoes and followed the creek to where it entered the Great Bear River. There is nothing quite like the silence of winter, surrounded by snow-coated spruces. A pause to listen reveals silence all around and a keen awareness of one's own breath and heartbeat. The snow was deep and the sky perfectly clear and sunny with a slight wind blowing out of the north, chilling an unprotected face. Once we reached the river, steam was visible in the distance, created by open water exposed to that crisp, cold air—sea smoke, essentially. This was an example of why the Great Bear River is not used for winter travel. It is narrow and deep, with a fast current that keeps portions of the river open even in extreme cold. A deadly beauty emanated from the tendrils of steam backlit by the afternoon sun.

The next day was a bit warmer, and dogs and people were ready to move. We were keen to reach the remote community of Deline on Great Bear Lake. Cirrus was still not bearing weight on her paw, so she would be a passenger for the day. Although she squirmed and protested as we loaded her into the sled bag, the instant the sled was underway, she fell asleep and remained in her little cocoon all day. Spray-painted orange paper plates on wooden stakes appeared every eight kilometers, and our countdown to Deline began. Catching glimpses of the river from the road we observed trees encrusted in a thick layer of hoarfrost from the dark patches of steaming open water.

A short, steep hill flung us onto Great Bear Lake's vast frozen expanse. The dogs picked up speed and trotted happily down the wide ice road plowed across the eighth largest lake in the world. Ahead of us a plow truck was battling the wind's constant attempt to cover the road in drifting snow. The faint outline of rooftops and buildings dotted the shoreline five miles across the bay. With the temperature hovering around negative 43 degrees Fahrenheit during the warmest part of the day, we were looking forward to resting in Deline for a couple of days and awaiting slightly warmer temperatures before continuing our journey.

A truck heading toward town rolled slowly past us, and we waved at its smiling occupants who were pointing and staring at us from the cab's bubble of warmth. Soon vehicles were driving out from town in a steady trickle to wave and take photos as we approached. A red truck slowed to our pace, and several members from the tribal council welcomed us to town. They explained that everyone there had two-way radios in their houses and vehicles, and the first truck that passed us had announced our arrival, so everyone in Deline knew we were coming. When we asked them if there were any good places to camp on the edge of town, they didn't provide much of an answer before driving away. "Boy, they sure seemed surprised when you asked them about camping. Maybe someone at the school will have some ideas," Van exclaimed as he skied along next to Ellen's sled.

Minutes later another truck passed us taking photos. The truck turned around, slowed to a crawl, and a cheery couple rolled down their window. They asked where we were planning to stay, and we said, "We don't know; do you have any recommendations for where we could camp near town?" They glanced at each other and said, "How about you stay at our house? We are leaving town in about an hour to drive to Fort Good Hope for a volleyball tournament and will be gone all weekend. You will have the house to yourselves, and you can stake your dogs out in our yard." We asked how to find their house. The woman with a twinkle in her eyes behind dark-rimmed glasses said, "I'm Verna. This is Bruce. Everyone knows where we live; you could ask anyone in town. But we'll show you the way." Soon they were leading our dog teams through the streets of Deline with their flashers on. A myriad of smells, a smattering of barking dogs, and trucks filled with curious residents out for a drive in search of the dog teams made for an exciting trip down the icy roads with twelve amped-up sled dogs.

Before long we had the dogs staked out and Verna and Bruce were instructing us to help ourselves to anything in the fridge. Bruce also pointed out a pile of frozen lake trout in a shed out back that we could chop up and feed to the dogs. Once inside we realized that we had met Bruce a few months earlier when we were paddling up the Mackenzie River. He was out hunting moose and had stopped to chat with us briefly as we slowly paddled upstream. A few minutes later we were alone in a warm house, sitting in stunned silence, a little unsure what had just happened. "Well, that was awesome! I am going to make some tea, does anyone else want some? Who is going to take the first shower?" Ellen beamed.

Deline's five hundred residents are physically cut off from the outside world for much of the year, but winter roads made it relatively easy to travel between the communities scattered throughout the Sahtu Region for a few months. Deline is the only community on Great Bear Lake, which is smaller than Lake Michigan but larger than Lake Erie, so opportunities to visit friends and family in the handful of communities within a day's drive over the winter roads are cherished.

We saw mostly the kind, generous, happy aspects of the remote communities like Deline, but just under the surface, and sometimes in plain sight, these communities struggled with poverty, substance abuse, and domestic violence. Our hosts were so generous and trusting to invite total strangers with twelve sled dogs to overrun their house while they were away, but at the same time, we were doing them a favor by occupying their house and ensuring there weren't any wild parties or other acts of mischief in their absence. Like the land around us, the divide between joy and sorrow is often very sharp in the north. However, we were constantly surprised by the warm people we met who were filled with knowledge and love for their communities and land.

The dogs were as happy to rest and eat as we were. Barking, spinning, lunging, drooling, they worked themselves into a frenzy as we used an axe to chop the rock-hard fish into two-pound chunks, which they quickly devoured. On our first full day in Deline we took Maddalen to the school for her first assembly. Since she is a total princess, she absolutely loved all the attention and the students loved her.

We stopped by the white, metal-sided ENR building to pick up our resupply. A uniformed man with buzz-cut jet-black hair greeted us at the door with a smile. Leeroy had been expecting us. He invited us into his office to talk about our upcoming route across Great Bear Lake. In his khaki shirt with the polar bear logo on the sleeve and brown work pants, he was short but strong and slightly older than us. Leeroy's smile, accentuated by a short-trimmed goatee, never faded. The only prompt Leeroy needed was Van placing our maps on his desk. "I grew up here—hunting and trapping by dog team in the winter and motorboat in the summer," he began. We tried to envision Leeroy out in a small boat on the vast expanse of Great Bear Lake during the brief summer when it is ice-free. He talked about streams we would pass and small, crystal clear lakes filled with whitefish that hardly anyone visits anymore. He explained, "You'll be dogsledding through the heart of the caribou's wintering area, so I'm pretty sure there will be Ski-Doo tracks from local hunters."

Having covered the necessary logistics about our route, the conversation shifted. "Sled dogs have all been replaced by snow machines, but caribou remain an important source of food for the Dene." Leeroy explained that the caribou numbers have been steadily declining, leaving scientists and locals alarmed. Things were changing so fast, and the loss of caribou seemed like another slash at the Dene's cultural fabric. Looking up from the map, Leeroy said, "When you travel by dog team you see every rock, every tree. The land speaks to you. You can hear the land." His eyes took on a glossier sheen as he continued, "Now the young people always have their headphones on and they're staring at screens—TVs and playing video games. When they go outside they race around on Ski-Doos or in trucks. They can't hear the land, and so they feel lost. They have lost their purpose. I have been a hunter all my life. Being out on the land, bringing back food—that's my purpose, that is what I know. When I was a kid, if we had a couple fish hooks and a little string, I felt rich. We would spend all day out fishing and were proud to bring home food." He took a sip of tea before saying, "Things have changed so much."

Before we left, Leeroy offered to haul supplies to us about a week after our departure from Deline. "I'll be heading out that way on my Ski-Doo to look for some caribou anyway," he said. It would take us about three weeks to reach the next town, so having a few hundred pounds of supplies hauled out to us would be a huge help. Leeroy hoped to harvest a few caribou for the community after he dropped off our supplies. We all looked forward to seeing him again. We had started this journey with our eyes focused on the vast swaths of wilderness we would cross, mountain ranges, and ribbons of water that connected everything together, but people like Leeroy made us realize that the people we met were having just as profound an impact on us. In addition to hearing the land as we traveled slowly through it, we heard the land through the stories people in places like Deline shared with us.

The next day we harnessed up one dog team, comprised of our mellowest and best-behaved dogs, and offered dogsled rides to anyone who was interested. The first riders were adults, mostly teachers from the school. Eventually, kids got curious as word around town spread. Fennel and Tally got to know the route well, looping around the arena behind the school over and over again. Despite the cold everyone was smiling and having a great time. Leeroy's words about listening to the land kept running through our heads. It seemed so ironic that we were a bunch of white people from the United States giving Dene kids their first dogsled rides. Forty years ago there were five sled dogs for every person in Deline, and now there were hardly any. Snow machines and prefab houses make life easier, but do they make life better? If the caribou don't come, famine is no longer a real risk, but First Nations people in communities like Deline are two times more likely to be diabetic than the general public. The local store is filled with chips, soda, and other sugary drinks that are more affordable than milk or fresh produce. We had no answers, but the collision between a nomadic, subsistence lifestyle and the industrial world still seemed fresh here. Colonization, forced resettlement, influx of new diseases, drastic changes in diet, residential schools precipitating a loss of language and culture—all were part of a brutal and unfair history that we had only read about in books until now.

As we walked back to Bruce and Verna's that night, the northern lights were out in full force. Beautiful ribbons of green danced in the sky as we trudged four blocks across town through squeaky, negative-forty-degree snow with our breaths rising in clouds around our heads. But lying in our sleeping bags on the living room floor in

Bruce and Verna's house that night, we finally realized what scared us most about Leeroy's words. Here 80 percent of households still eat wild foods and practice some form of subsistence; in many ways they remain tied to the land (or deliberately returned to the land). Down south, in our communities, elders with a memory of a nomadic existence are long gone. The land has been carved and smothered, polluted and transformed into an unrecognizable shadow of itself. It had been more than ten months since we loaded our kayaks and set off from Washington. Millions of paddle strokes, several hundred nights sleeping under the stars, immersed in the solitude and silence of some of the world's wildest places, had slowly allowed us to start hearing the land and understanding that humanity is rapidly consuming our only planet. Clean water, nutritious food, shelter, companionship—these are the basic building blocks that we need to survive. In the city even the stars are smothered, and true silence is an unknown. Our people are lost, and as a result, all life is paying for it. The earth is crying out, but society just can't hear it. At least here there were still people like Leeroy who could hear the land and were trying desperately to get the next generation to listen.

* * *

THE DOGS ALL eyed us carefully as we loaded our sleds. Cirrus was putting weight on her paw and seemed to be back to her old, ornery self. With nearly five hundred pounds of food stacked in the bottom of the sleds it was hard to fit everything in. Our sleds had never been this heavy, and the deep cold caused sharp, fine snow crystals, which squeaked under our mukluks and made it feel like we were pushing the sleds across sandpaper as we maneuvered them into place. "It's a good thing the dogs are well rested," Ellen said as she leaned into the handlebars of one of the sleds.

"Yep, and we are eating thirty-five pounds of food a day, so that adds up fast," Van said as he grabbed the front of the sled to give a hand.

Once the harnesses came out the dogs went crazy; it was time to go. The teams rocketed through town on the icy roads, but once we hit Great Bear Lake the work began. Traveling across the lake was like walking on an uneven sidewalk. The wind had packed the snow into a hard surface, and our skis, paws, and sled runners barely dented the snow, but it was far from smooth. Ridges and troughs like shallow moguls of a ski slope stretching for miles caused the sleds to tilt and lurch across the uneven surface. The dogs couldn't pull the heavy sleds with the added weight of a person, so the guys jogged next to sleds while the women skied. Driving the sleds was hard work. Every minute or two a sled would stall on a big drift. Pushing as hard as he could, the sled driver would yell, "Ready, dogs, hike! Hike! Hike!" The dogs would lunge into their harnesses in unison to start the overladen sled, but once the sled was moving, they happily chugged along, leaving the musher to jog next to the sled.

Several days out of Deline we were moving along efficiently—back in the rhythm of traveling and camping, not to mention the fact that we had eaten enough to bring the sleds down to a more reasonable weight. The weather was unseasonably warm, with a high of 28 degrees Fahrenheit. The abnormal warmth was our first clue that something big, meteorologically speaking, was about to happen. The trail was well packed and fast. We marveled at how well the sled runners and skis glided due to the warmer temperature.

We had taken two days to travel across a large peninsula that jutted into the lake. The wind was picking up as we reached the other side, so we stopped for lunch just before making our exit onto the wide-open lake in a large bay called McVicar Arm. Here we had to decide between three options: (1) Camp where we were and wait to tackle the lake the next day, (2) head out onto the lake and hug the shore around the big bay, taking more time (probably several days), but playing it safe, or (3) cut straight across the bay, a distance of about twelve miles. We decided to go for it even though we would be pushing the limits of daylight. The first two miles were a trudge as we worked through deeper drifts in a small sheltered cove before reaching the wind-packed snow. Suddenly, a substantial tailwind developed, and our world was engulfed in white.

Ellen led us toward our approximate destination based on a compass bearing and then aiming toward a clump of trees on the distant shore. As the blowing snow increased, the trees disappeared. The skiing was effortless, but the navigating was nerve-racking. We didn't even have to move our feet to propel ourselves as we were pushed along by the steady thirty-five-miles-per-hour wind. The dogsledding became much more labor-intensive as the blowing snow accumulated in irregular drifts. Van held up his jacket as a sail, attempting to aid the dogs. Dave's sled was the smaller one, which had a load that was piled high and therefore was more top-heavy. So he strapped on snowshoes and spent most of his time pushing and working hard to prevent the sled from tipping.

Eventually each skier attached a length of rope to the gangline of the dog teams, looped it over one shoulder, and began acting as a seventh dog. For several hours all we could see was white. We later heard that Norman Wells had recorded gusts up to eighty-seven miles per hour (hurricane strength). The blizzard would shut down the winter road and knock out power for days as crews worked overtime, and a couple of roofs were blown off farther north. We also heard the sad news that an elder perished in an attempt to snowmobile from his cabin back to town.

Fear did not really enter into our thought processes. We were all gripped in an intense focus on the task at hand: get across the bay and stick together. Nothing else mattered. The only real danger we perceived was if an individual, human or dog, became separated from the group. In these conditions tracks would disappear almost instantly, and finding your way back to the group would be nearly impossible. Trust was paramount. We were moving as one—thinking, reacting, navigating together. There was no room for doubt.

Within a couple miles of our destination the blowing snow lightened. We still could not see directly in front of us, but patches of blue sky appeared overhead. Eventually treetops were visible above the blur of white, and with the telltale scent of land in their nostrils, the dogs picked up the pace. The sun set behind us, briefly illuminating the dog teams in a rose-colored haze.

We skirted the dark mass of shore until a little indent appeared. Ellen skied in and surveyed it with the beam from her headlamp to confirm that it was sheltered enough for our needs. We staked the dogs in the woods and pitched our tent on the ice. In the dark we could hear a chorus of lapping and smacking lips as the dogs wolfed down their kibble before curling up into contented, tired balls for the night. Once our chores were done and a quick dinner consumed, we did the same inside blissfully puffy sleeping bags. As we closed our eyes, it didn't take long for our ears to grow accustomed to the dull roar of the wind that pummeled the stunted spruce trees outside our tent. The temperature plummeted overnight, and the storm raged on.

We would be pinned in this spot for the next two days, only venturing out of the tent to gather more water and firewood or to tend the dogs. This was the perfect time to fry up a batch of doughnuts. Ellen also baked an elaborate bacon-and-cheese bannock. This extra downtime provided an opportunity to work on a website update and answer emails from students. Most of their questions were about the dogs, but some students asked about how we dressed for the cold or about the animals that lived in the region. It was odd to think of them in their climate-controlled classrooms or computer labs as we typed on a laptop, warming fingers over the woodstove. Fortunately, we were able to transmit our communications through the canvas, with the satellite terminal set up inside the tent as the blizzard continued.

Once we were able to move again, we revolutionized our method of travel by hooking all twelve dogs together to pull both sleds in a train. What we came to call the "mega team" was the ultimate in efficiency. In a team of six, if one dog hesitates to pee or sniff something, that dog slows all the others down, sometimes even resulting in the entire team stopping. With the big team, the momentum of eleven other dogs would keep even the most distracted dog moving. We could also decrease the weight the dogs pulled by having just one musher and three skiers. The blizzard had aided our travels in a way we hadn't expected—although more snow had accumulated, it was impressively wind packed. Travel on this densely packed snow with our mega team was ideal. From now on, anyone we encountered would ask us two questions: "Have you seen any caribou?" and "Where were you during the storm?"

Within a few days it was time for a resupply. Leeroy snowmobiled out from Deline to us, with our boxes of food piled into a yellow sled that he towed behind. The place we had chosen to camp was set back from the snow-covered ice, tucked in a small stand of spruces. Wanting to make sure Leeroy could find us, Van procured the yellow Voyageur Outward Bound flag that he had brought along for the occasional photo op. This would be the perfect thing to call attention to our camp from a substantial distance across the white expanse of lake.

We tried not to think of the fact that Leeroy had just left Deline that afternoon, traveling in a few hours the same distance that had taken us over a week. Rosy cheeked and dressed in a substantial fur hat, a sweatshirt, and bib snow pants, Leeroy beamed as he explained that he had a surprise for us. On his route he had tracked us and spotted each of the places where we had camped before. Since we seemed to always produce a bit more firewood than we needed, we had left it in little piles at each old camp. Leeroy had extra room in his Big Boggan sled, so he threw it all on top of the load. Our chores for the evening were made much easier with this ready supply of cut, split firewood. As he sipped tea in our warm tent, we quizzed Leeroy more about his life and experience on the land. He shared with us a couple of rules that he lives by in the cold weather. "Move slowly in the winter," he told us. "If you move too fast, you'll overheat and sweat—and then you get dangerously cold." He also told us, "Never travel at night."

Leeroy went on to explain how vital caribou are to the Dene. "From a young age, Dene children are taught the importance of respecting the caribou and the environment and only taking what they need," he said. "We use all the parts of the caribou—from the hooves to the brain and everything in between. It all has a use." The meat is eaten as well as most of the organs and bone marrow. The hide and bone can be used for clothing, tools, artwork, sleeping mats, and hundreds of other things. Traditionally the Dene made their houses out of caribou skins. Leeroy explained that the blood of the caribou is often saved and can be made into a soup or a drink. "Drinking the blood is supposed to make you strong and give you lots of endurance."

Leeroy imparted one last thought before we all turned in for the night: "We have long believed that a massive heart beats at the bottom of Great Bear Lake, pumping its clear water through the world's rivers and oceans—and it's the job of Dene elders to protect it."

Knowing the sky was clear and the temperature would drop to negative 30 degrees or so that night, we offered a spot in our tent, but he opted to sleep out in his Big Boggan. Opening the door, the warmth of the tent briefly escaped in a puff of white that was illuminated by the full moon and countless stars. As Leeroy settled into his sled, we checked on the dogs. They were a neat row of multicolored balls, curled tightly on the sparkling blue snow. Clouds of white rose above each of them like the smoke from a row of chimneys. The dogs had been perfectly silent all evening.

In the years between 2011 and now, remarkable progress would be made in Deline, and Leeroy would play a key role. In 2016 Deline would become "the Northwest Territories' first self-governed community—and the first self-governed community in Canada to include both Indigenous and non-Indigenous people." This was twenty years in the making. Earlier in that same year, Tsá Tué Biosphere Reserve would be created, giving the Great Bear Lake region UNESCO biosphere reserve status. We were not surprised to learn in 2018 that Leeroy was elected chief of the Délı̨nę Got'ı̨nę in their first self-governing general election. Actually, *chief* is not the right word to use; he was Ɂekw'ahtı̨dǝ́ (pronounced "e-kwah-tee-day"), which means "highest honest leader" in Délı̨nę Got'ı̨nę.

* * *

WE MADE GOOD progress with the mega team and enjoyed the clear sunny days. In the wide-open space of Great Bear Lake, both dogs and people grew accustomed to the frosted landscape that lay before us. We became connoisseurs of sastrugi. As we moved, we studied the spots where waves froze alongshore, forming smooth mounds of ice evenly spaced.

We took a turn that led us deep into a bay in preparation for portaging away from the lake, and discovered caribou tracks. One set of tracks soon multiplied into many. Laid over the top of the ungulate tracks were those of several large canines, and we envisioned a pack of wolves tailing the caribou. The dogs, with the scents of caribou and wolf in their nostrils, picked up the pace. We bid goodbye to the open expanse of Great Bear Lake and left an offering of tobacco as a sign of respect and gratitude for keeping us safe even in the throws of the blizzard. Our first portage led to Touchay Lake and through a series of smaller lakes, eventually leading to Hottah Lake.

Ski-Doo tracks left by caribou hunters converged on the portage. Leeroy had told us about some guys who traveled the route three weeks earlier, and we had been concerned about how much snow had piled up since then. In the woods, the trail had maybe four inches of snow drifted in. Not bad for a stretch of the route that we had been mentally preparing to break open. The mega team blasted through the portage enthusiastically. After the monotony of the wide-open lake, the dogs were almost drunk on the abundance of new smells that lingered in the forest. There were objects to pee on, too, interfering with the territorial markings of wolves.

It took a couple of days to reach Hottah Lake. The weather warmed to a more comfortable temperature, and the incremental increase of light resulted in us making more miles each day. The sleds were getting lighter with each passing day, so we decoupled the "mega team" and returned to our normal routine of six dogs pulling each sled. The caribou and wolf tracks became commonplace, almost expected, on the trail. A new, five-toed track was a great source of excitement when we realized its creator—a wolverine—was ambling across the lake's wind-packed surface a hundred yards ahead of us. This iconic predator once roamed parts of Minnesota, Wisconsin, Michigan, and even Illinois, Indiana, and Ohio, but they have been extinct in the Midwest for many decades. Watching its dark form lope across the snow reminded us that we were in a truly wild place. Wolverines require an expansive range, which has been incessantly encroached upon farther south. Spotting one of these members of the weasel family, with their distinctive short frame and dark brown fur with tan striping, gave us hope that this land would remain wild.

As we popped out onto Hottah Lake, we were greeted by the view down a white swath surrounded by snow-covered hills. We followed the western shore to the point where we were planning to meet our next re-supplier—Joe from Gameti. Rounding a granite outcrop, we looked for camp in a sheltered bay and tucked the tent into the woods, with the dogs staked out alongshore to bask in the sun.

The next morning, after sleeping in and a leisurely breakfast, we played cards. At some point Van walked out to get more water from the ice hole, but abruptly ran back to the tent, shouting for the rest of us to come out. A line of caribou had just begun ambling across the bay. The leaders tentatively emerged from the rocky shore to the north and aimed for the next point of land.

In the winter, Barren Ground caribou generally stay in small groups as they search for lichen, their primary source of food. When the snow is deep, like it was this year, they have to work to access their food while also staying alert for predators. One by one the caribou lumbered across the bay, heads slowly bobbing with each step. Silently marching in place to ward off the cold, we watched forty caribou stream by. In the winter the caribou are scattered over hundreds of thousands of square miles where they find shelter and food in the boreal forest. Come spring, something will spur them to migrate north across the Barrens to their calving grounds near the Arctic Ocean, continuing an ancient cycle. The caribou's densely packed, hollow hairs protect them from the brutal cold that sent us scurrying back to our warm tent.

Hoping Joe would arrive with more supplies soon, Ellen decided to bake a special treat for our guest. She spent hours rehydrating dried broccoli in warm water and coaxing dough to rise overnight in her sleeping bag in preparation for the feast. We were all sure that fresh pizza baked under our woodstove was going to knock the socks off Joe as the aroma of baking cheese and dough filled the tent. As the cheese began to bubble and brown, the faint whine of snowmobiles broke the silence, and a few minutes later Joe joined our little world.

Slim and weathered, it was clear he spent much of his time out on the land. His twinkling eyes scanned our tent, stopping on the mukluks drying along the ridgeline. "Nice mukluks. What is on the bottoms?" he asked. Joe seemed to ration his words, but we quickly discovered that if we listened carefully, we could learn a lot. "They are made by Steger Mukluks in Ely, Minnesota, the town where we live. I worked at the factory, but I don't know what the rubber is on the bottom. It's a company secret!" Van explained. Turning one in his hands, Joe flexed the sole and admired the stitching, but he preferred to harvest his own moose and have his wife or sister sew mukluks for him and his family with the hide. "Would you like some pizza?" Ellen exclaimed. "We just baked it as a special treat!" A bit confused, Joe politely ate a small piece, but markedly less enthusiastically than we had all predicted.

The conversation drifted to caribou, and we told Joe about the herd that had crossed the bay the day before. "Hunters have been coming up to Hottah Lake for several weeks now," Joe said, "because the caribou chose to winter here this year." He explained that throughout the Northwest Territories the caribou's numbers had declined. "This winter hunters from as far away as Yellowknife are driving up the winter road to Gameti, towing their Ski-Doos. When I was young, elders told stories of times when the caribou would stream for days across the frozen lakes in the spring as they migrated north to the Barren Grounds. Other years, the caribou didn't come, and people went hungry." Traditional knowledge has taught the Dene that the caribou populations ebb and flow, but, Joe explained, "This latest decrease seems different."

Scientists aren't sure what is causing their decline. Some people blame wolves, others blame overhunting. Joe wondered if fires were making it hard for the caribou to find food. In the summer he worked on a crew of firefighters from his community who were deployed on wildfires across Canada, and he explained that climate change is causing fires in the boreal forest as well as farther north on the tundra to become larger and more frequent. "The lichen the caribou eat takes one hundred years to grow; when a fire burns through, caribou change their migration routes. There have always been fires, but things are changing, and everything is connected. When I was a boy we would chisel holes through seven or eight feet of ice to set our nets," he said. "There is less than four feet of ice this winter. The winters are getting shorter and warmer, and the summers are hotter; many of the animals are acting different, but no other animal can provide for us like the caribou."

Hottah Lake and the route we were following between Great Bear Lake and Great Slave Lake is the traditional wintering grounds for two caribou herds, the Bathurst herd and the Bluenose-East herd. In 2010 the Bluenose-East herd was estimated to be 120,000 caribou, and in 2018 there were only 19,000. The Bathurst herd has fared far worse. In the 1980s the herd was nearly 500,000 strong; by 2021 there were an estimated 6,240 caribou left. This sharp decline is being seen all across the Arctic, where millions of caribou once roamed. In the last three decades caribou numbers have plummeted by 70 percent. A study conducted by NOAA in 2018 found that only one out of the world's twenty monitored caribou herds has a population near historic high levels. In Canada, the population of nine Barren Ground caribou herds has declined so dramatically they are now nationally listed as threatened, and two herds in eastern Canada are now considered endangered.

A hunting quota has drastically reduced the number of caribou subsistence hunters like Joe can take. While hunting pressure is often pointed to as a possible cause for the caribou's decline, the majority of the caribou that hunters like Joe harvest are males, which should have minimal impact on the caribou's ability to reproduce. New research is pointing to the construction of roads, mineral exploration, and mining-related activities scattered across the North as the major driver in caribou population decline and found that overall communities that rely on subsistence hunting have voluntarily harvested fewer animals during times when caribou numbers were down to help ensure the health of the herds. In the face of this, governments have put limits on caribou harvest while actively expanding roads and mineral development across the North.

In every community we'd traveled through since we left Dawson, caribou were a common thread. They are an important food source and perhaps the most culturally significant animal for many of the Indigenous people in Canada. The world's caribou populations have declined by 56 percent, from "4.7 million individuals to about 2.1 million individuals over the past two decades." Visiting with Joe, feeling the radiant heat of the stove warming our tiny canvas cocoon, rays of sunlight casting shadows of black spruce branches on the tent walls that swayed in the breeze, it was clear that more than the caribou themselves were at risk. For many Indigenous hunters like Joe, caribou are like water and air. They are synonymous with life. Caribou are food, shelter, and survival all rolled together. Today Joe can buy food trucked in over winter roads—chips and soda, white flour, and sugar—but it was clear his identity is closely tied to the land, and caribou are at the center of it all. Indigenous people like the Dene, whose ancestors have relied on caribou for centuries, have endured so much.

Colonization, displacement, forced settlement, and residential schools have battered cultures across the north. A recent study predicts the caribou in southern and eastern Canada, including the George River and Leaf River herds, which historically contained over one million animals, will lose 89 percent of their habitat by

2080. In 2022 the George River herd's population was estimated to be just 7,200 animals, a 98 percent decline from approximately 385,000 animals in 2001. For communities like Fort Good Hope, Deline, and Gameti, the projections are better but still stark. Climate modeling suggest that without major reductions in greenhouse gas emissions, caribou habitat will decrease by 60 to 70 percent across Western Canada over the next sixty years.

With the broccoli pizza gone and several rounds of tea consumed, Joe was ready to head out in search of caribou. We thanked him profusely and agreed to stop by his house when we reached Gameti. We gave Joe a lake trout we had recently caught—and his eyes lit up. He was much more excited about this fish than the strange pizza we had just fed him.

The hundred-mile journey took Joe less than a day on his Ski-Doo but would take us nearly a week by dog team, which Joe understood because he'd traveled this route many times with dogs in his youth. As the sound of his machine disappeared and winter's cold silence engulfed us, we stared across the bay to where the caribou had disappeared into the forest the day before. Hunters had stalked caribou for tens of thousands of years in an intricate dance between predator and prey. Life and death hung in the balance on both sides, but now the scale had shifted. All of humankind now seemed to have its thumb on the scale as our global thirst for resources mushroomed. Returning to the warmth of the tent, we couldn't help but dwell on the idea that, regardless of what is causing the caribou's decline, the Dene and the caribou are inextricably linked.

On March 12 we crossed paths with a group of caribou hunters on Ski-Doos. In addition to the usual line of questioning, they had major world news to share with us. An earthquake and tsunami had struck Japan the day before—the most powerful earthquake ever recorded in Japan. A nuclear power plant, Fukushima Daiichi, had been damaged. The death toll and extent of the damage to three nuclear reactors was still unknown, and we parted company wondering what sort of nuclear catastrophe would unfold on the other side of the world in the coming days.

The timing of this news was sadly fitting given the region that we were traveling through. For much of the dogsledding leg of the journey, we had been wowed by the vast wild landscape around us. This land that appeared so untouched by man actually held a dark secret that was only evident to those who knew where to look. While in Deline we had heard of Port Radium and the Eldorado Mine on the eastern shore of Great Bear Lake. Our route had taken us relatively close to the old mine site, but we didn't visit it.

Although we had considered taking a detour to the site where many people from Deline had been employed in the 1930s, another uranium mine lay in our path. We were at that very moment approaching the remains of Indore Mine at the south end of Hottah Lake. As we neared the shoreline, the dark figures of several large, dilapidated buildings came into view. We parked the dog team and trudged into the knee-deep drifts to poke into several of the closest buildings. We found the old mine shaft elevator and some of the houses used by the miners. From the skeletal remains of the buildings surrounding us, we tried to imagine what the mine would have been like during its heyday of operation in the 1950s. Now snow drifted in the mess hall, and the sole inhabitants seemed to be snowshoe hares.

In 1929 and 1930, silver and pitchblende were found on the eastern shore of Great Bear Lake, at what became Port Radium. What had been a very remote place became a bustling tent city. Barges ran from east to west on Great Bear Lake carrying ore from the mine across the lake and down the Great Bear River to the Mackenzie River. Ore had to be portaged around dangerous rapids. Workers (many from Deline) loaded and unloaded sacks of ore by hand, and much of the dust filtered through the sacks onto the men hauling, thus exposing them to high levels of radon gas and radiation during their employment. We were even told that sometimes the retired sacks were sewn together to make tents, in which entire families camped near the portages while the men were working.

Many people involved in the mining and transport of pitchblende developed cancer and died. They had not been warned about any dangers of being in contact with the radioactive ore and therefore hadn't taken any precautions against exposure. They would also later learn that uranium ore from Port Radium was used in making the first atomic bombs that were dropped on Japan during the Second World War. This awareness drifted in our minds along with the news of Fukushima we had just heard.

While the old mining structures are slowly returning to the earth and the place felt nearly as remote as it must have prior to the discovery of pitchblende, Dene exposure to radiation is unfortunately not over. The source is both ironic and tragic, a classic example of bioaccumulation in a major food source. Radiation travels with air currents and ends up concentrating in lichen, which thrive in wild areas. Lichen filter the air as part of their life cycle and therefore concentrate airborne particles—including radioactive particles. Caribou are one of the only animals specially adapted to eat lichen, and they eat a great deal of it. Consequently, caribou end up concentrating abnormally high levels of radiation in their bodies. In fact, "The reported concentrations of radioactivity in caribou and reindeer have been higher than in any other large terrestrial mammal."

Joe stopped by again on his way back home after a successful hunt. "We got seven caribou," he said with a beaming grin. "We eat all parts of the caribou. I find myself craving it when I'm away from home." He left us with a large bag of caribou dry meat. As we ate it over the next week, we enjoyed it immensely but wondered what the health implications would be if we relied on it like the Dene do, consuming it for our entire lives.

* * *

AS WE APPROACHED Gameti, the wind picked up from the southwest—a headwind, but the dogs didn't seem to care. The trail was well packed and the dogs were running fast, easily pulling light sleds. After nearly a month of traveling across the south shore of Great Bear Lake and then down through a series of remote lakes, we were all eager to spend some time in town. We traveled in silence, each of us lost in our own fantasies of various foods, meeting new people, showers, and clean laundry.

A truck pulled up, disturbing our respective reveries, and two women (one with a camera in hand) wasted no time in quizzing us about our journey.

"Where are you coming from?"

"Did you do okay in this recent cold snap?"

"Did you see any caribou?"

We followed their directions to the school—about three blocks away. One of them mentioned the time and we chuckled as we realized that the time had changed for daylight saving time a while ago and we had no idea. We promptly changed our watches and rejoined civilization after weeks out on the land where sunrise and sunset had been the only times that mattered.

We were eagerly welcomed at the school. Matt, the principal, had been expecting us and showed us an ideal spot for the dogs behind the school. Once the dogs were settled in and fed, we wandered in for coffee and a conversation. Stripping off many layers of outdoor clothing, we were soon aware of our own body odor, which was not helped by the fact that being in a heated building felt uncomfortably warm.

We would meet the kids the next day. In exchange for our planned presentation and dogsled rides, Matt had offered for us to stay at the school. After school let out, we had the building to ourselves, and we quickly hauled in our gear and food, hung stuff to dry, set up the tent in the gym, and then eagerly jumped into the locker-room showers.

We would spend several days in Gameti as had become the norm for our stops in these remote First Nations communities, the original goal being to give a presentation at the school and dogsled rides to all the kids, but as frequently happened, we were invited to dinner at teachers' and nurses' houses, and tea with community elders. Gameti, like Norman Wells, Tulita, and Deline, was accessible only by car in the winter—over the frozen winter roads. The rest of the year the town was accessible only by airplane. Our first full day was a busy one, filled with presentations and dogsled rides for all the students at the school.

We came to appreciate the facility—a brand-new gym with a massive projector screen that lowered from the ceiling with the push of a button, and the new state-of-the-art projector that we easily connected to our laptop. There were carts full of laptops charging; each student had a set of brand-new gym shoes and cross-country ski equipment. Mornings were filled with the scent of freshly baked whole wheat bread as bread makers churned out nutritious loaves for the students. There was buzz among the students about the upcoming trip to Italy. How could this school be so well-appointed and its students given such opportunities? We found out the principal was a skilled grant writer, and the relatively nearby diamond mine was the source of most of the funds. In fact, the diamond mine was a major source of employment for much of the town. Workers flew out to the mine to work for several weeks at a time.

On our second day, we dogsledded over to Joe's house to pick up another resupply he had stored for us since January. After looping around on the icy, snow-covered streets we pulled up to Joe's house. His dog, Bluenose, alerted him to our presence with a hoarse howl. His wife was in the kitchen, in the midst of cutting and hanging strips of meat on racks, preparing caribou dry meat.

As we hauled our boxes of food out of Joe's shed, we couldn't help but notice and ask about a few items that hung on the walls. He had several traditional drums in various stages of construction. They were beautiful. Joe explained how they would be used for playing hand games. Joe and his wife would be heading out of town later in the day, along with most of the town really, for the Dene hand games tournament in Behchokǫ̀. During this traditional guessing game, individual players or teams of players hide objects in one of their hands. As elaborate gestures and bluffing unfold to the sound of a beating drum, the other player or team must guess which hand the object is in.

Joe also showed us a decorative dog harness with a large padded collar resembling what a horse might wear for pulling a heavy load. It had bright pink, blue, green, and yellow tassels and long white straps that ran along either side of the dog. The traditional configuration for dog teams here was single file—better for pulling a toboggan through narrow wooded trails. Joe gave us the harness and a frozen caribou leg. He also offered Bluenose, to give us more dog power, but since we did not know if Bluenose would be accepted by the other sled dogs, we decided it was best to leave Bluenose with Joe.

As we left Gameti humans and dogs squinted into the brilliant white landscape capped by the iridescent blue sky. We released the snow hooks and paws dug in. From Gameti, our goal was to head south through a series of lakes and rivers toward the north arm of Great Slave Lake. Our route to Whatì was on the winter road, which was for the most part a true ice road, cutting dark bands across frozen lakes and rivers. Our skis and sled runners glided across clear, dark ice surrounded by chest-high berms of plowed snow.

At our camps we had plenty of daylight in which to do our chores, and we ate like royalty—sawing thick steaks off the frozen caribou leg. The character of the forest was gradually changing around us. On higher ground we found tall poplar, gnarled jack pine, and the pale green bark of young aspen. We celebrated our first wedding anniversary with more caribou steaks.

We rarely encountered any vehicles, but when we heard one approach, we pulled the dogs over until the vehicle passed. One semitruck pulled over for us, however. To our surprise, the driver hopped out and gestured for us to pass him as he snapped pictures on his little digital camera. José, who was sturdily built and dressed in navy blue coveralls without a hat or gloves, hardly let us get a word in edgewise as he invited us to stay at his place once he learned we would eventually be passing through Behchokǫ̀, where he lived with his brother, Mauricio.

We arrived in Whatì several days later, just as school was getting out. The usual formula of presentations and dogsled rides ensued the next day. The kids, however, had a special treat for us. They showed us how they play traditional hand games, with the sound of drums reverberating off the walls of their gym. We gave the rest of our caribou leg to the school, and the teachers invited elders to prepare it for a special dinner.

From Whatì we had only about one hundred miles to Yellowknife. We now had all the daylight we could possibly want, stopping well before sunset every day. Our headlamps were forgotten in the bottoms of our packs. The days were warmer too. The dogs no longer had the voracious appetites they did at the beginning. Some would politely take their daily chunk of lard and then secretively bury it in the snow. Fennel grew wise to these buried treasures. Animated barking from the victim would alert us to another lard robbery as Fennel scurried off to his nest to devour his prize.

Behchokǫ̀ is really three communities—Rae, Edzo, and Frank Channel—and the largest community of Tłı̨chǫ Dene in the Northwest Territories. It was the first community along our dogsled route that was accessible by an all-weather road. We tracked down José in Rae and set up our tent in the woods near his house. He had found out from the Wilderness Classroom website that we had traveled in South America and was excited to share some traditional foods from his home country of El Salvador with us. We ate our fill of homemade pupusas, yucca, and even a mango that was somehow available at the grocery store in Yellowknife. However, our most memorable treat was the piece of wedding cake we had packed in with our resupply to find us around our first anniversary. It was fun to split the piece of cake six ways so everyone got a bite, but everyone insisted that we eat the pastry swan that had miraculously survived.

The trail out of Behchokǫ̀ meandered through streams and bogs filled with whimsically shaped black spruce trees, and their elongated shadows cast cool blue stripes on the snow. We had heard we were in wood bison territory. Genetically distinct from plains bison, the larger and heavier wood bison once roamed much of the boreal forest, from Alaska to Saskatchewan. Hunting dropped their numbers so much that they were assumed to be extinct in the early

1900s. They're on the rebound thanks to a massive restoration effort, so we kept our eyes peeled for the gigantic animals as we passed through their territory, but we only ever spotted their tracks and massive piles of dung that we struggled to keep the dogs from eating.

After several days of warmer temperatures, the trees shed their snow, revealing the deep and varied greens of their needles that had been encrusted in white for most of the winter. Sled runners and skis glided better than they had all trip on that warmer snow. We were all quite comfortable, our bodies adapted to temperatures well below zero now operating in the teens and twenties. We shed layers like crazy—skiing without jackets, hats, and gloves. Lunch breaks had shifted from a frantic attempt to shovel in enough calories before fingers and toes got dangerously cold to an event to be enjoyed as every dog contentedly sprawled out to nap in the sun and we humans carried on a conversation while casually eating handfuls of trail mix and cheese. The early April days were growing luxuriously long, and we were making good progress south.

We were excitedly closing in on Yellowknife, the capital of the Northwest Territories. A sure sign we were getting close was a cabin with a bunch of dog teams parked outside. After a brief chat with a guide we found out they were on a day trip and had stopped for lunch. They were just leaving, so we parked our teams and prepared for potential chaos as multiple teams of Alaskan huskies passed our motley crew of Canadian Inuit dogs, malamutes, and polar huskies. Our dogs were excited and lunged toward these unfamiliar dogs, but we had driven our snow hooks in well enough to anchor them in place. They seemed like untrained brutes in comparison to the eight teams of Alaskan huskies that trotted toward us and then made a ninety degree turn onto the trail as if we weren't even there. We laughed about it over lunch and concluded that we appreciated the heartiness and personality of our dogs.

Our route was on a dogsled highway of sorts from there, eventually popping out onto Great Slave Lake south of town. Just before reaching the lake, we crossed a road, and a lanky man with wild curly blond hair stopped his truck to chat with us. His name was Max, and he had a kennel of Inuit dogs himself. He offered a place for us to camp—just across the bay from Yellowknife. We thanked him and said we might just show up there in a day. That night we opted to camp in the shelter of a rocky island and would deal with the big city the next day. It was warm enough to forgo the tent, so we fell asleep to the sight of the northern lights dancing overhead and the discernible glow of Yellowknife emanating from the north.

* * *

IN THE MORNING we followed the lakeshore right up to downtown Yellowknife. After traveling by dog team for a couple of months passing through small remote communities, we were excited and a little intimidated. We were accustomed to the occasional trapper's cabin or at most a row or two of single-story houses. A rugged, cliffy, and rock-strewn hillside dotted with buildings rose up to our left. The main street—Franklin Avenue—could be identified by the density of tall buildings surrounding it as it ran straight down the hill to the peninsula we were aiming for. The stark and angular forms of multistory buildings signified an entirely different world than the wild one we had grown used to. We parked the dogs near the ENR office, where we would retrieve our resupply, and then walked up the hill into the midst of pavement and tall buildings. It didn't take long for the scent of Chinese food wafting from a restaurant to tempt us into eating out for lunch. At the table we peeled off layers of winter clothing, trying not to feel too self-conscious about our appearance and body odor. In the end, no one seemed to care, and we happily gorged ourselves from the all-you-can-eat buffet.

After gathering up our resupply we cut across the bay to Max's place to experience his warm hospitality in a rustic log cabin and meet his pack of Inuit dogs. He invited us in for tea and we perused his shelves of books about Arctic adventures and trapping. He shared with us several tales of his own dogsledding and kayak ventures, having just returned from a dogsled trip to Artillery Lake in the Barrens. With a twinkle in his piercing blue eyes he explained in a Swiss accent how he ran dogs in a fan hitch in the Inuit tradition, pulling a large komatik that he built. "It was a good trip," he said. "I was worried about the pressure ridges, but there were only a few." A wolf pelt on the wall drew Van's attention, and Max explained how he ran a trapline in British Columbia in the fall and winter. "I take my dogs. Not many people run their traplines with dogs anymore, but that's my favorite way to do it. Their scent on the trail gets the animals curious. I trap more whenever I use the dogs."

The view from Max's place encompassed the city as well as a swath of completely bald granite to the north. Not even lichen grew on those rocks because they were downwind from the smokestack of a gold mine. For over fifty years, the Giant Mine operations polluted the surrounding landscape and waterways with arsenic trioxide, sulfur dioxide, and hydrocarbons. The worst of the pollution, however, is buried underground—237,000 tons of arsenic trioxide. One teaspoon of this stuff is enough to kill a person. The current solution for containing this toxic nightmare is to keep it perpetually frozen. One might assume that this wouldn't be too difficult in a northern climate, but melting permafrost in the Northwest Territories is already a major problem for public infrastructure and will only get worse as climate change increases. The Canadian government is in the midst of a four-billion-dollar, taxpayer-funded program to remediate the site, piping coolant throughout fifteen underground chambers and then keeping it frozen with thermosiphons.

We departed Yellowknife under a sunny, cloudless sky. With just over one hundred miles left to go, we were all feeling a mixture of confidence, excitement, and anxiety. The temperature hovered in the upper thirties, approaching the upper edge of the dogs' comfort zone. They were still happily trotting along, but we were concerned by their panting. Our days from here on out would include many short stops so they could eat snow and roll around to stay hydrated and cool. We slathered our own faces with sunscreen and quickly realized that our pink-nosed dogs—Cirrus and Tally—needed some on their noses too.

We worked our way east and south along the cliffy shore of Great Slave Lake as it tapered, debating when to venture out across the lake. We got far enough east that the crossing could be broken up by a clump of islands. The monotony of the glimmering white surface was broken by a couple of pressure ridges. These spots where sheets of ice collided, like tectonic plates forming mountains, presented a new challenge and potential danger. Weak ice or even open water can form around these ridges of jumbled ice. We approached with caution, and both skiers prodded the ice with poles as they scoped out the smoothest route across for the dog teams.

The overcast sky darkened just as we made it to a cluster of islands. The dogs were staked out and the tent up just as precipitation of an unfamiliar sort began to fall. Rain. That, more than anything, seemed to be our cue that it was time to finish dogsledding. It would take us a few more days to reach Fort Resolution, trailed by a curious lone wolf.

As we skied and sledded, we reflected on this stage of the journey. Many of the elders we had recently met were born in tents and spent their young lives traveling by dog team, hunting, fishing, and gathering most of their food. Trips to town were rare, and they are some of the only people on the planet who understand what it is like to spend weeks and months living out of a tent, traveling across the winter wilderness in the old way. These people had traveled by dog team and lived off the land because their daily survival depended on it. When listening to their stories, it was clear the freedom and simplicity afforded by a life without walls had deeply affected them. These memories were often shared with big smiles and animated gestures. A new glimmer of light burned in their eyes. Oftentimes stories would end with a long pause and a wistful glance out the window or a slow sip of tea as smiles faded and laugh lines relaxed before another memory they cared to share bubbled to the surface. They had found a willing audience in us as we sat, enraptured, attempting to imagine each scene they described.

People often asked us why we were on this journey, befuddled by the idea of living out of a tent with only the things we could carry with us, especially in the winter. We rarely gave a satisfactory answer because even we didn't really know. Deep down, there is just something that draws us to the land, to wild places. Reflecting on Leeroy's wise words, we realized that, at the most basic level, we were there to listen to the land.

On our final day of travel the dogs picked up on our excitement and were flying along despite warm temperatures. Upon reaching the Fort Resolution ENR building on the outskirts of town, Dave went to retrieve the Suburban and trailer. The dogs napped in the shade after devouring hot dogs, and we sat munching cookies, celebratory treats from the nearby Northern Store. The dogs woke up and soon went nuts once Dave rumbled up with the trailer. They apparently still remembered the vehicle that transported them north despite months spent on the trail.

The drive south served as a gradual introduction back into civilization. In the following week we made our way back to Minnesota and returned the dogs to their respective homes, but Cirrus would stay with Ellen and Van, and Fennel would stay with us. Back in Ely as we unloaded Chris's six dogs from the trailer, they enthusiastically jumped out and happily returned to their old dog houses, sniffing and scratching the recently thawed ground. All except one dog seemed happy to be home. Porky made eye contact with us; his brown eyes conveyed a look of deep disappointment. He preferred to be out on the trail, spending each day in a new place. We could relate. The adventure, for now, was over.

# 4

# Canoeing to Lake Superior

## *Fort Resolution, Northwest Territories,*
## *to Grand Portage, Minnesota*

### 2,750 MILES

OUR MONTHLONG HIATUS from the expedition consisted of
a whirlwind school assembly tour in Illinois and Minnesota inter-
spersed with brief visits with family and friends, our newly retired
sled dog, Fennel, in tow. Fennel settled right into the role of solo
pet. He also quickly became the star of our school assemblies,
during which we shared stories from the dogsledding journey with
the kids. We drove around with a dogsled on top of our Toyota
Yaris, generating lots of befuddled stares from other motorists in
Chicago traffic. The dogsled and Fennel were a key part of demon-
strating the importance of teamwork to the students. That sled
would move only once a critical number of student volunteers
came onstage to help pull it.

We created an online poll in which students decided that Fennel
should join us as we paddled and portaged from Great Slave Lake
to Lake Superior. He would pull his weight by carrying a little backpack on portages and "writing" a weekly blog entry called *Fennel's
Field Notes* on the Wilderness Classroom website. We were excited
to have him along, but we weren't sure where he would fit, or even if
he would make a good canoe dog.

An awareness that our time in the city was finite inspired a frenzied pace. Our school assembly schedule combined with a nearly

daily battle with Chicago traffic left little time to recover. We struggled to sleep despite a growing sense of exhaustion; the sounds of cars driving by, a train in the distance, even the hum of the furnace or a fan were now foreign to us.

By the end of May we found ourselves back outside the school in Fort Resolution, packing forty days' worth of food and installing our North Water spray deck on our gorgeous new nineteen-foot Wenonah Itasca canoe. This was the canoe we had hauled on top of the dogsled trailer to swap out with the heavier Wenonah Cascade that had safely carried us through substantial white water on our way north. The lightweight Itasca would be much easier to portage. After a trial run of packing the canoe on a patch of soft grass outside the school, it became clear that all our gear, food, and a 105-pound sled dog were not going to fit.

For the next five months we would be following dozens of waterways that were explored and mapped by the voyageurs in the 1700s and 1800s. Their canoes were filled to the brim with trade goods on their journeys into the vast Canadian interior and furs on their return to Montreal. Space was at such a premium that men taller than five feet eight were considered to take up too much room in the canoes, so they were not hired as canoemen. We could not change each of our five feet, ten inches of height, but we could remove the front seat of the canoe and sit on a pack as the voyageurs did.

That night we were once again ensconced in our familiar yellow tent on the outskirts of town. Listening to the hum of voracious mosquitoes outside and Fennel's rhythmic snoring from the vestibule, we settled in for a restorative, deep sleep. In the morning we would begin our travels south, meandering 2,750 miles through interconnected lakes and rivers through the heart of Canada down to Minnesota. Our time back home had certainly been worthwhile, but as we nestled into our sleeping bags, a feeling of contentment settled in, and we realized that a nomadic existence suited us.

The next morning a gentle current pulled us down the main channel of the Slave River. Spring had exploded while we were gone, fueled by nearly twenty-four hours of daylight. A river otter poked its head out of the water and huffed at us with curious alarm. Fennel lurched to the right when he caught its scent, sending the right gunwale dangerously close to the water. "Fennel! Sit, Fennel, sit!" The water was only a few degrees above freezing; Fennel was going to have to learn some canoe manners quickly. As we savored these few miles of easy downstream travel, we watched mergansers, tundra swans, various kinds of ducks, and terns floating in the shallows and resting along the river's muddy banks and bars.

Within an hour the temperature began to drop, and the river became more braided as we approached Great Slave Lake. The river's silt-laden waters resembled chocolate milk, making it impossible to judge its depth. Time and again we grounded on shallow, muddy sandbars, which forced us to hop into ice-cold muck in search of deeper water. Then, rounding a bend, we spied the vast frozen expanse of Great Slave Lake emerging from behind the stunted willows. Glimmering white pack ice stretched as far as the eye could see.

At first we were able to dodge small icebergs, but we quickly found ourselves surrounded by a slurry of broken candle ice. We pushed, paddled, and pulled our way through to the constant racket of ice scraping and breaking against the hull. After a quarter of a mile we reached a sliver of open water running along the shore. The ice-free lane was too shallow to paddle through, so we took turns walking alongshore, regaining sensation in cold toes while the other waded in the shallows hauling the canoe with a rope. We were wearing dry suits and thick neoprene boots, but frigid water sucked the heat right out of our feet and legs.

A small crescent-shaped patch of sand called to us, so we gathered driftwood for a fire and set up the tent. We rarely build campfires, but the radiant heat felt glorious on our numb fingers and toes. Our journey had just begun, but already our bubble of consciousness was narrowing in focus. Warmth, food, rest—these were the things we craved and cherished. Would the wind shift overnight and slam the sliver of water that made travel possible shut, or would we be allowed to continue? This seemed like the only question that really mattered. We had thirty more miles of Great Slave Lake's ice-choked waters to traverse. Locals had warned us we could get stuck for weeks depending on the whims of the wind, but we didn't have the luxury to wait. The lake typically isn't totally ice-free until the second half of July, and during the last few days of May it was still 90 percent covered in ice. Tired and sore after our first day, we were just happy to shed the modern world's dizzying pace.

Dawn revealed little change in the ice pack, and we followed the same thin strip of open water eastward. Fennel spent most of the day swimming, wading, and running after us as we slowly paddled and waded fifty yards off a sandy shoreline. Eventually he started whining, so we let him ride in the canoe as we dragged it through the icy shallows. A huge, dark gray wolf came trotting down the shore. Once it saw us, it stopped and stood there for a long while, staring and sniffing. We had never seen a wolf this close before; its long, thick coat ruffled in the breeze as we peered at one another.

We slowly clawed our way eastward by wading, paddling, and occasionally portaging when the ice was too thick to paddle through. It was slow, cold, physical work slogging through a frigid, ice-choked watery wilderness, but it was exciting and challenging. Out here life was simple. Discomfort and inconvenience were common, perhaps the norm in a nomadic existence, forcing us to focus our energy on the things that truly mattered and highlighting the smallest accomplishments and comforts. Reaching a point to finally take in the view beyond was cause for celebration. The radiant heat of a campfire never felt so good. Nestling into a sleeping bag, surrounded by the natural sounds of water lapping against ice and wind blowing through naked tree branches, triggered immediate and satisfying sleep for both of us.

Reaching the mouth of the Taltson River, we turned south and left the ice of Great Slave Lake. Hundreds of miles of mostly upstream travel awaited us. Paddling upstream was easy in comparison to the unknowns involved with a mostly frozen lake. We were, however, on a less-traveled path. Most who have crossed this region have chosen the much larger Slave and Athabasca Rivers—and they have paddled from south to north, with the current. By heading up the Taltson River, we were avoiding the Alberta tar sands, which flank the Athabasca River just south of the western corner of Lake Athabasca. Although that route may have been easier and more straightforward, we simply couldn't bring ourselves to knowingly paddle through such a fresh, deep wound in the earth—not to mention miles of river where the water was undrinkable. The tar sands, also known as oil sands, are "a mix of sand, water, and a heavy, viscous hydrocarbon called bitumen that can be converted to oil." Alberta, Canada, is home to Earth's largest-known oil sands deposits and third-largest proven oil reserve at 170 billion barrels, underlying about fifty-four thousand square miles of boreal forest. The tailings ponds are some of the biggest human-made structures on Earth—large enough to be seen from space. According to *National Geographic*, "They contain a toxic slurry of heavy metals and hydrocarbons from the bitumen separation process." The oil sands produce nearly 75 million tons of $CO_2$ emissions annually, about 11 percent of Canada's total emissions.

Instead, for the next month we would be traveling deep into rugged country laced with rarely visited lakes, rivers, and streams. Spruce, birch, and jack pine abounded, and the shores were lined with deadfall. We would rely heavily on geologist and explorer Charles Camsell's account of his journey though the region one hundred years before us. His 1916 book, *An Exploration of the Tazin and Taltson Rivers, North West Territories*, was the only comprehensive written account we could find for these waterways.

Fennel was usually content to ride in the canoe, napping with his head resting on a gunwale or thwart. But if he got squirmy, it was time for him to run. We would pull over to let him hop out. The miles passed faster when we could paddle while watching him bound over downed trees, through the mud, up the bank, and through the woods. After a few hours, he would swim after us, signaling he wanted back in the boat. Fennel also began to associate the fishing pole with a meal. If we cast from shore, Fennel sat at attention right by our feet. Fishing from the canoe became nerve-racking as we wondered if Fennel would jump in after any fish that were caught. Once a fish was on the stringer, Fennel trembled with excitement, drooling and never taking his eyes off the fish as we paddled.

As we climbed up another rise of granite on our third portage, the river split into many different channels and cascaded down over bedrock and boulders. It had taken us a week to settle into the rhythm of wilderness travel. The dark cloud of concern and self-doubt abated and was replaced by bright rays of sunshine illuminating a landscape of endless possibilities. We could happily remain here, watching the water flow over the rocks and the light changing throughout the course of the day and the comings and goings of beavers and white pelicans. What would this place tell us if we were to remain for a week, a year, indefinitely just listening? In our brief stay it simply told us that we as humans need wilderness.

A few days into the month of June, cold weather surprised us. The sky clouded over, and a north wind blew cool air down from the mostly frozen surface of Great Slave Lake. Tiny spurts of a drizzle came now and again. Large moose tracks showed us the way across our first portage of the day. We used our sail when we could to take advantage of the tailwind. Lunch was especially chilly; the rain began in earnest. We ran up and down our little sheltered beach repeatedly to warm up. Paddling would have been cold enough, but the immobility involved with sailing was worse. We sailed for another hour or so before noticing a cabin tucked in the woods to our right. As we were admiring its new green roof, we noticed that smoke was coming from the chimney and decided to stop in, with the excuse of asking the inhabitants about the upcoming dam at Twin Gorges.

A large man with a booming voice and firm handshake greeted us at the door. Wayne invited us in, introducing us to his wife, Linda. Her warm smile and sparkling eyes made us feel immediately welcome. They had been dropped off at their cabin by floatplane a few days earlier. We dried out by the woodstove and sipped hot cups of coffee laced with sugar and real cream while we explained our trip to them. It turned out that Wayne used to work at the Twin Gorges hydroelectric dam, so we poured over maps, determining the best approach and how to portage around the dam. Wayne had been retired for thirteen years, but he told us stories of power outages, encounters with other wilderness travelers, and about the workings of the dam. It had supplied power to the Pine Point mine, but now the power went to Hay River, Fort Smith, and Fort Resolution. As we talked Wayne kept adding logs to the fire while Linda refilled our cups and fed us cheese and crackers. When we finally left, dressed in our layers that had dried by the stove, the rain had turned to snow.

Snow flurries persisted through the night and into the next day. We built stops into our day to run around on a beach to get circulation back to our chilled feet. We paddled through a narrow passageway lined by high cliffs and past several nesting pairs of Canada geese—not even realizing they were perched on granite ledges until the geese burst out of the nest. One goose proceed to flap and skim the water—pretending to be injured, instinct driving it to lure us away from its goslings. Keeping our distance while peering up at the ledge, we could see little yellow heads peeking out of the nest.

Leaving Tsu Lake, we entered a vast area that had been burned in a forest fire. The charred remains of jack pines stood towering over the young green saplings below. Our second portage of the day was a mile long. For the first quarter mile we stumbled our way through the tangle of charred, toppled trees and jack pine saplings. We managed to find signs of a trail—first just spots where alders had been cut and then actual blazes on the trunks of jack pines and birch. Relieved to have a trail, however old and unused, we tramped on. Instead of doing the full mile with one load and coming back for the second, we did little shuttles back and forth. Crashing through the woods, watching our steps on lichen-covered granite and on moss and duff, over countless downed trees. Fennel seemed to enjoy himself, finding the occasional fish skeleton or animal turd to munch on or roll in.

After paddling and portaging for a couple more days we crashed through the woods and popped out onto an old gravel roadbed filled with aspen saplings below the much-anticipated Twin Gorges dam. Soon we were greeted by two barking dogs with tails wagging—one of which was a sled dog pup and the other a short-haired indiscernible mix with a porcupine quill sticking out of its swollen cheek. Shortly after our meeting with the dogs, Yves, the lonely dam keeper, appeared. His big smile and giddy nature made it clear that he rarely had visitors. He invited us to stay the night—offering up abundant food and a warm shower.

As we paddled away from the dam the next morning, the dogs howled a farewell to Fennel. Looking down into the water, we could see that we were hovering over black spruce treetops. This had all flooded when the dam was built, and the ghostly trees remained standing under the water. We paddled with our eyes trained downward, trying to imagine this place before the dam existed.

* * *

SEVERAL DAYS LATER we were portaging around Napie Falls and spotted a large white blob hanging above the rumbling cascade— snow and ice clinging to the cliff in the shade. It was June 8. The days seemed impossibly long and sunny. How could snow and ice still be holding on?

Two weeks after leaving Fort Resolution we reached the Tazin River and were immersed in a rugged, untrammeled landscape ruled by water, fire, and rock. Our days were filled with a mixture of paddling, portaging, and lining. More often than not summers pass without a single party traversing the Tazin River, making the portage trails largely game trails with the occasional bits of colorful flagging or weathered saw marks left by fellow travelers in years past. We were thankful to find clues that we were headed in the right direction, but at the same time ribbons of pink plastic fluttering from gnarled jack pine branches seemed out of place.

Trees are caught in a constant battle for survival here. They endure long, dark, brutal winters, clinging to a windy, rocky land scraped bare by the glaciers. It feels like a new land starting to spring up, even though the last glaciers receded more than ten thousand years ago. Add to this the massive fires that periodically thunder through these stunted forests and it is easy to understand the harsh beauty of the Tazin River. Portages typically involved less of a trail and more picking our way over beds of caribou moss and lichen-covered rocks, not to mention crashing through dense willows and tightly packed pines. It was hot, buggy, hard work, but we drew strength from the wildness, urged forward by the wonder of what lay ahead.

We encountered places so beautiful that beckoned us to linger, but we often rushed by due to a keen awareness that fall's storms and cold were only a few months away. Occasionally our logic would be overpowered by a place that inexplicably gripped us; at one such place, Nolan Falls, Dave cast a red-and-white Dardevle spoon into the cold churning water at the base of a small rapids and plucked a three-pound northern pike from the water. The next nine casts produced nine more almost identical northern pike, which were carefully released. It was great fun and quite the streak—ten fish on ten casts.

While it wasn't easy, every day we had been able to catch one or two lake trout or northern pike to keep Fennel well-fed and provide us with a few nice fillets to supplement our diet. It felt good to harvest our own food, and very little was wasted. In the beginning we had wondered how Fennel would do on this diet of whole fish—skin, fins, bones, and all—but over the coming months we watched his health and energy level improve and realized he was thriving.

\* \* \*

PADDLING DOWN SOULIER Lake a few days later, we were trolling a deep-diving Rapala lure, the sun shining through the aquamarine water to dance off boulders thirty feet below us. A helicopter, flying low, buzzed overhead and disappeared over the next ridge. In the same moment, the rod doubled over, and line began whizzing off the reel. After several minutes a ten-to-twelve-pound lake trout spun far below us, peeling line off the reel in powerful bursts. Fennel watched patiently as we carved off beautiful fillets, and he quickly inhaled the belly fat and other tasty tidbits tossed at his feet. The thick orange slabs of meat would make a perfect dinner.

Just as we were getting back in the canoe, we heard the sound of an engine—the helicopter starting up. It had apparently landed nearby, about half a mile away. As we continued, we noticed a man with a canoe and a dog out on a gravel beach. The man was loading the canoe as the medium-sized gray dog scampered up and down the shore. Minutes later, we landed and enthusiastically greeted Tim, a thin, tall man dressed in Carhartt jeans and a plaid flannel, and his dog, Scout, a German shepherd / husky mix. We had been communicating with Tim for several months over the phone and by email because he was the only person we found contact information for who had paddled through this area. From our conversations we had learned that he would be out here around the same time, and so we had hoped to run into him. He appeared to be a bit younger than us, with his short brown hair tucked under a wide-brim hat. We were surprised by his lack of enthusiasm or even a wave of greeting as we approached. Without a word, he sat down a few feet above the waterline to roll a cigarette, occasionally glancing up at us, squinting into the sun as we approached.

A few years back Tim had built a log cabin on Hill Island Lake, several hundred miles from the nearest road or town, using only hand tools. He was now paddling back to Fort Smith, the nearest town.

"So did you just get some ice-cold beer helicoptered in?" we said, attempting to break the ice as Fennel jumped out of our canoe to flirt with Scout. "No," was all he said at first. "Those guys just hauled away a black bear I shot," he explained as he pointed to a gut pile down the shore that was still oozing streaks of red into the water. Tim had been stalked by a predatory black bear, and he was still visibly shaken by the ordeal. He had packed up camp and was ready to leave, but after visiting for a few minutes we all decided to camp there together and cook up a feast of our trout and Tim's potatoes, onions, and garlic.

As we cooked and ate, Tim's story slowly unfolded. He explained that this campsite had been used by people for a long time. Nearby he showed us bits of flaked stone left from ancient people making tools. He also pointed out one of the pounding rocks. But not all the human signs were ancient. There was evidence of more modern use, too, such as racks for hanging moose and an aluminum boat stashed up the bank.

"Something didn't quite feel right when I landed here last evening," he explained. "I felt kind of spooked, and Scout was acting strange, but I told myself it was just my imagination. This is a great campsite and people have been stopping here for so long." He had found a golden eagle feather on the beach and placed it near his tent. "Since I had the bad feeling about the place, I walked around my tent four times and gave an offering of tobacco, asking for protection.

"That evening, Scout sensed something in the woods nearby, something that raised her hackles and made me fearful. She stuck really close by me and was eager to get in the tent for the night. Then, early this morning, like at four o'clock or so, I woke up with a start because I heard splashing in the water. I poked my head out of the tent and—ho-ly lipton!—a big male black bear charged out of the water and ran up the beach directly toward my tent." We walked to the water's edge, where the bear's massive prints were still etched in the soft sand.

"I let Scout out of the tent to buy some time—enough to grab and load my shotgun. Scout ran straight at the bear but then turned and ran off as the bear chased her. I fired a warning shot. Instead of being scared away by the loud noise, that big bear spun around and ran back toward me!"

Crouched in his tent, he took aim at the bear, but the gun jammed and the bear stopped at the door of the tent, sticking his face in. "The bear was just staring at me, drooling. I froze, staring back—I was really scared," Tim explained. "I tried to think of what I had in the tent—what I could use to defend myself. My Leatherman was at the back. Could I reach for it in time? I'll never forget the look on that bear's face and the drool. His breath stank!" Tim's face scrunched up in disgust.

"Then, instead of coming in after me, the bear moved around to the side of the tent. I was able to unjam the gun by banging it on the ground, and then as I crawled out of the tent, the bear charged right at me." His first shot hit the bear in the shoulder, and the bear backed up and sat in the bushes. Then Tim fired again—a gut shot, and the bear ran into the water. His third shot killed the bear.

He explained how he had called the ENR office in Fort Smith on his satellite phone to report the incident. The helicopter had flown in to pick up the bear. Tim had spent the rest of the day skinning it and preparing it to get flown out. The hide and meat would get used by someone in Fort Smith. The ENR guys brought tobacco and more ammunition for Tim, along with news that a forest fire was burning near Hill Island Lake.

Once the dramatic story was complete, we all sat in silence, digesting the gravity of the situation our new friend had just been in before the conversation turned to more lighthearted topics. Tim asked us about previous trips and shared some of his. We talked about the land, climate change, history of the area—even through the evening wave of mosquitoes and into the semidarkness of midnight. Staring into the fire's glowing embers, Tim said, "This land likes having people travel through it. It especially loves the sound of our paddles in the water." He told us that he liked our attitude—humble and asking questions, not assuming we had all the answers already. He was maybe twenty-five and still figuring out his place in the world, but in many ways, he was wise beyond his years. His knowledge and love of the land ran deep, and spending time in the bush helped ground him.

We could relate because we were struggling to figure out where we belonged and how we could give a voice to everything we had experienced over the last fifteen months. Out here our lives seemed so full and rich; we were truly alive. Hell, Tim had almost been eaten by a bear the last time he slept. In the morning we loaded our canoes and said goodbye. Like Tim, we were slowly paddling home. It would just take us another four months.

* * *

A COUPLE OF days later we woke up from the heat of the sun beating on the tent fly. Smoke from a distant forest fire had created a haze and acrid scent we had grown accustomed to. We'd just packed up and carried our packs down the beach to the canoe when a black bear ambled out of the woods. It was a decent-sized bear but didn't seem to pay any attention to us. Fennel, ever the curious dog, trotted over to it, tail wagging. We were, of course, nervous about that and excitedly called him back. The bear ran toward him, causing us to shout louder. Fennel, tail now between his legs, ran back to us. The bear backed off and continued on with its morning wanderings.

As we paddled, distinct plumes of smoke appeared on the horizon. Smoke engulfed both sides of the river ahead, making the channel dark and ominous. We nervously joked about how we felt like we were paddling into Mordor. Fortunately the wind was at our backs, blowing the smoke away from us. By lunchtime massive plumes of dark smoke rose directly in our path. We pulled out the satellite phone and called the ENR in Fort Smith. The man who answered the phone, Rick, said there was a fire near the Northwest Territories–Saskatchewan border on Tazin Lake and another near Lake Athabasca. Since the fires were supposedly in Saskatchewan, he didn't know too much; he was just keeping tabs on them in case one crossed the border into his jurisdiction in the Northwest Territories.

After another mile and a half a wall of smoke rose to the east, and our first sighting of flames high up on the hillside gave us pause. We were still five miles or so from the Saskatchewan border and could now confirm that the fire had reached the Northwest Territories. We paddled "into Mordor" for a bit, wondering if we would be able to continue forward. Before the smoke got too thick, we turned around and paddled back to a gravel bar with minimal vegetation in the middle of the river.

We set up the tent and cooked a meal while watching the line of flames creep down the hill upriver. A light speck appeared in the flames and billowing clouds of smoke across the way, and suddenly, a whitish bird rocketed out of the miasma, crash-landing on our little island. It took off again and struggled to gain altitude in the headwind. We thought it was a gull at first, but as it came closer, flying at about head height, it appeared to be a northern harrier. It came within thirty feet of us, still at head height before it caught a gust of wind and awkwardly shot up into the sky, flying to the opposite side of the river and up beyond the ridgeline.

By seven thirty that night, a dancing orange-and-yellow wall of flames had crept all the way down to the bank of the river. We watched in silent awe as all the trees were engulfed in the blaze. Not only did flames rise from the burning trees, but the occasional ball of fire also shot into the air. We could feel the radiant heat from a quarter mile away. The sound grew in intensity from that of a distant rumble to the all-encompassing din of a large waterfall, ending with a thunderous roar punctuated by the popping of exploding trees and cracking trunks as they fell. It was shocking how quickly that stand of jack pines disappeared. Healthy trees one moment, orange flaming torches the next, and then black smoldering trunks. In that brief moment when those trees had been starkly silhouetted, they were a row of black skeletons, backlit by pulsing brilliant orange, red, and purple flames.

By nine o'clock we began to worry about our position in relation to the movement of the fire. We hurriedly packed the canoe and spent another half hour waiting and watching. Eventually the smoke did start to bother us. Relatively sure that it would soon get significantly worse, we roused a sleepy and confused dog to backtrack about a mile to a rocky point on the west side.

Fennel's frantic barking woke us at five o'clock the next morning. The fire? A bear? What was it?! We peered out of the tent to see Fennel with quills sticking out of his muzzle, barking at a cornered porcupine. Rushing from the tent, we dragged Fennel away from the bristling creature that chattered at us and eventually waddled off. We immediately set about removing the quills from Fennel's mouth, chest, and paws with a forceps. Fennel tried to wriggle away from us, so we took turns holding him down while the other pulled out quills. We had heard that the quills work themselves in over time and were glad to have the chance to pull them out so soon after the incident. Fennel's pain seemed to abate the second the last quill was removed from his face; he was instantly back to his happy-go-lucky self, showing no sign of the ordeal he had just been through.

The fire had crept to the southwest overnight, and the northeast wind had held steady, blowing any smoke away from us. We hemmed and hawed about what to do. The urge to continue was strong as we didn't know whether more fire was on its way from the east, but we had no idea how far the fire extended along the riverbanks upstream. The wind increased to fifteen to twenty-five miles per hour as we packed up the canoe. It was time to call Rick again. He said he would receive a weather briefing soon and told us to call back at 11:40 a.m.

Apparently our observations proved to Rick that the fire had indeed crossed the border into the Northwest Territories, prompting a helicopter flyover. "If you can find a good spot, the pilot will try to land and give you the lowdown on what he saw. You can expect the helicopter sometime between two and three o'clock, and give me a call back if you don't see it by four." So we packed up again—and backtracked again—to a promising gravel beach three quarters of a mile away.

We read a book to pass the time—Bill McKibben's *Eaarth*. It was eerily fitting that we would happen to experience something we were reading about, and we contemplated how this fire fit into the bigger picture. It undoubtedly started in a natural way: lightning. And fire is certainly a normal part of the boreal forest life cycle, with any given portion of the forest expected to burn every fifty to two hundred years. Wildfires help forests regenerate; they return nutrients to the soil and create openings in the trees for animals like moose and deer to graze. Some plants, such as jack pine, won't grow until after their seed cones have been in a fire. However, wildfires in North America are becoming bigger and more numerous thanks to warmer, drier weather and insect infestations due to climate change.

In *Eaarth*, we read: "As with hurricanes, it's not just more fires but bigger ones. On average, large fires now burn four times as long as a generation ago, and in recent years three-quarters of the bad fires across the West came in years when the snow melted well ahead of schedule. 'We're getting in a place where we are almost having a perfect storm' for wildfire, said one Forest Service official. And, of course, it all feeds back on itself." Canada's 2023 wildfire season was the most destructive ever recorded. As of September 5, 2023, almost forty-one million acres had burned. Until then, their annual average was six million acres. The fires in 2023 were widespread as well, "from the West Coast to the Atlantic provinces, and the North." By mid-July, there were twenty-nine mega-fires, each exceeding two hundred acres.

About halfway through the 2023 Canadian fire season, the area burned was roughly double what is normally burned during an entire season. By the time the wildfire season ended in October, Canada's wildfires had generated more than 529 million tons of carbon emissions, equivalent to 1.9 billion tons of $CO_2$—five times the country's average for the past twenty years.

A quarter past three o'clock in the afternoon, we heard the *dub-dub-dub* of rotors. The helicopter circled and, to our great amusement, landed on the beach one hundred feet away from us. Fennel hid in the woods. The pilot shut off the engine and we walked over to talk. Two fire management officers in yellow jumpsuits hopped out and explained that the fire had burned out along most of the river and that the "head" of the fire had moved several miles west. They handed us a packet of papers—the latest weather report—and advised that we paddle through the recently burned area right away because the winds were predicted to change overnight, which meant the intact forest we were currently standing in could all go up in flames. We thanked them profusely, and just like that, they were back in the air and gone.

Despite the fact that it was now four o'clock, we decided to put in as many miles as we could. Paddling through the burned area seemed like traversing a war zone. Charred trees lined the eastern banks while fresh smoke rose from the green trees on the west side. Every once in a while we heard a tree drop to the ground. Fresh smoke rose from an island, and a tree burst into flame. We were quiet, taking in all that we saw—the destruction, the opportunity for regrowth. How long would it take for this stretch of river to be green again? When would the animals return?

The smoke and charred trees transitioned back into healthy forest somewhere after we crossed into Saskatchewan. We paused to make dinner but continued paddling afterward. The temperature dropped with the sun and the river narrowed down. At some point we had to portage along an almost-dry stretch of rapids, carefully stepping from boulder to boulder as the sun's final rays blanketed the rocks, trees, and water in a golden glow. Reaching Thainka Lake, we floated past shores lined with sand reflecting on the lake's mirror-smooth surface. Twilight was premature due to cloud cover, and we paddled on into the growing darkness. Eventually we spotted an island that would make a good campsite and finally crawled into our sleeping bags by two o'clock in the morning, exhausted.

We would later learn that this particular fire burned over 20,000 acres (300 square miles). That summer, hot, dry weather contributed to the growth of several wildfires near the borders of Alberta, Saskatchewan, and the Northwest Territories in late June. There was also a much bigger fire burning to the southwest of us along the banks of the Athabasca River. The Richardson fire had begun in mid-May and ultimately burned 1.7 million acres (2,656 square miles)—the largest fire in Alberta since 1950.

As we made our way south and east up the rest of the Tazin River and then through a series of lakes to Camsell Portage on Lake Athabasca, we saw the forest through new eyes, aware of what portions of forest had burned and when. Charred trunks surrounded by bright green new growth stood out to us in patches that we guessed had burned within the last five years. Younger birch, aspen, and jack pine told us that another fire had burned maybe ten to twenty years ago. We would no longer look at a landscape and just see a blanket of forest; these trees, young and old, had a story to tell, and their locations and sizes now spoke volumes to us. Fire has always played an important role in forest health, but climate change is rapidly throwing the forest balance out of whack.

After three weeks of clawing our way up the Taltson and Tazin Rivers, we hollered and hugged as we set down our packs on Lake Athabasca's stark ledge rock shore. We assumed this would be our last portage until reaching Stony Rapids 140 miles to the east. Athabasca's cold, clear depths and jagged shores reminded us of home, and we imagined this is what the North Shore of Lake Superior must have looked like a couple hundred years ago, before roads and development.

How novel to paddle for hours over a layer of undulating glass stretching to the horizon. We fell into a rhythmic trance as the miles slid by, but in the morning we awoke to the sound of wind and waves crashing on the shore. We had hoped to cut across a six-mile-wide bay and around a massive peninsula jutting into the lake, but staring out over the churning lake as we ate our oatmeal, it was clear today was not the day for an open water crossing. Studying the map we noticed a stream and a couple of small lakes that might serve as a route across the peninsula. There appeared to be a network of roads around Uranium City that we hoped would help us connect the stream with the lakes and ultimately spit us out on the east side of the peninsula.

Uranium City was established in the 1950s when a series of mines sprang up. Close to 2,500 people lived there in 1982 when the largest mine closed. Only accessible by boat or airplane in the summer, or by ice road in the winter, this remote community hummed right along until the mines closed. The town's population plummeted, basically becoming a ghost town within a decade. If the creek was deep enough, we hoped to follow it to the outskirts of Uranium City and portage past the largely abandoned town.

The stream got smaller and portages more numerous. When the stream became too shallow to paddle up, we decided to go with plan B and lugged all our gear up a steep one-hundred-foot bank and popped out onto a gravel road. We portaged down a wide road in the middle of nowhere, but if our map was correct, in half a mile we would reach a small lake. This surprisingly well-maintained road was part of a small network surrounding Uranium City with no connection to the outside world except for a few months of the year when a hundred-mile-long ice road was plowed to the east end of Lake Athabasca. As we approached the lake, warning signs about radiation stating "Do not stop or get out of your vehicle" frightened us, but what were we to do, turn back? Metal poles with clear glass jars hanging from them were scattered across acres of barren ground. We assumed they had something to do with monitoring pollution from the mine waste.

Both of us had a strong urge to keep moving and get out of there as quickly possible while skirting around an ominous gray slope surrounded by tattered orange fencing. The pale gray soil seemed to flow into Nero Lake, which we were about to paddle across. The water looked different—a bright turquoise. Perhaps even more disconcerting was the ring of dead spruce trees around the edge of the lake and the distinct lack of fish, aquatic plants, or even algae. In that moment we were hesitant to breathe, wondering what horrible toxins we were inhaling. We struggled to load the canoe without touching the water, while Fennel was tethered to a dead tree to keep him away from the water until it was time for him to hop in. We paddled as quickly as we could across the lake, trying to keep water from splashing off our paddles onto us or our gear. Fennel stared at us sheepishly after we scolded him for trying to lap up a drink of water from the lake.

An imaginary Geiger counter was blaring in our ears as we crossed the lake. A short portage brought us to Beaverlodge Lake, which looked normal. Uranium City lay a few miles to the north, but we just wanted to get as far away from there as we could, so we set out across the lake. We paddled about five miles into a stiff wind and portaged three quarters of a mile along another section of road to emerge back onto Lake Athabasca. Rolling whitecaps greeted us so we paddled into a cluster of nearby islands to set up camp. It was after nine o'clock at night, but there was still enough light to navigate and we didn't care how late it was; we just wanted to get as far away from Nero Lake as possible. Before setting up camp we plunged into the cold water and scrubbed our bodies and our clothes.

Over a giant pot of mac and cheese with extra dried peas and corn we couldn't stop talking about the surreal moonscape we had just portaged and paddled through, concerned that we had been exposed to radiation and perhaps other nasty things. However, we were mostly struck by this massive scar on the land, which, because of its extreme remoteness, appeared to be just left there. For months we had been confidently drinking the water right out of the lakes, but back there, we were scared to even touch the water, or breathe for that matter.

Headwinds and big seas rolling across Athabasca's broad expanse caused us to advance in fits and starts as the summer solstice made one day stream into the next with only a few brief hours of real darkness. The winds would build in the heat of the day and ease as the sun dipped toward the horizon, inspiring us to paddle at night. We whiled away the day resting, breaking camp after dinner. The wind was beginning to ease, and the lake's undulating surface was no longer laced with whitecaps. By midnight the stars were winning their struggle with the sun's final glow. In these last moments of twilight, silently gliding over the lake's windless surface, we crept past a bald eagle nesting on a little rock island.

Paddling into the night, we ruminated on a thought that had been forming for quite some time. Why were we here? What was our purpose? Everywhere we looked we saw beauty and wonder, but along with it was a horrible and confusing mess of human-inflicted scars. From garbage-strewn beaches and calving glaciers to climate change and radiation, we were left feeling confused about our role in the world. We had set off with the purpose of introducing thousands of elementary and middle school kids around the world to the plants, animals, and people we encountered through the Wilderness Classroom, but the thought that we might want a Geiger counter while paddling across a potentially radioactive lake never crossed our minds. Watching our bow wake ripple through the heavens' reflection didn't provide any immediate answers. Eventually fatigue quieted our minds. As dawn approached, we set up our tent and crawled inside as a faint breeze broke the stillness.

After about a week of evening paddles on the vast waters of Lake Athabasca we reached the eastern corner of the lake and the tiny community of Stony Rapids. We cruised across shallow Stony Lake and then up the river, spending the day paddling, portaging, and lining. The next day we began a 3.5-mile portage to Black Lake. We found the beginning of the rough road at a boat launch of sorts in the sand and horsetails. Trash was scattered around, including several foul-smelling diapers. The portage was easy, strolling down the sandy road lined with spruces. The amount of human debris (trash) increased as we got closer to the end. So did the number of tree stumps from firewood harvesting. The sky clouded over and darkened as we walked. We came out onto Black Lake and launched the canoe amid a cloud of mosquitoes.

We reached the town of Black Lake around lunchtime and the start of the rain, casting a somewhat depressing shadow over what was already a rather dreary scene. Small houses in various states of repair stretched from the waterfront up a gradual rise. We left our canoe tied to a large wooden dock but hauled our paddles and packs with us up to a small gazebo where we found shelter from the cold rain. Someone in Stony Rapids had told us that Black Lake was kind of a rough town, so we checked on the canoe periodically. Maybe it was the weather, or comments about Black Lake, but we just wanted to leave this bubble of humanity and return to the river's churning waters and rugged forests.

After picking up three weeks' worth of food, we hauled the first load down to the canoe—only our canoe wasn't there. We had checked on it so many times! How could it be gone? It had been tied off, right? Then we thought the worst: maybe someone had swung past with a truck and hauled it away without us noticing. Dropping the packs, we looked up and down the shore to find it being paddled away by young kids about 150 yards away. They were using an assortment of boards as paddles. We yelled at them, "Hey, that's our boat! Could you please bring it back here?!"

Caught red-handed, they landed and scrambled out of the canoe, ran up the gravel bank, and disappeared behind the nearest row of houses. One kid in a blue shirt—the smallest of the group—hesitated and ran back to the canoe. Was he thinking of paddling it back to us? Or was he going to be extra nasty and push it out into deeper water? As we ran down the shore we resigned ourselves to the idea of swimming after the canoe. But the boy actually pulled it up on the rocks, assuring that it wouldn't drift away—what a considerate thief.

* * *

THE NEXT DAY we realized the burden of our brim-full packs as we portaged half a mile around a waterfall. After that we commenced more upstream travel on the Fond du Lac River, encountering a mixture of flat water that we paddled and rapids that we lined. We made slow progress wading in the water, working the canoe through shallow spots or strong current. It was awkward and slow. Layers of creamy, undulating sandstone lined the riverbanks.

We spent ten days slogging upstream for the one hundred miles to Wollaston Lake. Stumbling on slippery rocks that we couldn't see as we waded through waist-deep water, clutching the canoe tested our resolve and our relationship. Our lower backs ached from the bent-over posture required of dragging the canoe up the numerous rapids. A glimmer of hope lay in the knowledge that after Wollaston Lake, we would once again be paddling downstream to Reindeer Lake and then Lake Winnipeg.

When planning canoe journeys people typically choose routes that allow them to travel down rivers because it is, of course, faster and more fun, but when crossing a continent, both upstream and downstream travel is inevitable. To be fair, there were easier routes that we could have chosen. We tried to remind ourselves that easier isn't always better in the end. We had decided to travel up the Fond du Lac River because it allowed us to remain in a vast, roadless wilderness longer than easier routes to the south, but wading up rapids was wearing us down. The Fourth of July was one of our toughest days—twenty-three miles plodding through a drenching rain and squirrelly wind. We were paddling through a recently burned area, and there was no shelter anywhere—just little islands topped with grasses and willows. Our forearms were wet from rain dripping down the sleeves of our raincoats. Working against the current was unforgiving. Fennel was unhappy, too, not wanting to lie or sit in the water that accumulated in the bottom of the canoe.

Grumpy, stiff, and sore, at times we had to push thoughts of quitting out of our heads. It would have been so easy to turn and point the canoe downstream. After a bit more wading on a sandstone ledge, we rounded the corner and the rumble of a waterfall was palpable. We skirted past the wave train at its base and found the portage trail by following footprints on a little sand beach. Soon we were setting up camp above the Manitou Falls.

This spot warranted a day off, and the tension of the previous couple of days melted away. While Fennel napped at our feet, we spent hours sitting under our tarp, sipping tea, admiring our commanding view of the falls, and reading from a worn journal that was kept in a cairn near camp—it was full of entries written over the past few decades by passing canoeists. Gary and Joanie McGuffin mentioned finding this journal in their book *Where Rivers Run*, which details their six-thousand-mile unconventional honeymoon by canoe across Canada in the 1990s. The journal also contained a photocopied account of David Thompson's trip down and back up the Fond du Lac in 1796. We might have been tired and cold, but we never experienced a situation as dire as his.

Thompson, trying to find a shortcut from the Mackenzie Basin to Hudson Bay, paddled down the Fond du Lac River from Wollaston Lake to Lake Athabasca—but then turned around and traveled back. Although the trip downstream was filled with adventure, the trip upstream was when the party almost perished. Just upstream from our campsite, Thompson happened to be in the canoe, steering as two other men lined the canoe from shore. They lost control of the canoe, resulting in the canoe and Thompson tumbling over the falls. The party lost all of their food and most of their equipment. They miraculously kept a means to start a fire (flint from the gun and his steel knife). They nearly starved, and when they did manage to kill two young eagles, they suffered life-threatening dysentery. Thompson was walking and wading up rapids barefoot, suffering from a major wound, clothed only in some fabric from their tent. Had they not stumbled across a Dene family upriver, they most likely would have perished.

We continued our slow, steady progress toward Kosdaw Lake despite a stiff headwind. In the early evening we were working our way slowly, wading, when we saw a person fishing onshore. Our surprise at seeing anyone else in this remote spot caused us both to rub our eyes and take a second look. Fennel, who had been happily trotting alongshore ahead of us, got to the man first and, being the large, black dog that he is, startled the man, who thought Fennel was a black bear. A minute later we reached two guys loading up a backpack and petting Fennel. Not seeing a tent or boat, we asked what brought them out here. They were geologists—waiting for their ride home from work. Before we could ask any more questions a helicopter appeared overhead. "Hold onto your canoe!" they shouted over the roar of the helicopter as it descended and whisked them away. What a commute! We wondered what they were looking for—uranium? Gold? Even if they found something substantial, would building a mine way out here ever actually happen? Watching the sun set behind the tops of jack pines, we reflected on our terrifying experience near Uranium City and hoped that this river and surrounding forest would remain as it was in that moment, free from backhoes, roads, and power lines. Aren't there places on this earth worth keeping as they are regardless of the resources they contain? Surely our civilization is at a point where we can be selective about what gets mined or logged or developed.

A Bonaparte's gull swooped low and darted past the bow of the canoe, welcoming us to Wollaston Lake. The scorching rays of the sun reflected off the lake's glassy surface. It was hot, without a puff of wind to cool us; the canoe slipped silently out into the middle of the lake. The Fond du Lac had been a real challenge—slow, grueling work paddling, lining, and portaging up what would have been such a delightful trip downstream. The lake's vast, calm expanse was just what we needed. Thirty-five miles of island-hopping lay ahead. Wollaston is unique in that it is a bifurcation lake—actually the largest in the world. In other words, the lake has two outflows. It is the source of both the Fond du Lac River, which flows to the Arctic Ocean, and the Cochrane River, which flows to Reindeer Lake and the Churchill River system, ultimately emptying into Hudson Bay.

To the southwest an industrial hum could be heard from the Rabbit Lake uranium mine, the longest-running uranium mine in North America, which is owned by the second-largest uranium company in the world. Little did we know the impact the Fukushima disaster would have on this corner of the world as demand for uranium plummeted; in 2016 the mine was shuttered and five hundred people lost their jobs.

As much as we tried to relish the satisfying sensations of our paddles rhythmically gripping the water and the canoe surging forward, we couldn't help but wish tomorrow and the next day would be just like this one. Two more calm days and we would leave Wollaston in our wake. Had we been pushing too hard? The struggles of our upstream travels had gotten us wondering why we were always rushing toward the horizon rather than living in the moment. But then again, the days were already getting shorter, and August, with strong winds bringing fall storms, was not far off. Scattered marshmallow clouds and pine-studded islands appeared to float on the water's glassy surface. Our final night was on a small beach where Sigurd Olson and his party had camped in 1957. We spent our time wondering how much had changed since the night our conservation hero had pitched his tent here.

Nine portages lie between Wollaston Lake and the Blondeau River, ranging in length from a tenth of a mile to one mile. Progress was slow as we picked our way through bogs, searching for blazes, checking the map and compass, feeling our way forward, literally, with our feet. Stepping into dark puddles, we never knew if we would hit the firm bottom an inch or a foot below the surface. Trudging through wet muskeg and sphagnum moss was like walking over a giant uneven sponge. A couple of times we sunk thigh deep. *Splorsh.* "Shit!" When this happened, you had to toss the canoe off your shoulders, struggle to climb out of the muck without losing a shoe, drag the canoe to firmer ground, flip it back overhead, and crash on.

It had been raining all day, and everything was wet and muddy by the time we reached the ninth and final portage. We dropped our packs in a small stand of jack pine partway across the portage and quickly set up camp, our weary muscles urged on by a steady drizzle and clouds of mosquitoes. All day we had experienced an intense level of focus on the simple tasks involved in finding and completing each portage, tackling each challenge as it arose. Bellies full, warm and dry, listening to the light rain drumming on the fly, snug in our sleeping bags, the day's discomfort melted away.

\* \* \*

IN THE MORNING we portaged the rest of the way to the Blondeau River under overcast skies. What a feeling to climb into the boat and have it immediately start moving in the direction we wanted to go! After weeks of upstream travel, we were finally paddling with the current. We twisted and turned, snaking our way on this winding, small river, gliding by spruce and tamarack perched over willow-coated banks. Few parties travel this route from Wollaston Lake to Reindeer Lake, but signs of humans were becoming more prevalent. Reindeer Lake's rugged, island-dappled expanse was our transition from a wilderness rarely visited by humans to a landscape lightly sprinkled with fish camps, dams, towns, roads, and bridges. We had yearned to visit Reindeer Lake for a long time, to explore the many bays and channels between islands. Approximately a hundred and fifty miles long and about thirty-five miles wide, chock-full of islands of granite covered in thick stands of spruce and pines, we could spend a whole summer exploring Reindeer Lake's nooks and crannies. We both seem to be drawn to large bodies of water. Perhaps it is the clear cold water or the expansive views. They possess the potential for big waves to build, resulting from tumultuous storms. Yet the calm moments generate possibly even more awe—that such a massive body of water can lie entirely still.

The Sturgeon-Weir River began as a small winding creek, with wild rice growing in the shallows and blueberries carpeting sunsoaked islands. The water was high, especially for early August. Shortly after Scoop Rapids we were making our way through a fairly long flat-water section. That is where we encountered the Trans CanEAUda crew—eight people and one dog in four canoes paddling in the opposite direction from us. They had begun their journey in Ottawa and were raising awareness about the importance of watershed conservation in Canada. Camping together, we spent an evening swapping stories, route advice, and discussions about gear. They were a bilingual group (*eau* means "water" in French), and their conversation transitioned fluidly between English and

French. Like us, they were on a tight schedule, with a goal of reaching Inuvik by the middle of October.

We set off at seven o'clock the next morning, sad to part ways with such great company but left in awe of our surroundings as the sun rose, piercing the fog with its golden morning light. The land was still and silent except for the water dripping off our paddles as they skimmed over the river's smooth, dark surface before grabbing the water for another stroke.

By traveling northeast up the Goose River from the Sturgeon-Weir River over to the Grass River, we were deviating from the main route to avoid more populated areas and access the remote eastern side of Lake Winnipeg. On Tramping Lake numerous ocher images decorated the pink granite cliff face. Caribou, moose, people, trees, a serpent? One image reminded us of Mishipeshu. Some were faded and indistinguishable. Others looked like they had been painted yesterday. A little farther on we found a smaller cliff lined with countless handprints. To show our respect, we left an offering in a crack in the cliff.

The Grass River widened, and true to its name, large swaths of grass lined either side before it opened up to a series of small lakes. As we paddled in a cold, drenching rain, we spotted through the mist the heads of two caribou swimming—our first woodland caribou sighting. Like the Barren Ground caribou to the north, the woodland caribou population has declined in recent decades, making us especially excited to see these elusive, ghostly animals in the fog. The pair swam into the grasses on our left and clambered onto higher ground before disappearing into the trees.

After crossing Setting Lake we pulled into a large campground and walked around what seemed to be a ghost town. Most of the sites were taken up with RVs, but no one was around at half past six o'clock on a rainy Thursday evening. We held back shivers as we walked, longing to dry off and climb into warm sleeping bags. The campground was three miles from Wabowden, Manitoba, where we would resupply and pick up our portage wheels at the post office. The wheels would aid us on a long road portage to Sipiwesk Lake, where we would begin paddling up the Nelson River to Lake Winnipeg. We would only experience a small portion of the upper reaches of the Nelson River, which flows four hundred miles from Lake Winnipeg to Hudson Bay.

At Dwyer's General Store we chatted with the owner who put us in touch with the local natural resources officer—Pat. We tracked Pat down to discuss our route, and he suggested hiring a truck to drive us to Sipiwesk Lake, explaining that the Nelson River was in flood—nine to ten feet higher than normal. We listened to his description but took it with our usual grain of salt. So many people had told us we couldn't do countless portions of this route—and we had—so why should his naysaying be any different?

The next day we strapped our loaded canoe to the portage wheels and started walking. Fennel's sled dog instincts kicked in, and he was a great help in pulling the canoe. The day was sunny and dry. We were on pavement, only pulling onto the gravel shoulder to let the occasional car pass. Our pace was a little over three miles per hour. Pat drove by, offering us a ride that we declined, and he gave us bottles of water.

In the late afternoon, we had walked about eleven miles and were nearing the intersection where we would turn off the main highway. We heard a sickening crunch and the canoe lurched to the left. The wheel had come off! While we were surveying the damage, along came Pat. "Uh . . . remember that ride offer? We'd like to take you up on it now," we said sheepishly. Admitting defeat, we loaded everything into Pat's truck and were whisked off toward Sipiwesk. The parking lot had flooded, so the dock was just sort of at the end of the road, with a couple of large fishing boats tied to it. The water was up into the trees. Pat's expression conveyed an "I told you so," but he never said it out loud as we moved our canoe and gear from his truck to the water's edge.

Paddling through this flooded landscape was disorienting. Cutbanks dropped into the water. Dead, gray trees dotted shorelines, along with jumbled trees where banks had collapsed. We paddled to an island to find a campsite. Land features looked significantly different from the map, as points were underwater, peninsulas became islands, and some islands just weren't there.

We paddled through white spruces to land the canoe, reminded of the flooded forest of the Amazon. After dinner we again surveyed the damaged wheel—a bent frame and a cracked hub. The website said this thing could carry 350 pounds. The instructions said it had a max load of 300 pounds. But, in fine print, the tires said 110 pounds. We figured we came close to maxing it out but thought we were still within its limits. Regardless, the portage wheels had lasted less than a day.

A cool morning greeted us, and the day gradually heated up as the sun rose higher in a cloudless sky. Leaving Sipiwesk Lake, we resumed paddling upstream on the Nelson River. We worked to avoid a prominent eddy line by hugging the inside of a turn. Then we were stuck heading against the main current as it ran through the trees. We ducked under branches, trying to stay as close to the side as possible for about a mile. Eventually we hit a current that made us feel like we were on a treadmill, so we pulled over to eat lunch and assess the situation. The current was much faster than the Mackenzie River— more like the Yukon River flowing against us. We still had about a hundred miles to Norway House. Lining was impossible due to the high water because we'd be winding our way through flooded trees and tangles of underbrush. Many narrow spots and rapids stood in our way. If we continued to plod our way through, we'd be lucky to do ten miles a day. We were doubtful of our ability to even approach rapids and portages if the current became any stronger than it was right in front of us. Pat had been right.

Paddling up a creek would take us back to the road, where we could try our luck portaging about twenty-five miles to the Jenpeg dam. After spending the night camped by the side of the road, we awoke to the sound of a car passing. Our packing was hurried— dancing to evade mosquitoes. We repaired the portage wheels as best we could. The sun rose higher, warming the pavement as we began walking. As we crested a hill we heard a familiar thud and the canoe lurched. This time the wheel not only came off but bent in an irregular shape, and all of the ball bearings tumbled onto the pavement. We had gone only about a mile. Defeated, we sat down to wait for a passing truck, wondering who would pick up the world's most encumbered hitchhikers ... canoe, lots of gear, and a hundred-pound dog. Cars passed.

Then a truck coming from the other direction stopped. Two guys, both named Joe, were on their way to work. The driver actually recognized Fennel from a previous Wilderness Classroom expedition, when Dave and our friend Adam had dogsledded through Cross Lake about eight years before. Joe turned the truck around and took us all the way to the Jenpeg dam. After unloading at the landing above the dam, we exchanged addresses, and they gave us a little Canadian flag to mount on the bow of our canoe. We were incredibly grateful and astounded at the odds of crossing paths with someone Dave and Fennel had met so long ago. During the drive Joe and Joe had filled us in on Cross Lake news. It wouldn't be until we returned home that we'd learn about the full extent of the destruction of their community's land caused by Manitoba Hydro and the provincial government.

When Dave dogsledded through this area in 2004, local people explained that developers looking to build the dam had come to their community promising jobs and prosperity. They said the dam would not change the landscape or affect the hunting, trapping, and fishing on which they had relied for generations. "We were told the water levels would never change more than the height of a pencil," an elder named Edwin had explained to Dave in his trapper's cabin deep in the bush outside Cross Lake. In reality, major fluctuations of water levels and other disturbances have severely impacted the landscape and the First Nations communities throughout the Nelson River Watershed.

The hydro project flooded more than twenty-five square miles of Pimicikamak (also known as Cross Lake) land and caused severe damage to hundreds of miles of shoreline, but it was nearly forty years after the dam was built and only after a major protest led by First Nation people that the Manitoba government formally apologized. By protest, we mean an eviction of Manitoba Hydro employees and a six-week occupation by Pimicikamak Okimawin at the Jenpeg Generating Station. In addition to the apology by the Manitoba premier, Greg Selinger, negotiations included revenue sharing, a shoreline cleanup, and help with residential hydro (electricity) bills.

The Jenpeg dam had devastating effects on the surrounding ecosystem. "Changes in silt levels have made Cross Lake's water undrinkable, and sediment has affected the spawning patterns of local fish populations: now the sturgeon, the whitefish, and the pickerel are gone. And without the fish, the muskrats, the wolverines, the bears, and the beavers are gone too; there's no more trapping and there's very little hunting."

As Jackson Osborne, a local elder and historian, told author Kazim Ali, "The lake is an essential part of our identity here . . . The water is as sacred to us as the land. It is a part of our lives as much as the earth and the sky. The water is the blood that sustains us. It must flow for our land to be healthy."

The Nelson River above the dam was vastly different from below. As we launched our canoe where the Joes dropped us off, we observed that the high-water mark along the banks was about six feet above the current water level. Our upstream progress would be challenging, but at least we were back to manageable water levels.

We didn't realize it at the time, but we were in a region that had been suffering from historic flooding since the spring thaw. "High soil moisture at freeze-up, above normal winter snow, additional snow and rain during the spring, heavy summer rains and several severe wind events all combined to form the 'perfect storm.'" The 2011 "super flood" created the highest water levels and flows in modern history across parts of Manitoba and Saskatchewan. "In all, 7,100 Manitobans were displaced from their homes, with 2,700 still evacuated at the end of the year." On May 9, the Manitoba government declared a province-wide state of emergency. The Assiniboine River and Lake Manitoba bore the brunt of the flooding, with the Assiniboine "estimated to be at levels experienced once in 330 years. And on Lake Manitoba, engineers called the flood a one-in-2,000-year event. Governments at all levels spent close to $1 billion on flood fighting and victim compensation."

To protect valuable properties surrounding the city of Winnipeg, the province diverted floodwaters onto reserve land. "The community of Lake St. Martin was evacuated and subsequently destroyed by the floodwaters. For six years the lost town's nearly fifteen hundred residents lived in temporary housing in Winnipeg. Only in 2017 were some of the residents finally resettled back in Lake St. Martin; ninety-two elderly members of that community had died in the intervening years. As of early 2020, approximately 314 families were still waiting for housing to be built so they could return home. Those who had already returned were still lacking jobs, healthcare facilities, and social services." We were learning firsthand about increases in extreme weather linked to climate change, considering that during a matter of months we had paddled from a massive wildfire to extreme flooding.

* * *

LAKE WINNIPEG HAS many moods, and our guts were filled with nervous tension as we left the steady pull of the Nelson River's powerful current and paddled south into a two-foot swell. The voyageurs considered this to be the most dangerous of the hundreds of lakes they crisscrossed, including all the Great Lakes. Fierce winds blowing off the prairies to the west often build quickly, and most of the lake is extremely shallow, which causes the waves to be steep, so we were forced to paddle a mile or more from shore to avoid dangerous shoals and breaking waves. For 250 miles we would follow the lake's largely uninhabited eastern shore, of which the first 150 miles were roadless, with few islands to break the brunt of the wind and waves.

September usually brings stronger winds and cold—and the next day was September 1. Sure enough, twenty miles down the lake we were stuck in our tent for twenty-four hours by thirty-five-mile-per-hour winds and waves thundering against the shore a stone's throw from our tent. Tucked in a dense stand of snarled spruce, we read and ate and tried not to think about how often this might happen as we worked our way south. Once the storm blew itself out, we paddled on in fits and starts. The land was majestic and uniquely austere. Shallow bays rimmed with sand were interrupted by small rocky points, which offered ideal lunch stops and campsites.

Flocks of white pelicans perched on smooth rocks rising slightly above the lake's surface waddled nervously, turning in unison away from us as we paddled by as if to say, "I can't see you, so you can't see me." They are such silly, awkward-looking birds on land, in contrast to their silent grace in the air gliding just above the water surface.

The land remained raw and wild, but something was not right with the water. Our campsites were filled with the pungent smell of decaying algae, and we found ourselves paddling through miles of foul-smelling, swirling blue-green swathes of algae so thick our paddles would completely disappear as they pierced the surface. Its increased viscosity slowed us down—like paddling through pea soup. We didn't understand what exactly it was, but we had no desire to drink the water, so we kept our eyes peeled for tiny streams to fill our bottles.

When we asked one of the locals about the algae-laden water, we were told, "Don't even let your dog drink it." They explained that in the summer and early fall the lake is often covered in massive blooms of blue-green algae, which produces a toxin that will make you sick. You can't boil or filter the toxin out, so our only choice was to gather water from streams entering the lake. With this new knowledge we scrounged up four, two-liter soda bottles to increase our water-carrying capacity.

After paddling out of Berens River, we set up camp in the protection of the river mouth, ready to try our chances on the brooding lake once more. Lake Winnipeg is, after all, the seventh-largest body of fresh water in North America. Staring out over thirty miles of churning brown waves to the west as the last rays of sun painted the clouds in a golden hue was like watching the sun set over an ocean. The lake was so vast that we couldn't quite wrap our heads around the dark thought *"Don't even let your dog drink it."*

Phosphorus and other nutrients flushing into the lake are the major cause of massive algae blooms like the one we encountered. Much of the water feeding Lake Winnipeg comes from waterways like the Red River, which flows for hundreds of miles in Minnesota and North Dakota farm country. Runoff from farms and towns in the United States is responsible for about half of the phosphorus that enters Lake Winnipeg. Old timers explained that the blue-green algae has always been in the lake, but these massive blooms have become much more frequent during their lifetimes, often covering vast portions of the 250-mile-long lake for weeks or months each summer and fall.

Half a week later not a ripple disturbed the water as we paddled through the narrows separating the large northern body of Lake Winnipeg from the slightly smaller and more protected southern section. One hundred and fifty miles lay behind us and the final one hundred miles contained a few more bays and islands to hide behind. Fennel was constantly panting and fidgeting in the heat, and we were drenched in sweat. We all would have loved to stop, but this glorious July-like day in the middle of September couldn't be squandered. It was perfect except that the stifling heat enhanced the foul smell of blue-green algae, which seemed to grow thicker the farther south we went. Plus, it was thirty miles to Loon Straits, where Dave first visited by dog team nearly a decade earlier.

Before motorboats and snowmobiles, fishermen checked their nets with row boats in the summer and by dog team or horse-drawn sleigh in the winter. Travel was hard and slow, so there were tiny communities like Loon Straits scattered all along the roadless shores of Lake Winnipeg. As life grew faster these tiny settlements, often consisting of just a handful of families, slowly disappeared or became summer cottages for city dwellers. But Edgar and Doreen have stayed on in Loon Straits, choosing a quieter, simpler life.

Dave and Frosty had stumbled into Loon Straits in the winter of 2003 when they were traveling on skis with two of Fennel's brothers pulling toboggans from Cumberland House, Saskatchewan, to the south end of Lake Winnipeg. This older yet very fit and active couple had stuffed them with hamburgers and walleye that they helped Edgar pull from his net. They must have each eaten five hamburgers and a plate piled high with fish. The temperature hadn't risen above 0 degrees Fahrenheit in a month—plus skiing all day, every day, required the consumption of about six thousand calories each day. But Doreen didn't blink an eye; she just kept churning out more steaming plates of food. Eating and talking late into the night, Edgar and Doreen shared stories of their lives and their deep knowledge of the lake. It was an encounter with a way of life that is all but gone, so we were anxious to find out if Edgar and Doreen were still around.

Things looked quiet as we approached, but soon we spotted a woman sitting in front of a rustic but neatly painted cabin. The woman was reclined in a comfortable-looking lawn chair, her attention focused on a book. She was full-figured, dressed in a pink-striped button-down shirt, with a matching headband pulling back curly brown hair from her face. She appeared to be maybe ten years older than us. As we paddled within an audible distance she put her book down, flashed us a jolly smile, and asked where we had come from. Soon Lynda invited us to land in her yard and quickly produced ice-cold water and slices of delicious pizza. We sat in those comfy lawn chairs and chatted, and eventually we mentioned that Dave had been here eight years ago and had gone out in a bombardier to retrieve fishing nets with Edgar and enjoyed the ensuing feast. As it turned out, Edgar and Doreen's house was only a hundred yards away, and they came walking over about the same time Lynda's husband, Richard, arrived.

Richard was a large man who seemed very excited to have two wayward paddlers land in his yard. As he bustled around the yard assembling the necessary items for a fire, he peppered us with questions about our journey in a loud, deep voice. Soon we all sat around a blazing fire and carried on three conversations at once. Edgar, in a short-sleeved plaid shirt and worn jeans, a broad smile on his weathered face and brown eyes shaded by a trucker hat, talked about the algae on the lake and fishing, and Doreen, with her short, curly gray hair and sunglasses, asked if Dave could still bake bannock the way she'd taught him. We roasted hot dogs over the fire, drank beer, and talked until the stars came out.

After a brief sleep in our tent set up on Lynda and Richard's lawn, we wandered over to Edgar and Doreen's for coffee and breakfast at six o'clock the next morning. Edgar cooked sausage and potatoes while Doreen made toast and kept our cups full of coffee. We absorbed more stories about their grandkids, fishing, and life at Loon Straits. Doreen packed us a bag of tomatoes and onions from her garden, plus sliced cucumber and peppers, oranges, apples, and cookies before we could stop her As we packed our canoe we reveled in a warm glow of their generosity, thinking about which of the treats we would consume first.

With lots of well-wishes, hugs, and waves as if we were parting company with friends we had known for years, we said goodbye before turning to paddle into a headwind and one-foot chop. Doreen shouted to us, "If you get around the point and see it's too rough, you could always come back." It sure was tempting; we could learn so much from them and wished we could stay for a month. Well, it wasn't too rough—just hard work and slow going, so we put our heads down and dug in. There was a storm churning across the plains that was forecast to reach us in a few days.

The morning before the storm, we woke up to a pre-sunrise pink sky. It was hazy from the smoke of a wildfire burning somewhere to the north. The wind had switched in the night to northeast—an offshore tailwind. We paddled with a purpose and were boosted by the steady wind. By the time we stopped for lunch around one o'clock, we had paddled a little over twenty miles. We were only thirty-five miles from the mouth of the Winnipeg River where we would leave the lake and find protected water. The impending storm motivated us to aim for the river mouth, but we weren't sure if we had a fifty-five-mile day in us.

We threw more bars in our pockets and kept going. Five hours later we stopped on a small rocky island at dusk to grab our headlamps and jackets and take a pee break. A full moon rose in the east, casting a welcome glow across the small waves that pulsed under the canoe from stern to bow, pushing us toward our goal. We rounded a point only to see that another lay ahead. It was hard to judge progress as the sky darkened around us, but it seemed tediously slow. Passing the next point, we saw yet another before us. On and on. The wind shifted and we found ourselves paddling into a growing headwind and against the current as the river mouth finally drew near. We were so close, but our progress had slowed to a crawl.

On we went into the darkness, lulled into a trance by the rhythmic motion of our bodies propelling our paddles. Fennel, who had succumbed to the strong pull of his circadian rhythm long ago, lay comatose on the bottom of the canoe, snoring softly. We made the mistake of checking the time at 1:42 a.m. It was so late, and we were exhausted. Fifty-five miles turned into fifty-nine as we looked for a campsite in the dark. Then a point covered with tall grasses and no nearby houses appeared. We worked our way in, landing as quietly as we could on a tiny patch of gravel. We crawled into the willows and alders, set up the tent, and crashed—contentedly tired and relieved to be done after eighteen hours of almost continuous paddling. While we were dead to the world the gale arrived, but we were securely out of its reach. With Lake Winnipeg behind us we felt as if we were nearly home.

* * *

THE REST OF our route for this stage of the journey was up the Winnipeg River to Lake of the Woods and then up the Rainy River to Rainy Lake, through Voyageurs National Park, and finally through the

Boundary Waters Canoe Area Wilderness to Lake Superior. The prospect of reentering the United States in addition to reaching our home turf reenergized us, or maybe it was the onset of cooler fall weather.

After our final push on Lake Winnipeg we were slow to get going the next morning, but we felt a need to get someplace we could hunker down for the strong wind. It had already picked up out of the northwest, but we felt okay to proceed on the relatively sheltered Winnipeg River. We sailed until it became too hard to control the canoe while surfing steep waves. At the town of Powerview, we decided that a hotel was our best option. We had planned to stay just one night but woke up the next day to a gale warning—thirty-to-thirty-five-knot winds blowing on the river. It was then that we learned of the Pagami Creek Fire burning in the Boundary Waters between Ely and Isabella, Minnesota.

A call to our friend Jason in Ely left us better informed—and worried. In northern Minnesota they were also experiencing high winds out of the northwest. A little lightning-ignited wildfire in the BWCAW had exploded from eleven thousand acres to seventy thousand acres—advancing fifteen miles in one day. As Jason gave this description over the phone the hair on the backs of our necks stood up. Sawbill Canoe Outfitters and a nearby parcel of land that we owned—our home of the past five years—were in the path of the fire. If it kept burning at its current rate, the outfitters and then our home would be engulfed within twenty-four hours. It was hard to comprehend, sitting in that dumpy hotel in Powerview. After a sleepless night we learned that the wind had shifted, meaning Sawbill and our home were no longer in immediate danger.

The rest of our route involved a strange mix of wildness and development. By the end of September, we crossed the Manitoba-Ontario border on a beautiful stretch of river. The abundance of exposed granite reminded us of home. Numerous motorboats were out and about fishing. On a cold, rainy day we saw white pines for the first time since we left home. Frost on the tent fly became a common occurrence, and the daylight was noticeably decreasing.

Power lines and hydro dams signified our approach to Kenora. We wound our way through islands and stopped at a dam, landing on the beach beyond a barbed wire–topped fence and began portaging. Soon "the big city" was in sight. Although the population of this town is only fifteen thousand people, the waterfront filled with apartment buildings, motorboats, and the high-rise Best Western hotel was an entirely foreign scene to us.

A couple of days off in town meant showers, frantic website work while we had access to Wi-Fi, pizza, sushi, and produce from the grocery store. When we did leave, we paddled through a maze of channels between numerous islands filled with immense "cottages" on Lake of the Woods. We camped on a rock, high above the water, and admired the sunset during dinner. There was a "cottage" across the way from us—which we later found out belonged to Goldie Hawn.

We reached the Rainy River on Dave's birthday (September 28). To our right was a shoreline crowded with wooden docks and buildings on the United States side, and to our left were oak trees and grass on the Canadian side. We saw a United States Coast Guard boat, bristling with guns, and waved them over to ask how we could check in with the United States Customs and Border Protection. They got on a cell phone to call the customs office and told us to pull up to the dock in Baudette and walk up to the customs building. "They'll be expecting you," they said. It sounded like they might even have someone waiting at the dock, which we really hoped wasn't the case since we still had ten miles to go in a canoe. It was three o'clock in the afternoon, so we had our work cut out for us to get to Baudette before dark. We got in around six, a little nervous about the Coast Guard's announcement of our arrival, but we found no customs officer on the dock, and in the office they took down our canoe's license number and that was that.

We camped near town in a thick grove of cedars, with the boat stashed near the water. Given our proximity to the customs office, we joked about how we hoped no one would spot us and consider us a threat to the US Department of Homeland Security. Sleep was a challenge as the night was filled with man-made sounds that had become unfamiliar to us—trains ran somewhere nearby periodically, big trucks braked on the road as they neared the international bridge, and an industrial hum buzzed in the distance.

October greeted us with a hard frost and gorgeous fall colors as we entered Voyageurs National Park. Tensions flared while windbound on Lake Kabetogama for several days. Being in the park so close to home, we were anxious to get there, but all we could do was wait out the strong northwest wind that was riling up whitecaps out on the lake. Even though we had two hundred miles to go, the rugged landscape around us told us we were home, and our heightened emotions were testament that we had been missing it.

We reached Handberg's Marina with just enough time to set up camp before Amy's mom rolled up in her teal station wagon with Bryan's black solo canoe perched on top. Bryan, our longtime friend and paddling companion from Grand Marais, would join us for the remainder of the trip to Lake Superior. Also a professional photographer and Wilderness Classroom board member, he was here to help document the end of this stage of the North American Odyssey. When he was looking for a ride to the put-in, Amy's mom jumped at the chance to see us after months apart. Catching up over burgers in Buyck was not enough time.

The next morning Amy's mom stood on the dock waving as we paddled away. After she disappeared from view behind, we settled into easy conversation with Bryan paddling next to us, happy to have someone familiar to talk to. A couple of years older than Dave and a similar height, Bryan was fit and well-equipped for cold-weather paddling. His short brown hair was hidden under a hat most of the time, but his chestnut-colored eyes accentuated by laugh lines expressed happiness and mirth as our lighthearted banter, and joking continued from lake to lake. The day warmed up fast and we stripped off the extra layers that had seemed necessary at sunrise.

We paddled the Vermilion River, then Loon Lake. Setting up our tent in a BWCAW campsite at long last, our sense of belonging and homecoming was overwhelming. Everything was familiar—the sloping granite, the scents of white pine and cedar, the sound of water lapping against the rocky shoreline, the fire grate. Having a latrine at every site was a luxury we hadn't experienced for most of the journey up until this point.

We paused at the pictographs on Lac La Croix. Moose, handprints, some human figures, another four-legged animal. We had seen these before, in the winter a couple of years ago. For a moment time looped back on itself as these ocher images brought us back to a glorious sunny March day, the lake a solid sheet of snow-covered ice. The dog teams were parked nearby. We stood on two feet of ice next to these mysterious images where we now bobbed in a canoe.

That evening we sat by the fire for a while, taking in our view of the lake with the rising moon. Fennel lay within arm's reach. His paws twitched as he ran in his sleep. Wolves howled in the distance and our hearts were full.

The next afternoon dark clouds grew as we began paddling on the Basswood River, and then a clap of thunder reverberated around us. We pulled over at the nearest campsite and set up the tarp with every intention of waiting out the thunder and lightning before continuing. It was four o'clock, but the rain lasted well into the evening. After a bout of hail subsided, we decided to set up camp. We were glad to see the area get such a thorough drenching because it would relieve the drought conditions that had brought about the Pagami Creek Fire.

The rain continued all night and into the morning. Paddling kept us warm. On the Basswood River just past Table Rock, a high, lichen-encrusted granite cliff rose to our right. There was a slight overhang and water dripped down from the face of the cliff, creating stripes of red, white, and black. Here and there we spotted various figures—more pictographs. People in canoes, imaginary animals, a moose smoking a pipe, fascinating images that left us pondering their significance for hours. What was life like back then? Who painted these and why? How many generations of people had passed by here and seen these images?

Despite wearing rain gear all day, we were soaked and chilled. A couple of miles from our intended campsite we noticed a large stack of cut, split wood by the fire grate of another campsite. Although we would ordinarily not pilfer firewood, today we needed it. As we put a couple armloads into Bryan's canoe, we reasoned that our good fortune had resulted from wood karma. In the Northwest Territories we had frequently cut and split more wood than we needed for a night, so at most of our campsites we left a little pile, hoping that someone passing on their snowmobile might make use of it. Could it be that on this wet, cold October day, we were cashing in on that previously banked wood karma?

Although the Pagami Creek Fire was nearly out, its swath of destruction caused us to alter our route as we approached Ely. We headed for Jason's house on White Iron Lake, where three days off were filled with learning about the fire, reuniting with friends, re-supplying, and working on Wilderness Classroom website updates. We were able to visit the incident command center in Ely and interview our friend and US Forest Service ranger LynnAnne about her experience with the fire.

The fire had burned a total of 93,000 acres in and around the BWCAW. On the day we found out about the fire and its scary-rapid growth, six US Forest Service employees had been out warning campers to evacuate. The fire overtook them, and they had to deploy their emergency shelters to survive. Amazingly there were no fatalities. According to the Minnesota Department of Natural Resources, the Pagami Creek Fire was the seventh-largest fire in Minnesota history and the largest in nearly one hundred years. As *Northern Wilds* describes, "The powerful blaze vaporized trees and resulted in a towering 35,000-foot plume that created its own weather system. Smoke from the fire drifted as far as Chicago."

The primary reasons the fire spiraled out of control were the unprecedented weather conditions combined with the state's driest fall in 140 years. The total price tag for this fire would come to $23 million. While we were experiencing the impact of the

Pagami Creek Fire and the large fire we'd paddled through in the Northwest Territories firsthand, these fires are a minuscule part of wildland fires across North America and around the globe. As global temperatures rise, fire seasons are growing longer, and as scientists have been predicting for many years, the size and intensity of forest fires worldwide are increasing. In the years since the Pagami Creek Fire, forest fires in the United States have drastically increased in size—8.7 million acres burned in 2011, a record of 10.1 million acres in 2015, and near repeats of that record with 10 million acres in 2017 and 10.1 million acres in 2020, 7.1 million acres in 2021, and 7.6 million acres in 2022. Warmer temperatures and drier conditions are driving an eight-fold increase in annual area burned by high-severity fire across western forests in the last four decades. The US government spent $4.4 billion on wildland fire suppression in 2021 and $3.5 billion in 2022.

We reluctantly left Ely and began paddling across Fall Lake. In many ways our arrival in Ely had been a homecoming, but we were more than one hundred miles from our goal. As we made our way across the dark, tannin-stained water, snowflakes drifted in the air and snow geese migrated overhead. On the larger lakes we were seeing many loons. Their plumage had changed color, and they no longer made their signature call. Beavers had been busy storing branches in the water outside their lodges—food for the winter.

On the east end of Basswood Lake we searched for a familiar bay that contains an ancient cedar tree. Like popping in to visit a friend, we paid our respects and gave the impressively wide 700-to-1,100-year-old tree a hug. It took both of us to reach all the way around its trunk, overcome by a sheer sense of awe peering up through its weathered branches.

After Monument Portage—where there are three large United States–Canada border markers—we paddled past gorgeous, golden tamaracks that looked as if they were sources of light in and of themselves. Tamaracks turn golden well after the last maple and birch leaves have dropped. On Saganaga Lake we camped near the mouth of the Granite River. The site had experienced a forest fire a few years ago. Tall, skeletal jack pines and white pines stood like sentinels over vast tracts of granite and charred trees. The now decaying remains of trees that had died in the fire lay on the ground like pick up sticks. We wondered if this was what the forest that burned in the Pagami Creek Fire would look like in a few years.

By October 24 we were out of the BWCAW and working our way down a very shallow Pigeon River. Our camp for the night was at the old site of Fort Charlotte and the start of the Grand Portage. Camping in style, we set up our tents on level, wooden platforms and sat at a picnic table to devour a mac and cheese feast for dinner. By twilight we were sitting around the warm glow of a campfire sipping hot chocolate and reminiscing about the trip. Peering through the trees to the north, Bryan asked, "Are those northern lights or just clouds?" We thought clouds at first. A few minutes later the sky brightened in shimmering streaks of green and Bryan ran to grab his camera and tripod.

The dancing lights grew brighter and eventually filled the whole sky. They pulsed and swayed as we yelled, laughed, and ran around looking for the best view while the colors swirled across the sky. Keen to help Bryan find a good shot, we were scurrying around the campsite, shouting to Bryan, "Come over here!" and "They're really good here." The truth was that they were amazing everywhere. Green swirls intermixed with white and then red appeared—and grew brighter. Bryan had to increase his shutter speed to account for the brightness.

We would later learn that this aurora event had been seen as far south as Kentucky. As we trekked down the 8.5-mile Grand Portage the next day—and throughout the duration of the winter, really—the memory of those swirls of color dancing playfully across the night sky would keep us energized and eager to return to our travels. Fresh produce and indoor plumbing and all the trappings of civilization felt novel and exciting at first, but those northern lights reminded us that wide-open spaces were where we truly belonged.

***

TAKING A CUE from Gordon Lightfoot's classic song "Wreck of the Edmund Fitzgerald," we decided that the gales of November were not the best time to be traversing Lake Superior, so we spent the winter at home in northern Minnesota, guiding dogsledding trips for Wintergreen Dogsled Lodge, conducting Wilderness Classroom school assemblies, and planning the final year of the North American Odyssey. Over the previous eighteen months we had traveled more than seven thousand miles through some of the world's most remote wilderness. We returned home transformed by the people and places we experienced as well as by the stark examples of environmental destruction our species is inflicting on the planet.

Planning involved studying maps and contacting people who had kayaked portions of our anticipated route. The open water of Lake Superior, Georgian Bay, and the Atlantic Ocean would require the use of our seaworthy kayaks. However the same features that made these boats capable of handling open water hindered portaging— and between Georgian Bay and the St. Lawrence Seaway, we would have a lot of portaging to do. So we researched collapsible portage wheels and bought some that seemed beefy enough to handle loaded kayaks yet collapsed small enough to stow away inside kayak hatches. Seeking new sponsors and maintaining relationships with existing ones was an ongoing job as we sorted and edited photos to send in addition to compiling a list of items we needed.

With frozen lakes and snow blanketing the northland, we fell into a familiar seasonal routine surrounded by friends and the seventy-five Canadian Inuit Dogs we helped care for, along with a constant influx of guests of all ages and abilities who journeyed north to ply the winter woods by dog team. As the winter progressed, we began hearing rumblings about new mines being proposed in the area. At first we didn't pay too much attention because this region is known as the Iron Range and has a long history of iron ore mining, but these new proposals were for copper and nickel. As we learned more about sulfide-ore copper mining's long history of catastrophic water pollution, our concern began to grow. The first mining project, called PolyMet, would be located about twenty miles south of Ely, Minnesota, near the headwaters of the Partridge River, which flows into the Saint Louis River on its way to Lake Superior. A second project called Twin Metals was also beginning to gain momentum just a few miles from our winter home at Wintergreen Dogsled Lodge. The Twin Metals mine was proposed along the southern edge of the Boundary Waters Canoe Area Wilderness, and water pollution from that mine would flow north into the wilderness area.

We wanted to help but didn't know where to start or what we could possibly do. But then fate—in the form of Frank Moe—stepped in. Frank had represented the Bemidji area in the Minnesota legislature for several terms before he and his wife, Sherri, moved to a tiny cabin outside Grand Marais to devote more time to racing their sled dogs. In March 2012 Frank was planning to deliver thousands of petitions from northern Minnesotans opposed to copper mining to the governor, Mark Dayton, a project Frank called Sled Dogs to Saint Paul. If all went as planned, it would take him a week to mush the five hundred miles south. But Frank needed another dog team to meet him in the town of Finland with a set of petitions from Ely, which he would add to his load.

After we met Frank for coffee at the Blue Water Café in Grand Marais, we agreed to deliver the petitions. The proposed copper mines were a contentious subject in Ely, and we were concerned that taking a stance would alienate some members of our small community, making for uncomfortable interactions at the grocery store or even worse, losing good friends. Confrontation just wasn't in our nature. This task took us out of our comfort zone, but we cared too much about this place to remain silent. This land—our home—we realized, needed those who loved it to speak up in its defense if it were to stand a chance of survival against multinational mining corporations. Plus, our jobs and way of life depended on the health of these lakes and rivers. It seemed like everywhere we had explored on our meandering journey from Bellingham to this point, we found lands and waters being polluted, cut, abused, and silenced. We couldn't help but remember paddling and portaging past Uranium City and the folks in Bella Bella locked in a battle over the proposed pipeline. Now our homelands and waters were under attack, and Frank had shown us how we could contribute to the cause.

After spending the winter telling dogsledding guests and community members about the issue and gathering their petition signatures, it would take us two days to mush our relatively slow team of Inuit dogs from Ely to Finland, Minnesota, to hand off a backpack full of petitions to Frank. Most of our route would follow snowmobile trails, and as we prepared to leave Ely on a blustery day in March, there were rumors flying that angry locals might try to stop us from using the trail to deliver the petitions. We fumbled through a few interviews with local reporters and chatted with several dozen folks holding homemade signs with slogans like "We support clean water!" and "Clean water supports us!" before loading petitions into our dogsled and heading off across Shagawa Lake.

Leaving the crowd behind, we were enveloped by the steady jingle of the dogs' necklines and the swoosh of the sled runners gliding over the snow. Perhaps to the casual observer, dogsledding seventy miles to Finland was the hard part, but a sense of relief and calm washed over us. This part was easy; we had been running dogs for years. Perhaps this was how we could use our skills to be a voice for wild places. As the light began to fade and the dogs' pace slowed, we reached National Forest Lodge, a small cluster of rental cabins perched on the edge of a network of cross-country ski trails. The owners of National Forest Lodge had offered to put us up for the night and organized a gathering with food and music. Bellies full, relaxing in the warm lodge, we were struck by all the caring people from varied walks of life who had gathered to celebrate clean water and support Sled Dogs to Saint Paul. When we reached the Finland community center the following evening even more people were gathered, and we joined the crowd cheering Frank after his rousing speech. A few days later we drove down to Saint Paul to act as crossing guards as Frank and his dog team traveled the final few miles along bike trails and city streets to the state capitol. His dog team racing up the snow-dusted front lawn of the capitol made a dramatic entrance to the rally of supporters before delivering the petitions to Governor Mark Dayton urging him to oppose copper mining in Minnesota.

We returned to Ely empowered by the small role we had played in Sled Dogs to Saint Paul and all the dedicated people we had met who were speaking loudly for our land and water. Throughout the North American Odyssey we had felt the urge to speak out against the environmental injustices we were experiencing firsthand. Our work through the Wilderness Classroom was important, but we felt like we could do more, or should do more, yet weren't sure how. Sled Dogs to Saint Paul opened our eyes to environmental advocacy. It was a little scary putting ourselves out there for others to judge, but when push came to shove, not very many people yelled at us, or scowled at us in the grocery aisles. In fact, we encountered more smiles and expressions of gratitude upon our return.

# 5

# Kayaking to Key West

## *Grand Portage, Minnesota, to Key West, Florida*

### 4,900 MILES

OUR LAUNCH ON Lake Superior in early May was punctuated
by unseasonably warm, calm weather and an assembly at the
school in Grand Portage—the Oshki Ogimaag Charter School.
Afterward a tribal elder presented us with tobacco to use for
offerings along the way and all the kids accompanied us to the
water. There we made our first offering to the cold, clear waters of
the largest lake in the world and floated our brim-full sea kayaks
for the first time since Alaska. This time we were accompanied
by three friends for varying lengths of time. Bryan was with us
for just a few days to shoot some more photos, until Thunder
Bay. John, who had kayaked the Inside Passage with us, was on
a quest to paddle around Lake Superior and so would be with us
until Sault Ste. Marie, Ontario. Dan, our young, trim intern from
Brevard College, with dark curly hair and a scraggly beard, would
accompany us all spring and summer.

We rounded Hat Point, pushed along by a light tailwind, and
stopped for a brief visit to an ancient and weather-beaten tree growing out of the rock—Manido Gizhigans or the Spirit Little Cedar
Tree. Estimated to be three-to-four-hundred years old, this remarkable tree has spiritual significance to the Anishinaabe of Grand
Portage, and the land the tree lives on is considered a sacred area.
Whenever someone crosses the waters of the big lake, the tradition

is to pass by the tree and sprinkle some tobacco at its base as an offering to the Great Spirit in return for safe passage.

We passed through the Susie Islands and rounded Pigeon Point before hugging an unforgiving cliffy shoreline, seeking a familiar refuge—Hole in the Wall. What looked like a continuous cliff face eventually revealed a secret passageway—a ten-foot gap between granite sentinels. The sliver of deep, dark water spiraled to the right, ending at a sand beach, dilapidated dock, and rustic cabin, all nestled safely out of reach of any wave action on the main body of the lake. This stop was comforting in its familiarity, and we slept deeply as the night air dropped below freezing.

The next day we marveled at Lake Superior's glassy surface as we performed what would become our daily ritual of data gathering. We were collecting water-quality data for the nonprofit organization Adventure Scientists. This "Daily Data," as we came to call it, would provide the students with real numbers to graph and analyze over time. For a water-clarity reading, we lowered a Secchi disk on a thirty-foot cord. The point of this exercise was to record the depth at which the disk disappeared. But when we reached the end of the cord, the black-and-white disk was still clearly visible thirty feet below the hulls of our kayaks; we resolved to lengthen our cord for future readings of this cold, clear lake.

We were floating on the largest lake in the world by surface area, containing three quadrillion gallons of water—10 percent of the world's fresh surface water that isn't frozen in a polar ice cap or glacier. Concerns for Lake Superior in the coming years would involve surface temperature rise and a related insurgence of invasive species and algae growth, pipeline spills, as well as less ice coverage in the winter leading to increased evaporation, lowering the water level. Seeing that disk and recording the data daily had a transformative power that was linked to regularly gazing into the depths while moving across the lake's surface. We would confidently fill up our bottles and be refreshed by that ice-cream-headache-producing water. The intimacy with and appreciation for this body of water grew with each passing day, well before we would hear the phrase "water is life" being used as a rallying cry at pipeline protests. As Dan Egan says in *The Death and Life of the Great Lakes*, "Historically, on average, about a quarter to a third of the surface of Lake Superior, an area of lake roughly the size of Massachusetts, froze each year. But average ice cover for Superior declined by 76 percent between 1973 and 2011."

The days passed with relative ease; we had, as always, budgeted miles conservatively in the early weeks of this stage of the journey so we could ease our bodies into shape. After a night in the relative luxury of Thompson Island with its wooden dock and sauna, Bryan veered north to his car and a return to life as usual back in Grand Marais while the rest of us continued east to Pie Island and beyond.

Somewhere near Rossport our party of four stopped for lunch on a rocky beach. After nestling our feet into coarse, dark sand, we noticed some white mixed in. John picked up a handful assuming it'd be fish eggs. To our dismay the millions of tiny white balls scattered along this isolated beach were plastic. Where could they have possibly come from? Seeing this plastic pollution on Lake Superior, glistening in the sun like diamonds, felt like a personal affront. We crouched at the water's edge hoping to figure out what they were and why they were covering the beach. How could this be? A perfect wilderness beach laced with wolf tracks and tiny plastic balls? We would later learn these round bits of plastic are called nurdles, which get melted down and turned into a million different plastic items from lawn chairs to plastic forks. Somehow, rather than finding their way to a factory to be transformed into plastic bags, these nurdles had found their way onto a remote beach along the Ontario shore of Lake Superior.

Wilderness strips life to the essentials and heightens your senses. Air-conditioning, indoor plumbing, light switches, and walls have a way of leveling the peaks and valleys. Wrapped in wildness, the highs are higher and the lows lower. Thousands of nurdles brought us crashing down in a way that trash strewn on the streets of an urban jungle had never done. In the city we rush through filth with our earbuds in and blinders on. Weeks of rhythmic paddling, storms, cold, moments of terror, discomfort, and sunshine had peeled away so many layers that we finally saw these tiny translucent beads for what they really are: a toxic assault on our planet.

* * *

THE SKY WAS overcast, and a light wind blew from the southeast as we left Terrace Bay, Ontario. Our stomachs were rumbling by the time we had paddled eight miles from the mainland into the shelter of the Slate Islands. Suddenly our perspective shifted from being way out in Lake Superior to casually gliding through an inland lake.

Two caribou came running out of the woods. We had high hopes of seeing caribou, but never expected to see them this quickly. The caribou seemed curious about us, yet slightly wary. These animals were part of the southernmost population of woodland caribou. At one time, caribou lived as far south as the North Channel of Lake Huron, but the destructive influence of humans on their habitat forced them further north.

The caribou were first observed in the Slate Islands after a very cold winter in the early 1900s. Not kept in check by predation, the population fluctuated wildly depending on food availability. At its peak, the islands contained as many as 650 caribou. The resulting shortage of food caused their numbers to plummet. During our visit in the spring of 2012, there were about 100 caribou. In 2014, however, wolf packs made their way across the ice to the Slate Islands and Michipicoten Island, a large island south of the Slate Islands, causing the caribou population in both places to plummet. The wolves disappeared after a few years in the Slate Islands, but two male caribou were all that remained. Starting in 2018 an elaborate human intervention began. Before the last caribou were eaten by wolves on Michipicoten Island, the Canadian government captured fifteen caribou and moved six to Caribou Island, 25 miles to the south. The other nine caribou were transported 75 miles to the Slate

Islands. The goal is to reestablish herds on those islands and keep the genetically distinct Lake Superior woodland caribou alive. Caribou Island is very small and can only support about fifteen caribou, but it is almost 40 miles from the mainland, so it is very unlikely that wolves will reach the island. If the caribou population grows on Caribou Island, the Canadian government will likely move some caribou to Michipicoten Island to try and reestablish a herd there. In the distant past there were thousands of caribou not only on the islands of Lake Superior but also along the Ontario mainland, and the caribou could walk across the ice and repopulate remote islands on their own, but now the few dozen caribou on these far-flung islands are all that remain.

One might argue that since we are responsible for messing up an animal's habitat in the first place, we should take some responsibility for that animal's well-being by intervening. As climate change or, more broadly, the Anthropocene brings about the sixth great extinction, how do we choose what animals, insects, and plants to save? And to what extent do we go to save them?

*  *  *

AFTER WE MADE the crossing back to the mainland, several days of headwinds, rain, and waves greeted us. Our progress was slow but steady as we sneaked through channels between islands and hugged the shore whenever possible. As we neared Marathon, Ontario, we wound through a small channel that was very shallow, almost impassible even for our kayaks. Here we noticed a rise and fall in the water level. Partway through the channel, we had to stop because our boats had run aground. But we just had to wait a couple of minutes for the water to rise back up. As we continued, we puzzled over the cause of this fluctuation—the wind and water running between the islands? A seiche? But we thought those were more extreme and long-lasting.

When we finally stopped for lunch we decided to observe the phenomenon more closely. As we ate our tortillas and cheese we stuck a stick in the sand at the current water level. We all observed the water rise up the beach and then drop back down below the stick over the course of five minutes. Watching this rhythmic surge and ebb reminded us of blood coursing through veins propelled by a beating heart. We felt like we were watching the pulse of Lake Superior—or when you consider the size and location of this lake, the beating heart of the North American continent.

* * *

FOUR DAYS AFTER leaving the Slate Islands the sun finally reappeared as we skirted the rugged coastline of Pukaskwa National Park. We cruised past the stunning pink granite, boulder-strewn, cliffy islands and shoreline with grand, green topography behind. Twenty miles went by quickly, and we found ourselves paddling into a bay through channels between rocky islands in the early afternoon. A white-sand beach beckoned.

Without the context of the chilling air and water temps and coniferous trees, one might mistake this beach for a tropical paradise. The water was a stunning turquoise near shore, shifting to a rich blue in the depths. After pitching our tents, we hung our dry suits, long underwear, and spray skirts on tree branches and rocks to dry in the sun. Lady slippers bloomed in the woods near an impressive pile of bear scat.

The dawn of the last day of May served to remind us that it was not yet summer. A heavy frost coated the boats and John's tent. John had been the only one to reside on the beach that night, while the rest of us opted to sleep in the woods, experiencing a slightly warmer night. It was a morning for paddling while enjoying a mug of piping hot tea. There is nothing quite so satisfying as pausing every fifteen minutes to wrap your hands around that mug, thaw your fingers, and sip on a warm drink.

We paddled past several massive, steep cobble beaches made of rounded stones ranging in size from baseball to bowling ball.

Landing was difficult, but we paused a couple of times to explore unique depressions in the stones high up on the beach at the ancient level of the lake—Pukaskwa pits. No one really knows the purpose of the pits or even when they were constructed. It is thought that many of the pits were made between 1000 and 1500 AD. They could have been shelter for people, places to store food, hunting blinds, fireplaces, or even of ceremonial use. Perhaps they were used for young people on "vision quests." A more recent theory posits they were filled with ice and snow to be cold food storage long into the summer. Regardless of the purpose of their origin, we were left pondering how such basic structures could last for so long and what alterations to the earth our current civilization was leaving behind to be puzzled over several thousand years from now.

By mid-June we crossed a wind-tousled Goulais Bay and rounded Gros Cap at the east end of Lake Superior as the city of Sault Ste. Marie loomed ahead. We were sad to see John go but glad that he had his own journey ahead of him as he would continue west along the south shore of the lake and we would continue east toward the Atlantic Ocean. We dodged paddle wheel tour boats, fishing boats, and freighters as we made our way through the locks on the Canadian side and dropped twenty-one feet without having to portage. Here was a place significantly altered by humans. Shipping and the locks have changed the rapids that were once a gathering place for many Indigenous people to harvest fish in the spring and fall. In fact, it was called Bahweting, or "the Gathering Place."

* * *

AFTER ABOUT A month of paddling along the North Shore of Lake Superior, we meandered through the granite islands of Lake Huron's Georgian Bay. Where the French River enters Lake Huron, we would leave behind the wide-open expanses of fresh water we had grown accustomed to. The Great Lakes form the largest surface freshwater system on Earth, containing one fifth of the world's surface fresh water—six quadrillion gallons—and 84 percent of North America's surface fresh water. Only the polar ice caps contain more fresh water.

We made our way up a narrow rocky channel to the base of a small set of rapids flowing into Lake Huron. "Well, I hope we remember how to portage!" Dan exclaimed as we climbed out of our kayaks. We would spend the next two weeks paddling up the French River, across Lake Nipissing, and then down the Mattawa River to the Ottawa River. From here all the way to Montreal we would be following one of the most-used voyageurs' routes. Native people gave the river its name because of the French-speaking explorers, traders, and missionaries who used to ply its waters in the 1700s and 1800s.

Those early explorers had adopted the Anishinaabe's traditional craft, the birchbark canoe, which, while fragile, was as light or lighter than the most sophisticated modern canoes made of Kevlar or carbon fiber. By comparison our eighteen-foot sea kayaks were heavy and awkward to load, unload, and portage. For the majority of our journey to Key West, our kayaks were the ideal craft. They were fast, stable, extremely seaworthy, and could carry a large load, but traversing portage-strewn rivers like the French and the Mattawa was challenging. All of our food and equipment was stored in waterproof bags that we carefully stuffed into hatches in the front and back of our kayaks. When we reached a portage we could haul the kayaks over the portages without removing all of the food and gear, or we could unload them, haul everything across the portage in several trips, and then repack our belongings into the kayaks. Loaded with food and equipment, the kayaks weighted between 125 and 175 pounds each, but the time and effort it took to pack and repack them usually forced us to haul the loaded kayaks across the portages. With one person at the bow and another at the stern, we would heave a kayak up onto our shoulders and then move across the portage as quickly as possible. The boats were heavy, but the hardest part was negotiating rocky, twisting, narrow trails with what felt like an eighteen-foot log balanced between us, digging into our shoulders.

It was hot, difficult work, but the Canadian Shield's rugged, wild landscape reminded us of home, and our tired bodies were lulled to sleep each night by the silence that surrounded us. In many ways this journey along the voyageur's highway was a final respite of wilderness immersion before cities, roads, and human impacts gained an ever-increasing grip on us. Over the coming months we would often ponder: What would this place have been like before the Industrial Revolution? Many of the rapids along the Ottawa River that the voyageurs hauled their canoes and trade goods around have been swallowed by dams, and the riverbanks are now speckled with towns and cottages. As the weeks passed the landscape really began to change. Pockets of civilization and the hum of distant roads were steadily replaced by an ever-increasing urban landscape.

As we approached Montreal, for the first time in a long time it was hard to find a place to camp. With skyscrapers looming in the distance, we hauled our boats onto a small, muddy island in the middle of the river with the constant din of traffic and the faint smell of exhaust wafting from a massive highway bridge just downstream. Ducks floated in the shallows near a stand of tall marsh grasses, but everything felt dirty and industrial.

In the morning we paddled the final few miles of the Ottawa River to the confluence with the St. Lawrence River and into the heart of Montreal. The Lachine Rapids form the last major obstacle between Montreal and the ocean. Along the southern shore of the St. Lawrence River a large canal (the South Shore Canal) and two massive locks allow ocean-going freighters to bypass the rapids, but we followed the Lachine Canal, a much smaller and older canal containing five locks, through the center of the city.

During our transit of the Lachine Canal, we contemplated what an engineering marvel this must have been at the time of its completion in 1825. The Lachine Rapids had thwarted explorer Jacques Cartier's party from venturing any further up the St. Lawrence in 1535. However, it wasn't until 1959 and the opening of the St. Lawrence Seaway (including the South Shore Canal) that massive ships—730 feet in length with drafts of 25 feet transporting grain, iron ore, and other cargo—could make their way from as far inland as Lake Superior to the Atlantic Ocean.

The canal was lined with parks, big buildings, trendy-looking condos, and restaurants. How odd to be paddling *through* a city. In the late afternoon we were spit out onto the river after the last lock. Boats of all shapes and sizes buzzed around us. We passed a massive floating spa in the heart of the city and longingly joked about stopping. Our tired muscles were tempted by cozy deck chairs and white-robed people lounging in the sun. The river's swift current was carrying us into a whole new urban world.

The current coming from the St. Lawrence downstream of the rapids was intimidating. Big boats gunned their engines and man-handled their way through. We bounced around in wakes left by the larger boats. Jumbles of confused water pulled us downstream at eight miles an hour past huge docks. The current remained strong as we crossed the river and left Montreal in our wake.

It was six thirty at night when we found the island we had been hoping for. Low-lying and in the floodplain, it had escaped the reach of development. We set up camp on dirt-encrusted rocks just inches above the water. Wolfing down spaghetti, we watched a steady stream of container ships streaming up and down the St. Lawrence Seaway, pondering how they had replaced voyageur canoes. In a few days' time they would be pulling into Duluth. In contrast, it had taken us almost two months to reach Montreal.

\* \* \*

AFTER TANGOING WITH the tankers for a few days we entered Lac Saint-Pierre and could feel the ocean's presence for the first time. A small tidal change reminded us we would soon be dipping our paddles in salt water once again. We relished the opportunity to paddle along the edge of the lake away from the large commercial vessels, which were confined to the narrow deep channel that runs down the middle of the twenty-mile-long lake.

After finishing the day at a campground and chatting with a friendly couple, we found out that the lake had been used to test artillery, and we had unknowingly paddled right through a zone that still had unexploded ordinances in it! For nearly fifty years (until the year 2000) the Canadian military had used the lake as a firing range; an estimated eight thousand unexploded shells are scattered across the bottom.

We had seen a yellow buoy, but we had passed many yellow buoys before and didn't stop to read the sign that had tiny print on it. There was a channel marked with lots of sticks and fluorescent flagging. We had no idea what it was when we were paddling past it, even when a man in a motorboat waved one arm at us in a "shoo, get away" sort of motion. We assumed he wanted us to get out of his way. Apparently his gesture had much more meaning than that. Ironically Lac Saint-Pierre is also a UNESCO biosphere reserve, containing the largest heron habitat in North America and "wetlands with rare plant life, and a rich ecosystem."

Downstream from Lac Saint-Pierre the tidal fluctuation increased, so we began timing our paddling with the outgoing tide and resting or setting up camp when the incoming tide caused the river's current to reverse and flow upstream. The current was really hauling by the time we were fifteen miles shy of Québec City. Just drifting, we were moving at five miles per hour with the outgoing tide. At low tide we decided to stop near an island far from any houses to camp rather than fight against the incoming tide. It was hard work carrying our loaded kayaks through the marsh to our campsite, but we wanted to make sure they would be safe from the rising water. We set them down in a field of wildflowers and quickly set up camp in the woods just beyond. We assumed that the flowers wouldn't grow in a place that was covered by water at high tide, but we looped a rope though all the kayaks to secure them to a tree just in case.

We woke up to a faint but unusual clacking sound around midnight and peeked out of the tent. Shining our headlamps on the kayaks, we were relieved to see they were where we had left them—but then they moved, bumping against each other. In our sleep-induced stupor we slowly realized they were floating! Scrambling out of the tent without bothering to put on any clothes, we waded into waist-deep water without hesitation to save our kayaks from being flushed downriver. The wildflowers in the marsh were entirely submerged. We carried each kayak to a spot slightly uphill from our tent before turning in again, shivering and exhausted.

Paddling out the St. Lawrence Seaway was like dancing with the sea. To succeed we had to follow the ocean's rhythm. When the tide was high, we would launch our kayaks and paddle hard for six hours, flushed along by the outgoing tide. With the help of the tidal current we could often cover thirty miles in what amounted to little more than half a day. Then at low tide we would haul our kayaks several hundred yards over stinky, mucky mudflats and search for a place to camp. We bid farewell to Dan, who had to head back to North Carolina for the start of the school year. We would miss his good humor, hard work ethic, and skillful video production. The Gulf of St. Lawrence spread out before us, and the salty, seaweed smell of the ocean filled our nostrils. There was something satisfying about reaching salt water after so long.

* * *

AFTER FOUR DAYS we passed the tiny town of Saint-André-de-Kamouraska, Quebec, and spotted slick, dark heads popping out of the steel-gray water. Beady black eyes stared back at us with a wary curiosity. We lamented that we were leaving the ocean on the same day we had our first seal sighting. We then angled our kayaks up a small stream. It was already August, and we knew that paddling all the way out the St. Lawrence Seaway and around the coast of New Brunswick and Nova Scotia and would take too long. Instead we decided to follow a long-forgotten route over land to the Saint Francis River, which forms the border between Maine and New Brunswick as it flows into the Saint John River, which would eventually lead us to the Bay of Fundy and the Atlantic Ocean. On Google Earth it all looked simple, but on the ground things rarely pan out that way.

Our twenty-seven-mile portage to the Saint Francis River had been used since people first arrived in this region after the last ice age more than ten thousand years ago and was named the Grand Communications Route by the French in the 1700s. We began by following a tiny stream that was just barely deep enough to float our kayaks, sliding our boats over kelp-covered rocks and logs. Tall grasses gave us tunnel vision, and spiders clung to webs woven in the swaying blades, glistening in the afternoon sun.

Standing up in our kayaks, peering over the mud bank, we finally spotted the road. We slid our kayaks up onto the grasses above and scrambled up ourselves. We assembled the carts, changed our shoes from sandals to running shoes, and away we went, bumping along the gravel road.

The first half mile of the portage was on gravel, which was hard on our carts. When we reached pavement, we both breathed a sigh of relief. Slowly trudging along Quebec Route 289 we got funny looks from passing cars, bicyclists, and grazing horses. Up and up, out of the St. Lawrence River Valley, we climbed. Hauling our heavy loads uphill was slow and tiring work.

Our second day of portaging was primarily downhill. Just as our feet and shoulders were feeling weary, a man with sandy-white hair and wire-rimmed glasses pulled over, introduced himself as Martin, and invited us to camp at his place—Atelier Amboise. We arrived in Pohenegamook as it was getting dark and then walked just over a quarter of a mile up a road to find Martin's house. He and his wife had finished their dinner on the porch of their gorgeous house— containing all sorts of wood furniture and cabinets that Martin had made. They packed up some cherries, grapes, tomatoes, cheese, bread, mayo, and beer for us. Martin showed us to the spot beside a small waterfall and idyllic swimming hole. Rain started shortly after we climbed into the tent. Martin had said it hadn't rained in a month here. It felt special to sleep under the much-needed rain.

It was still raining in the morning. We gobbled oatmeal as we packed up camp before going up to the house to charge batteries and shower. Then we wheeled about a mile to an abandoned hotel on Pohenegamook Lake. The sun had come out by the time we launched our kayaks. At the end of the lake we reached the Quebec-Maine border, where the Saint Francis River began.

The river was narrow and shallow, with lots of twists, turns, and gravel bars. Aside from the occasional sounds of the road and the polluted scent of the water, it felt completely wild. We would frequently encounter mini rapids that required us to get out of our boats and wade through. Geese flew overhead, herons waded in the shallows, and kingfishers and bald eagles perched in tree branches above our heads. As it grew dark we gave up looking for a gravel bar or clearing and set up camp in thick brush along the bank. Good campsites are usually easy to come by, but when you camp in hundreds of different places, you are bound to end up with a handful of truly rotten ones. Tonight's certainly qualified, with an abundance of roots and rocks sticking into our backs and deforming the tent.

* * *

A SURE SIGN that we were nearing Fort Kent, Maine, on the Saint John River was the sudden presence of fishermen in little motorboats. We awoke at five o'clock to the sound of rain and a fishing boat trolling past our campsite. We later found out they were in search of muskie for the annual Fort Kent Muskie Derby. As the soggy day wore on and we couldn't shake the chill, we resolved to treat ourselves to a hotel room once we reached Fort Kent.

Of course, this was the first American town we had been in for a long time, so we had to clear customs upon arrival. We paddled through shallow water below the international bridge that was under construction and struggled to find a spot to pull off the river. After an awkward scramble up the steep, rocky bank, we walked into the customs office and realized that paddlers checking in here was an uncommon occurrence. A drug-sniffing dog inspected our kayaks before we were permitted back into the United States.

Little did we know that we had stumbled upon Fort Kent at its busiest, due to the annual fishing derby and Ploye Festival, which meant all the hotel rooms in town were booked. We paddled to the boat ramp and wheeled our kayaks up the main street in a downpour past carnival rides being assembled and a big top tent. Fortunately the manager at the Northern Door Inn was sympathetic to weary, damp paddlers. The hotel conference room would be our home for the night. The assistant front desk manager talked to us as we unloaded our boats. He called the local paper—the *Fiddlehead Focus*.

After an interview with the paper in the hotel lobby, we found the Chinese buffet. On our way back to the hotel we learned what a ploye was—basically a buckwheat pancake that you don't flip. It is rooted in the Acadian culture of the region. A crowd had gathered around a giant griddle—twelve feet in diameter. Coals glowed underneath and the griddle steamed from the rain falling on top. We were about to witness the creation of the world's largest ploye. Six people poured batter out of five-gallon buckets and a cloud of steam enveloped the crowd. More people used long-handled squeegees to spread the batter evenly. When it was cooked eight people moved the griddle off the coals and more people set to work scraping the ploye off the griddle and onto a picnic table where the bits would be slathered in butter and served to the crowd. As we stood in the evening drizzle eating our ploye pieces, we couldn't have been happier about the timing of our arrival in Fort Kent.

On our way out of town the next day we wheeled our kayaks over to a monument marking the northern terminus of US Route 1. As we posed for a photo and bought mile-marker 2,390 stickers, the perspective on our journey shifted. We were on our way to mile 0 of US 1 in Key West—just 2,390 miles away. Of course, we were traveling by water, so our route would be more circuitous—about 3,250 miles—and it would take us about eight months to paddle, compared to someone cruising US 1 for a leisurely week in a car.

We headed east and then south, following the Maine–New Brunswick border on a river that grew less wild every day. Passing industrial areas left us no longer comfortable drinking from the body of water on which we paddled. After all, the river basin is home to about half a million people. The Saint John River suffered from many sources of pollution for two centuries—pulp mills, timber harvesting, sewage, dams, hog and poultry farms, and potato processing. It may be on the mend, having improved in the last forty years, but it was apparent that it still had a long road to recovery.

Surrounded by civilization, we talked about how difficult it was getting to find a camping area for the night. We were living on the fringe, wondering if our identity would shift from that of adventurers to vagrants. Perhaps we needed to begin asking people to camp in their yards. We remembered our track record when we paddled the Amazon River five years before. While spending six months traversing South America by canoe and bicycle, we often found ourselves pulling up to a small town along the river and inquiring about spending the night. There were six of us, we hadn't showered in weeks, and we struggled with the language—and in every instance except one, people opened their doors to us. We slept in schools, churches, community centers, and—most often—people's houses. Our time in remote villages in Peru and Brazil affirmed the belief that most people are good at heart. We still had reservations that this approach would work in North America. The only thing preventing us from finding out was working up the courage to ask.

This discussion was taking place as we were nearing the end of our paddling day. We had gone thirty miles, and it was time to look for a camp spot. We were a couple of days away from Fredericton, New Brunswick, and finding a patch of nonprivate land seemed unlikely. We paddled past a nice yard with a man sitting on a bench near the water's edge and paused, contemplating asking him about camping in his yard. We hesitated and passed up the opportunity. What were we so afraid of?

As we paddled on, lamenting our cowardice, a man and his black lab pulled up in a little green motorboat. White-haired and in a plaid flannel shirt, Blake asked with a smile where we were from and if we were looking for a place to stay! He told us that if we headed back to his place with the gorgeous yard and the bench by the water, we could stay in his guesthouse. We were dumbfounded. Had he read our minds? Our concerns were allayed instantly by this generous act, and we stopped fretting about the rest of our route.

Blake and his wife, Elaine, who were both retired and extremely friendly, took us in; we spent two nights in their guesthouse before continuing on. This stop allowed us to catch up on producing content for the Wilderness Classroom website and submit a grant proposal that was due soon, in addition to chatting with Blake and Elaine over coffee each morning on their front porch overlooking the river. We savored stories of Blake's days of running a dog team and iceboating on the frozen river.

We rode a wave of hospitality and generosity the rest of the way down the Saint John River. CBC (Canadian Broadcasting Corporation) Television and Radio, and the Fredericton and Saint John newspapers covered our story as we arrived in Fredericton. Replenishing our food at the grocery store in Oromocto, country music was playing on the radio, until the news came on—and we heard our own interview on the CBC!

The next day we received an email from a man named Paul who lived along the river. He had read a recent article about our journey in the Fredericton newspaper and invited us to stay at his place. We decided to take this stranger's kind offer and battled a headwind all day as we slowly worked our way downriver toward Paul's house. We were greeted by a middle-aged man with a big grin who waved at us vigorously from the end of his dock as we paddled near. Paul helped us secure our kayaks and whisked us away to his restored farmhouse built in the early 1800s, where we met his blond and equally friendly girlfriend, Paulette. After luxurious showers and a delicious dinner of salmon, sweet potatoes, salad, green beans, and corn on the cob, we chatted late into the evening. Paul used to guide kayaking trips and had lots of good advice for us, in addition to several contacts farther along our route. He also worked for the Coast Guard. Reversing Falls and the Bay of Fundy were our next big challenges, and we were so glad to have a conversation with a man who was familiar with both. We took him up on his gracious offer to escort us through Reversing Falls.

* * *

THE NEXT MORNING we paddled through the largest city in New Brunswick, Saint John, and watched the shoreline change as we approached the ocean. Slowly the river surrendered its power to the Bay of Fundy's massive tides. Rock outcrops replaced sandy banks and our nostrils were filled with the smell of the sea as millions of gallons of salt water rushed up the river with each incoming tide. Reversing Falls had been a source of anxiety and wonder for us ever since we included the Bay of Fundy in our route. The tidal shift here is twenty-eight feet. Add to that a substantial river funneling into a narrow gorge and over underwater ledges. Water is forced through this gorge in roiling rapids one hundred thousand cubic feet per second. At low tide, the river drops in violent rapids into the Bay of Fundy. At high tide water from the bay rushes in, causing tumultuous rapids in the opposite direction, flowing back into the Saint John River. This means we had a small window of time to pass through safely at slack tide, when the ocean and river were at the same level— fifteen to twenty minutes.

After spending most of their lives in the ocean, Atlantic salmon, shad, and alewives ascend the Saint John River and its tributaries to spawn in the spring. These fish along with Atlantic sturgeon and American eel were an important food source for the region's early human inhabitants, the Wolastoqiyik. Paddling birchbark canoes through Reversing Falls during the fifteen-to-twenty-minute windows allowed by the tides, occurring roughly every six hours, would have been treacherous, so we were not surprised to learn of a traditional portage route. Our goal was to carefully plan our timing and paddle through the falls, but it was comforting to know that the portage (which would now involve zigzagging on several city streets) could be our plan B.

We planned our passage for high-water slack, when the shift would happen from the water flowing in to water flowing out. That way, we reasoned, if we were delayed, we would at least get spit out at the end instead of having to fight an ever-increasing current sucking us back in. Our tidal window would be early the next morning.

We were up before the sun and packed in an adrenaline-induced frenzy. By six thirty we were paddling against a slight current toward the roar of Reversing Falls. As we wound around through the river gorge, Paul and Paulette caught up to us in their motorboat to escort us through. We had to wait a while for slack, but it was better to be early than late. We floated in an eddy, watching cormorants as we chatted with our two new friends. The tide turned a little later than predicted because the river was low, so we had a few extra minutes to take in the surreal scene of the slowly diminishing rapids and the paper mill towering above the river.

Once we chose to start paddling, the roiling water had calmed down substantially, but we were still going against a little current. Our passage through the narrowest part of the gorge was on perfectly flat, calm water, but we did not linger to take it all in because we knew that calm would only last for a couple of minutes. Rock walls of billion-year-old light gray marble from South America on one side, five-hundred-million-year-old dark gray sandstone and shale from northern Africa on the other, towered above us. As we passed under the bridge, it became apparent that the tide was dropping and had been dropping for a while, as indicated by the exposed slime and barnacle-coated rocks. Safely in the bay, we said our thank-yous and goodbyes. They were off to an office party replete with face painting and bouncy castles. We were headed for a slightly different party, hosted by Neptune, and we hoped the sea god would be happy to see us.

* * *

ALONE AGAIN, WE smiled at each other wide-eyed. Here we were in the Bay of Fundy. Although we turned our bows south and still had many months of paddling ahead of us, in this moment, as our kayaks floated on their second ocean, we had achieved our goal of crossing the continent, from the Pacific to the Atlantic.

We moved with a sense of urgency as long as the tide was going out. After five hours we stopped on a pebble beach tucked in a crack of an otherwise jagged, cliffy shoreline for a quick lunch and pee break as the water began rushing back into the bay. Every few minutes we pulled our kayaks higher onto the beach to prevent them from floating away. The rocks were covered in dripping seaweed and barnacles, making us feel like we were eating lunch on the ocean floor. To our amazement, during our thirty-minute break the water rose several feet. The final few miles to Dipper Harbor felt like we were paddling up a fast-flowing river. We inched along the shore, trying to take advantage of every eddy and pool of slack water. In many ways it felt like paddling up the Mackenzie River, only the rugged, cliff-lined shore barred the option of lining our kayaks against the current.

Two and a half years earlier we had used this same technique when we experienced opposing currents along the Inside Passage, but there the intertidal zone was speckled with sea stars, crabs, urchins, anemones, and a whole menagerie of life. In many ways this coastline felt the same, only the ocean seemed relatively barren. We grew excited when we saw a single sea star or a lone crab. The water was cold and clear, the tides enormous, and the country rugged, but some vital ingredient seemed to be missing.

On our third day out of Saint John we paddled into Lubec, Maine, and said goodbye to Canada for the last time. As we paddled south the tides were growing smaller and the currents weaker, but we still had to carefully time our paddling with the tide. We left our final Canadian campsite in the dark with the outgoing tide. Phosphorescent plankton, excited by our paddle strokes, left a glowing trail, and even our bow wakes glowed as we pierced through the predawn stillness. The sun came up, a red-orange ball of fire, over our left shoulders.

Several bald eagles were hunting for fish as the day began. We parked at a dock in Lubec and walked through quiet streets to the customs office just as the town was waking up. Folks were out walking dogs, shops were opening, and an older couple sat on a bench overlooking the harbor.

Once settled into the local campground, it felt foreign to be surrounded by RVs in a sterile field of neatly mowed grass, but we would have to get used to a more urban adventure as we progressed south. Back in 2009 when we began tracing possible lines across a map of the continent, we surmised that paddling down the East Coast would give us a chance to meet more people and stop in schools all along the way to share our journey with thousands more students. This had been part of our grand plan all along, but we were still sad to leave solitude and remote wild lands behind. It felt like we were drinking orange soda instead of fresh-squeezed orange juice made from organic fruit we had picked ourselves an hour before. Wilderness is like a superfood, and its intangible values fill our minds, souls, and bodies with life in ways that land and waters trammeled by humanity's heavy hand can't do. Hours of paddling each day and the rhythm of setting up camp only to break it down as the pink sun greeted us the next day provided enjoyment and a sense of purpose, but there was something missing that only wilderness could provide.

In place of the stillness and solitude we would learn to savor the communities along our route and the hundreds of people we would meet from all walks of life. Our cheery campground neighbors in Lubec—John and Pat, who traversed up and down the East Coast in their motor home each summer, living life on their own terms— provided a glimpse of many such human encounters to come during our final eight-month push to Key West.

This journey had forever changed us, but as the end of the North American Odyssey grew closer, we began to wonder how we would fit in and what we would do back at home. John and Pat, though so different from us, shared about their own journey. They had left good jobs as an elementary art teacher and a college librarian for the freedom of the road.

The current swept us past the "spark plug" lighthouse and a handful of lobstermen checking their traps with their clunky, rumbling boats stopping, starting, and moving in unpredictable directions. There were so many multicolored lobster pot buoys in the water—thousands of them—that they were never out of sight until we reached Massachusetts. Looking out across the calm, dark water, the haphazardly scattered buoys reminded us of an Easter egg hunt. We rounded the weather-beaten rock point where the lighthouse stood and began scanning the shoreline for John and Pat. Soon, we saw John hiking on the trail with his walking stick. Pat emerged from the woods and pulled out her phone to take photos and video of us paddling by. One last wave and we were alone again, paddling down the Bold Coast.

Fog, wind, rocky shores, and lobster floats filled our days as we wound our way through Maine's labyrinth of islands and bays. We bobbed in the Atlantic's robust swell before gliding for hours through intricate protected channels that reminded us of a salty version of northern Minnesota. Paddling down one such channel we spotted two sea kayaks headed toward us. Recreational kayak sightings were common, but these long sea kayaks were weighted down with camping gear like us. Excited by the prospect of meeting some fellow travelers, we waved and glided to a stop. Steph and Jeff appeared to be similar in age and mindset to us. Both were brown haired and shorter in stature but very fit. They were out for a long weekend, paddling and camping among the islands. Jeff's smile was accentuated by his long but neatly trimmed goatee, and his eyes glimmered under his thick-rimmed glasses as he quizzed us about our journey. Steph, with her energetic personality and glowing smile, was a teacher at the middle school in

Exeter, New Hampshire, and before we knew it, plans were set for us to stay with them when we reached the New Hampshire shore in about a week and Steph was determined to arrange an assembly at her school. With both parties traveling in opposite directions, our meeting in the light ocean swell did not last long.

A few days later, true to her word, seven hundred sixth graders filed into the auditorium as we finished setting up our tent and arranging a kayak and an assortment of our gear on the stage. Stories and questions flowed, and you could hear a pin drop as we described paddling with humpback whales in Alaska and dogsledding through a blizzard in the Northwest Territories. The students' excitement and enthusiasm were contagious, reminding us why we had chosen to paddle down the East Coast. Over the next month we had a series of assemblies as well as adult presentations planned in Massachusetts, Connecticut, New York, and New Jersey. We were no longer traveling in the wilderness, but we could still advocate for it by sparking interest in young people.

In early October we had reached the Connecticut coast and determined that fall had officially arrived. We each put on an extra layer under our dry suits and cherished the brief moments of sunshine. One day we paddled under an oppressive blanket of gray clouds. It was raining around lunchtime, and we had been paddling along a seemingly abandoned strip of beach that we imagined had been bustling with tourists and sunbathers in the not-so-distant past of summer. We happened to paddle past a restaurant and quickly made the decision to stop in instead of sitting on a beach shivering in the rain, eating from our dwindling lunch bag. Some days we could empathize with homeless people living on the margins. Stopping for a warm meal to bask in a diner's warm, dry booth for an hour helped make up for the stress we often felt as the end of the day grew close and a place to camp seemed nonexistent.

We pulled our kayaks high up on the beach and tromped into the restaurant in our dripping dry suits. We attempted to avoid the funny looks of the customers and waitstaff as we extracted ourselves from the damp Gore-Tex. Our server was curious about how we arrived in this state, first guessing that we had arrived by motorcycle. She smiled when we said that we were kayaking and peppered us with questions about our journey as she took our order and then brought our hot food. This stop was just what we needed to buoy our spirits. We dried off and warmed up as we filled our bellies. The worst of the rain was over by the time we were paying our bill. The server returned with the receipt with a new grin on her face. She was nearly bursting with excitement when she exclaimed, "I can't believe your last name!" When we stared at her blankly, she spelled it out for us: "Freeman. You're on this crazy journey and you're free, man!" We kept chuckling about that as we crossed the state line into New York. We were indeed free.

Horseshoe crab sightings were frequent, and their recently shed dark, helmet-like exoskeletons littered the shoreline. These living fossils evolved in the shallow seas of the Paleozoic Era, millions of years before the dinosaurs. Some of their fossils have been dated at 360 million years old, and now they survive here on the ocean floor surrounded by New York City's urban sprawl and the filth of humanity spilling into the ocean. Like cockroaches, blue-green algae, and countless other ancient beings, it seems inevitable that the Anthropocene is just one of many global disturbances that they will humbly navigate during their long life as a species.

* * *

LONG ISLAND SOUND narrowed as the tall buildings of the New York City skyline came into view. The light pollution from the city was so substantial that we could see its glow for two nights before our arrival. Where to camp on the evening before we would enter the East River posed a far bigger challenge than the five-knot current rushing through Hell Gate in the heart of Manhattan at dawn the next morning. On the map, Hart Island looked promising—a relatively undeveloped island with no bridge to it. As we approached, we talked to a man in a motorboat who said, "You don't want to camp there. It's haunted." When pressed for an explanation, he said, "Prisoners bury the indigent out there." In other words, it's New York City's potter's field, run by the department of corrections. Inmates from Rikers Island were paid $0.50 an hour to bury bodies there. Reluctantly, we pointed our bows toward City Island, hoping that a plan B would present itself. Anything would be better than an island filled with unmarked graves.

As darkness approached along with a growing sense of panic, it felt as if we had reached a new low. Camping and urban areas don't mix. Surely we'd be thrown out of any sort of public park, and everywhere else was grimy and developed. We just needed a few hours of sleep because we needed to get up around four o'clock in the morning to time our approach with the tide. Our dinner that evening consisted of a few doughnuts at a dingy Dunkin' Donuts a couple of blocks from a run-down marina where we had left our kayaks.

In the end we procured permission to sleep on a boat, with our kayaks tied to the dock. Neither of us really slept in the cold, unfamiliar environment as a stream of worries about the next day cycled through our heads. What would the current be like? Would the wind be a factor? Would we be safe paddling in the predawn darkness? How many other boats would be out on the East River? Would they see us? And, most importantly, would we get through Hell Gate safely?

Hell Gate is where tides from Long Island Sound, New York Harbor, and the Harlem River meet, causing whirlpools, boils, and strong currents. Historically a key gateway to the Atlantic, this mile-long strait was treacherous for ships, thanks to a substantial whirlpool, rocks, reefs, and islands. Although many of the rocks and reefs that caused numerous shipwrecks have been removed, at peak flow the tidal current still reaches five knots. Our passage through Hell Gate was as concerning as Reversing Falls, perhaps more so, due to the volume of commercial ship traffic.

Although the sun would not rise for another three hours when we emerged from the musty-smelling boat, the glow of the city was so bright there was no need for our headlamps. We launched at five thirty and aimed for the illuminated skyline of New York City. Already we could hear its hum. The current carried us along so quickly that turning around to paddle against it would have been impossible.

The sun rose as we passed under the Hell Gate Bridge, and we were suddenly immersed in the hustle and bustle of the morning commute. A distinct hum grew louder and became a deafening buzz that we struggled to speak over. With the Bronx behind us, Manhattan to our right, and Brooklyn to our left, cars were creeping in one solid traffic jam alongshore and even overhead on bridges. People were running, walking, riding bikes on riverfront paths as we continued along down below. We wondered if anyone in their car saw us down on the river in our orange and green kayaks. Of course, there was an on-the-water rush hour as well. Ferries erratically zipped from one side of the river to the other. Tugboats pushing barges plodded up the middle of the channel, sending menacing wakes rushing toward the riprap and steel shorelines created to separate the ocean from the city. It felt like the kayaking equivalent to a game of Frogger, with far bigger consequences.

We proceeded under the Ed Koch Queensboro Bridge and along Roosevelt Island when the unmistakable spire of the Chrysler Building came into view on our right. Then the Empire State Building. The 104 stories of One World Trade Center towered above the rest of the city, gleaming in the morning sun. Still under construction, a dark top revealed the steel skeleton of a few unfinished floors as two cranes slowly moved like giant, mechanical rabbit ears. The last of the outgoing tide swept us down the East River past the southern tip of Manhattan as the Statue of Liberty came into view.

For months we had been looking forward to visiting a kind Russian family who lived in Sea Gate, near Coney Island on the tip of Long Island. The past winter Almira (Mira), Eugene, and their daughter, Liza, had gone on a dogsled camping trip with us. When they learned that our route would take us through New York City, Mira invited us to stop at their house. After the previous night's ordeal, we were especially thankful to have a warm welcome just a few miles from Manhattan.

We pulled our kayaks up onto a coarse sand beach. Plastic bags, wrappers, cups, dog turds, cans, and an assortment of other flotsam were scattered across the beach, partially embedded in the sand. We found a driftwood log to sit on as we snarfed a late lunch. How could this beach look like this? We were appalled by the amount of refuse from the city that ended up in the water and then washed up here. Why was there no effort to clean it up?

Mira, dressed in a pink hoody and exuding happy energy, walked up. When she saw our granola bars in hand, she looked hurt and shouted, "No, no, no! I have food for you! Come eat at my house!" We should have known. But it didn't matter that we had already eaten—we were still ravenous. Mira gave us each a big, welcoming hug and showed us where to store our kayaks at a neighbor's. She then helped us shuttle our bags across the street to her house.

At Mira and Eugene's she laid out a feast of amazing Russian food for us. We were still snacking when Liza came home from school and Eugene from work. Little did we know, we were in for a treat. They took us to a Russian bath, where we steamed in dark rooms until we couldn't stand the heat and then dunked in an icy bath—and then back to the steam room or jacuzzi and so on. Eugene talked Dave into doing it the traditional way, which meant a large, stern, hairy Russian man in a Speedo beat him with birch boughs as he lay in the steaming sauna until he couldn't take the heat or the pain any longer.

\* \* \*

As Adam Sobel describes in *Storm Surge*, on October 28, 2012, a "giant, misshapen hurricane made a left turn from its previous north-ward trajectory over the Atlantic Ocean and headed for the New Jersey coast." The following evening, the center of the storm, which followed a never-before-seen track, made landfall near Atlantic City.

The destruction sprawled far from there. A few days earlier, over the Bahamas, Sandy had crossed paths with another weather disturbance, a low-pressure system in the upper atmosphere. It took on some of that system's properties, including its great size. As it made landfall, it merged with yet another system, an extratropical, or "winter," storm that had come from the North American continent at the leading edge of a blast of autumn cold air. This merger gave Sandy a new jolt of energy, increased its size yet further, and completed its transition from a tropical cyclone to a mammoth hybrid . . . The size of the storm, like the track, was unprecedented in scientific memory . . . At its landfall, gale force winds covered a large fraction of the Eastern Seaboard and an enormous patch of oceanic real estate as well. To the north of the center, Sandy's easterlies traversed a thousand-mile-plus fetch before coming onshore, driving a massive storm surge: a giant, slow wave that dragged the ocean inland, on top of the high tide, and onto some of the most heavily populated, economically active, and valuable land on earth.

Oblivious to the brewing storm, we happily paddled through the tidal marshes of Barnegat Bay, New Jersey—twenty-five miles north of Atlantic City—on October 26. We were right on time to do a presentation for the local paddling community, hosted by New Jersey Kayak. Owners Bill and Carmen had invited us to stay at their house for a couple of days. "It looks like a pretty big storm is going to pass near us in a few days," Bill said after setting up our bed for the night—the pull-out couch in their living room. A hint of concern was apparent behind wire-rimmed glasses in the creases of his brown eyes. "Maybe you should stay here until it blows through; it could cause flooding, and you don't want to be stuck camping in a salt marsh someplace." Although we had known him for less than twelve hours, we had learned enough of his character to know Bill was quite practical and not one to be overly dramatic, so by the next morning, we had decided to heed his advice.

As the hurricane approached it became clear that we were going to get walloped. Bill and Carmen's kayak shop was located on the waterfront just a few feet above sea level, so we spent a day helping Bill lash down their kayaks on the racks and move important items from the shop to their house. On our final trip back to Bill and Carmen's house, a fire truck drove by announcing through a megaphone a mandatory evacuation by six o'clock that night. In that moment the reality of the impending danger sunk in. We lashed our own kayaks onto their porch and prepared to evacuate. Bill and Carmen were going to stay with family and arranged for us to stay with their friends, John and Joan. Before relocating inland, the four of us walked down to the water's edge. The wind was picking up and the end of the road had already begun to flood, pounded by erratic brown, foaming waves.

John and Joan, who lived several miles inland, welcomed us like family, and for the next eighteen hours we all waited anxiously as the hurricane approached. They also had a small, rustic, summer bungalow in Ortley Beach, which is on the Barnegat Peninsula, a long, narrow strip of sand separating Barnegat Bay from the ocean. Their family had been going there for generations, so the items John retrieved from the house were irreplaceable artwork and family photos.

Once the power flickered to a halt, board games and books took our minds off the storm raging outside. Around six o'clock at night on October 29, the howl of the wind briefly subsided, the sky cleared, and the full moon's rays illuminated the tangled branches of a large oak tree that had crashed to the ground an hour before. We ran outside into the surreal silent, dark street in front of John and Joan's house. A few minutes later the wind and rain returned from the opposite direction; the eye of Hurricane Sandy had passed over us. By the next morning the high winds and pelting rain subsided.

In the ensuing days Ortley Beach was among the many flooded coastal areas closed to everyone except emergency responders, but John's brother was able to reach the island by boat and called once he was safely back on the mainland. After John hung up the phone he wiped tears from his eyes and took a moment to compose himself before relating what he had heard. Despite his lifelong familiarity with the area, John's brother couldn't find their cottage because all familiar landmarks were gone—the roads were covered in sand, the street signs were missing, and most of the structures were destroyed.

Bill and Carmen retrieved us the day after Halloween, once the roads were clear. It was hard to put into words how grateful we were for John and Joan's hospitality. Like Bill and Carmen, they were stuck in a scary, stressful situation but chose to welcome strangers in need. By the next day the floodwaters had receded enough for us to drive to New Jersey Kayak. Some houses appeared unharmed until we spotted people hauling sodden furniture and carpet out. Piles near the curb grew on every street we passed. Houses closer to the water were completely ruined.

Bill was relieved to find all his kayaks on the property and the building still standing. As evidenced by the line of mud inside the office, about three feet of water had washed through. His docks and fences were ripped apart by the wind and waves. Several dump trucks full of debris—reeds, pieces of houses, docks, toys from a sandbox, pieces of boats, plus an old wooden twenty-foot motorboat—had been deposited by the storm. We dug in with shovels, rakes, and work gloves. Many people came to help Bill, including John and Joan. Tools and trucks were loaned without question. Neighbors supplied coffee and doughnuts on their stoop. When many bodies were needed to move larger objects, people gathered without hesitation.

We spent most of the week working on cleanup at the kayak shop. After many trips with the fully loaded truck and trailer, all the kayaks were relocated to Bill and Carmen's backyard. For the cleanup effort, we made three huge piles of debris. On the fourth day a front-end loader finally rumbled through the gate and took the piles away. Local government workers and first responders were stretched thin because of the widespread devastation Sandy had left in her wake. We were all thankful when the heavy equipment finally reached us. By the time the last pile was hauled away, we took in the view. What a relief to have all that junk out of there, but where would it go? The kayak shop was like one grain in a whole field of wheat. The utter destruction appeared to stretch for a hundred miles or more. And the reports from New York City were grim.

Having grown up in the Midwest, we had both previously only seen the headlines and news flashes with reporters standing in pelting rain as they talked about hurricane X, Y, or Z, but those glimpses had not prepared us for living through it and dealing with the aftermath. We felt strangely guilty about how we would paddle on with all our possessions intact while Bill, Carmen, and millions of other people were just beginning the long process of recovery.

We got word from Mira and Eugene in Sea Gate that their cozy basement where we had slept flooded to within inches of the ceiling and they had no idea when power would be restored. We were relieved to hear from them because news reports had shown snippets of the devastation in their neighborhood. During the storm Eugene had been at home, moving valuables and furniture out of the basement, while Mira worked at the hospital nonstop. Their car disappeared—washed away by the floodwaters. We wondered if a middle school in Queens we had visited a few weeks earlier was still standing as horrific images of the flooded and fire-torched Breezy Point neighborhood swept the internet.

Bill decided to paddle with us for a few days as we continued south to Atlantic City. The stresses left in the wake of the storm were overwhelming, and a few days on the water would help him clear his mind. Sadly, returning to the water didn't entirely allow us to escape Sandy's grip. Wreckage of all shapes and sizes littered the water, salt marshes, and shore: thirty-foot motorboats skewered on pilings, sailboats tipped over in boatyards, piles of rubble where houses once stood, and plastic garbage scattered by the wind.

Paddling through Sandy's wake at three miles an hour left us plenty of time to contemplate what we saw. For at least a hundred miles, the damage and debris were humbling. What would happen to all this junk? From plastic bags and pop bottles littering the marshes to water-logged couches and smashed vehicles, mountains of construction rubble, and hundreds of destroyed, half-sunken boats of all sizes and stripes, much of it would eventually be hauled to a landfill, but clearly unknown amounts of fuel and other toxins would continue to leach into the water as the sun, wind, and waves slowly broke the garbage into smaller bits to be scattered through the food chain.

We had thought that ocean plastics were the result of careless humans tossing their garbage overboard or into a nearby stream, which eventually carried the garbage into one of the world's oceans as its toxic chemicals slowly leached into the environment. But now we were experiencing plastic pollution that dwarfed anything we had seen before, even the plastic-covered beach we camped on in British Columbia near the beginning of our journey. This wasn't caused by careless acts of individuals; it was the product of the modern world colliding with a climate change–intensified natural disaster.

On the outskirts of Atlantic City, New Jersey, we slid past marsh grasses glistening in an unnatural oily sheen, dotted with plastic shopping bags fluttering in a headwind that was slowing our progress. Once Bill left, we continued to paddle on for days through a postapocalyptic scene.

In the coming months and years much of this would be cleaned up and the human footprint on the coast rebuilt and strengthened, probably with even larger houses and more opulence, but how long can this last? Climate change is already causing sea levels to rise and hurricanes to become more severe. The media headlines were focused on the human toll of Sandy and the billions of dollars required to rebuild, but surveying the damage from our kayaks left us to wonder what impact all the debris flushed into the ocean by the storm would have and how larger, perhaps more frequent, storms combined with sea level rise would fundamentally transform this coastline.

Before Sandy, sea level rise and climate change's amplification of severe weather remained distant and abstract to us, but now they were all we could think about. The kayaks we paddled, the tent we were sleeping in, the clothes we wore were all made of plastics; the food we eat is grown and distributed with machines that burn fossil fuels. Everything we do is, one way or another, entwined with the $CO_2$-belching fossil fuel industry that is leading to a world filled with plastic pollution and a changing climate. We have been rapidly transforming the earth in ways that will likely prove unsustainable for humanity. Our nomadic life had shown us that we could live with less, but Sandy caused us to reevaluate our carbon footprint even more.

As Elizabeth Rush writes in *Rising*, "Since the rise of scientific rationalism, our particular brand of western knowledge has lulled us into thinking that we are separate from nature: if we can design our way out of feeling the cold at the heart of winter, we can also simply raise our communities above the storm. But now climate change is calling us to attention, drawing us to the water's edge to ask with wonderment and fear whether there is, or ever really was, something that separates us from our environment."

\* \* \*

AFTER THE LIGHTS and buildings of Ocean City, Maryland, and the rolling dunes of Assateague Island we worked our way south toward the mouth of Chesapeake Bay. Duck hunters were out in force, hiding in their blinds with decoys scattered nearby. The air had a definite chill in the ever-lengthening nights. We followed a channel that snaked its way close to a barrier island, with the sound of surf pounding just on the outside. We managed to camp close to the northeast end of the Chesapeake Bay Bridge-Tunnel, which would be our point of departure from land for a seventeen-mile crossing of the largest estuary in the United States.

The red-orange orb of the sun appeared over the water shortly after we launched. The current of a flood tide was flowing into the bay and a ten-knot headwind was blowing. We angled toward the bridge tunnel and into the current. Our progress slowed to one and a half miles per hour at one point, which we feared would mean this crossing could potentially take three times longer than we anticipated. Our fortune turned around as we reached the first island. The Chesapeake Bay Bridge-Tunnel, a feat of engineering, allows cars to cross the mouth of the bay while accommodating massive tankers and navy vessels by having the road run under the water in two different mile-long stretches. The man-made islands were where the bridge transitioned into tunnel. We took a little rest in the eddy formed by the island, thought about trying to land and pee, but the seaweed-covered boulders didn't look very inviting, so we ignored our bladders and stiff legs and paddled on.

At the second shipping lane we paused as a large freighter passed. We saw another boat coming—a gray speck on the horizon—and decided to scoot across. Within minutes we dug in with everything we had as the gray dot morphed into a massive aircraft carrier moving at an alarming speed. We scurried across the center of the shipping lane in front of it and slowed to a more sustainable pace once we were safely out of its way.

We paddled to the Lynnhaven Inlet near Virginia Beach and awkwardly clambered out of our boats onto the sand, surprised by how stiff we had gotten from spending eight straight hours in our kayaks. The sun was getting low. Heading into the inlet, we crawled against the current under the bridge and then eddy-hopped as best we could. We inched past several Coast Guard boats, fishing boats, and dockside restaurants, trying to imagine this now deserted place in the summer—sprawling outside decks filled, people eating seafood and drinking mojitos. Two guys filleted their catch on the dock. One of them, with a T-shirt stretched tight over a beer belly and a camo trucker hat, asked if we had paddled across the bay because he had seen us out there along the bridge. "Yer crazy!" was all he said when we confirmed it was us that he saw.

\* \* \*

EIGHT BROWN PELICANS watched us as we paddled near shore with the aid of an eddy. We were contending with wind, but the bay narrowed down into a channel that got smaller and smaller until we were in a tiny canal that was occasionally crossed by bridges. We would be following the Intracoastal Waterway (ICW) for most of the way down to Florida from here.

This place reminded us of our training paddles in the Chicago suburbs. It felt like we might round the next bend and see our car at the takeout where we would drive to Dave's parents' house, ready for dinner and a cold beer. A bit homesick for family, friends, and the comforts of modern living, the nice fantasy helped the monotonous miles pass. The days were about as short as they were going to get. Temperatures were dipping below freezing at night. We were navigating a fine line between urban and wild pockets at a dreary and somewhat uninspiring point in the journey. What pulled us out of our funk was remembering that on those training paddles, we were always wishing we were on an expedition, wishing we could shove off from shore and just keep going. Now, here we were—going—living the dream. Not every day was sublime, like some carefully curated Instagram feed, but the good days still outnumbered the bad by a long shot. With only about a hundred days left, our perspective had shifted once again. Early on in the journey it had been necessary to focus on the moment when the going was tough, because the end was unfathomably far away. As our proximity to the end grew closer, mental images of the sun, white sand, and palm trees of Key West kept us going.

Once we entered the Great Dismal Swamp, we were alone in a marshy channel with cormorants, mallards, kingfishers, and herons. It seemed to us that by late December most of the sailboats and trawlers piloted by snowbirds heading south had already done so. In shortcuts off the main ICW channel, beaver activity slowed our progress—log jams filled with plastic debris, tires, algae. A sulfury smell rose from the brown water, especially when we got stuck and had to struggle to scooch forward off a floating log. We lost sight of defined banks much of the time, as shallow water persisted as far as we could see through the curvy, dark trunks and knees of cypress trees. It reminded us of canoeing through the Amazon rainforest in the rainy season, when you might not see dry land for days. For the first time in a long time the sounds of roads and urbanization were gone, held back by a vast swampy oasis.

We crossed into North Carolina and the red and green channel markers indicated we emerged onto the ICW again. Cypress trees gave way to golden marsh grasses, and we put in long days, driven to get farther south. Launching in predawn darkness and setting up camp several hours after sunset became the norm. We were hungry all the time, trying to compensate for the calorie deficit of our constant motion and the extra effort our bodies put forth to stay warm in the steadily dropping temperatures.

As we crossed the Albemarle Sound and entered the Alligator River, the only other boats around were small, camo-painted johnboats of duck hunters. The marine weather forecast's familiar robotic voice spewed from our handheld VHF radio, breaking the silence and monotony of the morning calm. Strong winds were in the forecast for the day after Christmas, so we attempted to get somewhere comfortable to hunker down. This meant putting in two thirty-plus-mile days.

On Christmas Eve, we contemplated stopping at a nearly deserted marina but decided to press on to Belhaven, North Carolina. This meant we would be on the water well into the night. But that was just as well because we didn't spot any dry land until we reached a tight canal. By then, the sky was completely black and occasional lightning flashed to the southeast. We had passed the inviting masthead light of a ketch at anchor in a bay to the north. A warm glow emanated from the windows, and we imagined a couple inside cooking dinner, eating, casually chatting, then settling into a warm bed. This led to reminiscing about Christmas with family; in any other year at this moment, we might be gathered in the living room, bellies full, looking at the twinkling lights and heirloom ornaments on the tree, opening presents, laughing.

We hugged the shore in the canal, trying to assess the camping potential with our headlamps. At first things did not look good—marsh grasses and tree trunks protruding from the water lined both sides. Eventually we could tell there were some pine trees to our right, signaling higher ground. Rain began just as we finished our spaghetti and climbed into the tent. With no cell signal, we couldn't even call home on Christmas Eve.

Christmas Day dawned cooler and windier than the previous day. We had just launched our kayaks into the narrow channel when the ketch we had seen at anchor came slowly motoring along. It was a large, blue, steel ketch named *Goose*. Just as we thought it would overtake us, they honked their horn at us, so we paddled over to say hi. We were greeted with an enthusiastic "Good morning" and "Merry Christmas!" from Allan and Mary Ann, a smiling couple in their early sixties who could have easily been our parents plucked from their urban lives and plopped on a sailboat. They were bundled up in slightly dated winter jackets, perhaps purchased when they were a few pounds lighter and a few decades younger, but their windblown, suntanned beaming faces made it clear they were following a dream. They asked us if we could pull alongside the *Goose* because they had something for us. Mary Ann handed down a napkin bundled around a dense, sticky object—fruitcake! Apparently they had just opened it. Allan had gotten it before they departed several months ago and kept it secret from Mary Ann in a paper bag marked "Don't open until Christmas." They were boater missionaries, heading to Honduras. Their destination for the day was the same as us—Belhaven.

We put in an easy twenty miles as a tailwind gradually increased. The *Goose* was already docked, and Allan walked over as we landed. Just then a car drove up. A local couple making the rounds, dropping off paper plates loaded with Christmas cookies to friends and neighbors, saw us newcomers and drove over. A beaming and energetic woman with short blond hair gave a plate to each of us as they inquired about our journey. Karen and Andy ran a bed-and-breakfast out of their home. Perhaps they held some affinity toward travelers because they themselves had arrived in Belhaven years ago aboard their Nordic Tug. Andy, who was boisterous with a graying goatee and glasses, remained in the back seat of the idling car as we chatted, because his leg was in a cast. They suggested a sheltered spot for us to camp on property they owned just a little farther down, right in the heart of town. We thanked them profusely and relocated to that spot to set up our tent for the night, well staked in anticipation of the coming storm. Splitting the remaining cookies after dinner, we marveled at our good fortune. Some moments might be difficult, but the reality was that we had everything we needed and then some. Nothing was quite as humbling and heartwarming as being welcomed into a strange town and given a place to pitch our tent—or strangers sharing their precious fruitcake that they had saved for months. The rain came in surges blown by the erratic wind, but we slept soundly. Our hearts were full on this most memorable Christmas.

\* \* \*

TO BE TOTALLY honest, before pouring over maps as we worked out our route down the East Coast, we didn't even realize Georgia had a coastline. In our minds we always thought of it as a landlocked state, but as the sun eased toward the western horizon on January 26, 2013, we pulled up to a worn floating dock in front of Old Daufuskie Island Crab Company. This sleepy little bar and restaurant next to a small mowed field speckled with guinea hens milling about was a welcome relief and our last stop in South Carolina. This laidback oasis provided the perfect transition to Georgia's wild, largely undeveloped maze of salt marshes and barrier islands.

Paddling past Hilton Head Island, South Carolina, an hour before, we had stared at multimillion-dollar mansions lining the shore. It felt like the natural world had been manicured and developed into oblivion, but here on Daufuskie Island, we set up our tent under the thick branches of old live oak trees cloaked in Spanish moss with a chorus of gentle songbird melodies drifting through the forest.

Georgia's coastline is just over one hundred miles long, but it remains one of the least-developed shores in the country in large part thanks to some of the wealthiest families of the nineteenth and twentieth centuries. Between the 1880s and 1930s, the Morgans, Rockefellers, Vanderbilts, and other ultra-wealthy families bought up many of the barrier islands, and then later generations sold or donated the land to a variety of state, national, conservation, and scientific organizations.

This wild oasis appeared much like we envisioned it would have prior to colonization. We camped on sand beaches speckled with sandpipers and plovers scurrying along the surf line that stretched for miles. These uninhabited islands were a world of crashing surf, blowing sand, and howling winds that made us feel raw and wild. It was a place we could have lingered, and maybe we should have, but we also felt a strong pull to keep moving. We were ready to be done, to move on to other things. Physically we were stronger than we had ever been. Adding an extra five miles to a thirty-mile day seemed easy. We constantly pushed ourselves to travel farther and faster, even through this beautiful pearl of wildness. To our daily routine we added a half-hour-long run because we felt like paddling for ten hours a day wasn't providing the cardiovascular exercise we needed.

Mentally we were struggling with the notion that this journey, which seemed almost impossible at times, was hurtling toward an end. Our whole married life had been consumed by following this random squiggly line on a map and beaming our experience along the way into thousands of classrooms. Our relationship had been pushed and tested countless times since stepping into our kayaks in Bellingham, Washington. Like a muscle that grows stronger with repeated use and strain, our love and trust had grown considerably, but it was clear that the constant stresses of not knowing where we would sleep each night and the physical and emotional toll of our nomadic existence were wearing on us.

\* \* \*

THROUGH A POLL on our website, we had asked students to vote on whether we should paddle the east coast of Florida or cut across to paddle the Gulf Coast. They had overwhelmingly voted for the Gulf Coast because that meant we would share our experience in the Everglades with them. Following their decision, we left our last campsite on the Atlantic Ocean and enjoyed the ride as the current of a flood tide flushed us up the Saint Marys River, which forms the Georgia-Florida border.

Our original plan was to take the Saint Marys River as far inland as we could, portage to the Okefenokee Swamp, paddle through and then down the Suwannee River. But when we called the park office to get permits for the Okefenokee National Wildlife Refuge, we learned that thru-paddling was impossible. Lower water levels and a large wildfire in 2011 and 2012 had left a large portion of the swamp impassable. More than 309,000 acres burned, and it took almost an entire year for the fire to die out thanks to the smoldering nature of burning peat.

Our route problems created by this fire were minor in comparison to the environmental ramifications it exemplified. Bill McKibben sums up the feedback loop that has been set in motion:

Peat covers about 2 percent of the planet's land surface, mostly in the far north—think moors, bogs, mires, swamp forests. They are wet places filled with decaying vegetation, a kind of nursery for what in many millennia could become coal. Because they're wet, they're very stable; the plants decompose very very slowly, so peatlands make a perfect "sink" for carbon, holding perhaps half as much as the atmosphere. But say you raise the temperature and hence the rate of evaporation; the water table starts to fall, and those swamps start to dry out. And as they do, the carbon in all that decaying vegetation starts to decompose more quickly and flood into the atmosphere. A 2008 study found, in fact, that "peatlands will quickly respond to the expected warming in this century by losing labile soil organic carbon during dry periods." How much? Well, peat bogs worldwide hold the equivalent of sixty-five years of fossil-fuel burning, and the expected warming will dry out enough of them to cause the loss of between 40 and 86 percent of that carbon. It's as if we'd conjured up out of nowhere a second human population that's capable of burning coal and oil and gas nearly as fast as we do.

In this passage from *Eaarth*, McKibben is just talking about peat drying up. Imagine that carbon sink burning. A dry swamp or bog is more likely to catch fire when lightning strikes. One study estimated that peat fires may produce emissions 75 percent higher per hectare than fires consuming standing vegetation alone.

Our plan B was a forty-mile portage on a road; good thing Florida is flat. We were a little nervous as we paddled the last few miles up the Saint Marys River. The river slowly got smaller and smaller, and the last ten miles were choked with down trees and sandbars. It was slow going, but at least we were paddling. We frequently spotted egrets and herons alongside the river. The closer we got to the start of our portage, the more difficult the paddling became.

We spent two solid days walking on the straightest, flattest road we'd ever seen. Our feet, more used to sitting in boats than bearing our weight, quickly got hot spots and blisters. A handful of people stopped to ask us what we were doing and offer us rides, but we were determined to walk the entire way despite the monotony. We gauged our progress by mile markers. A curve in the road was a big deal. We'd spot one five miles ahead and be ecstatic by the time we reached it and could see the next long expanse of road.

Near Fargo, Georgia, we launched into the brown, tannin-stained Suwannee River. Its sandy banks were occasionally interrupted by cliffy limestone outcrops. Cypress trees created a diversion as we studied their irregular shapes, burls, knees, and tangles of roots. The first alligator we saw (maybe six feet long) sent chills down our spines as it slipped off the bank where it had been sunning itself and disappeared instantly in the black water. How many unseen alligators were in the water around us? As is the case with most wild animals, if we didn't bother them, they wouldn't bother us.

We followed the Suwannee River Wilderness State Trail and felt like we were glamping (glamorous camping). There were campgrounds and "primitive" campsites along the river, many with amenities like screened-in shelters and shower houses. We would encounter various groups of paddlers on a regular basis and interact with kind campground hosts. After months of stealth camping, the anxiety of wondering where we would lay our heads at night was gone, allowing us to bask in our surroundings and enjoy our time on the river. We kept a daily tally of turtle sightings, sunning themselves on logs. Our record was 312.

As we pulled into the Peacock Slough campground at the end of a long day, a massive sturgeon jumped just a couple of feet from our kayaks. It must've been six feet long, rocketing overhead. We had seen warning signs about them earlier in the day—now we knew why. A jumping sturgeon could certainly kill a person zipping by in motorboat going too fast. The campground host warned us about wild pigs roaming around the slough at night. We fell asleep to the sounds of armadillos rustling below the floorboards of our screen shelter.

Farther downriver, we visited several crystal clear springs, and we weren't the only creatures that appreciated their warm waters. Paddling into Fanning Springs, we turned into a narrow channel off the main river and a large, gray object floated by. We were both awestruck and engaged in a frenzied hour of observing several manatees, taking underwater photos, and shooting video from our kayaks.

Early the next morning, we walked down to the springs again. A park ranger had told us that he saw manatees regularly in the morning and that at 7:30 a.m. they'd swim out to the main river channel. We easily spotted three manatees hovering in that warm, clear water. We kept our distance and just watched them eat. There were three adults and eventually a young one emerged from the shadows near shore.

After a few minutes, one manatee swam within an arm's length and surfaced to take a breath. Then with slow, powerful thrusts of their tails, the group swam out to the river together. We took a look at our watches—precisely 7:30 a.m.

Part of our excitement about seeing these manatees had to do the fact that our young online audience had voted for us to investigate them. Thanks to this encounter, we had some great content to share. We could just imagine how excited the students would be on Monday morning when they logged on and saw this video footage and a *Notes from the Trail* all about manatees.

We made our way out toward the Gulf of Mexico with manatees on our minds. These massive creatures are so gentle and vulnerable to boat collisions, development, and climate change. Every boat ramp we passed had warning signs about manatees and slow zones designed to protect them. Still, these slow-moving sea cows are frequent victims of boat collisions. We had even heard that boaters needed to check their propellers before starting their engines because manatees might be grazing the algae growing on the boat's bottom! The odds seemed stacked against them, and all the adult manatees we saw had scars on their backs. The threat of climate change on this species is multifaceted. Disrupted weather patterns can cause some waters to be too cold for manatees, leading to cold stress and pneumonia. A hurricane can devastate a local manatee population, so more frequent hurricanes means bad news for manatees. In recent years manatees have also fallen victim to algal blooms. Blue-green algae flushing out of Lake Okeechobee and the red tide that laid siege to the southwest Florida coast for fifteen months (beginning in 2017) had devastating effects on the manatee population.

A few days later we were flushed out the mouth of the Suwannee River and into the Gulf of Mexico. We were about 350 miles directly east of where the BP *Deepwater Horizon* Macando well had burst. Plying these waters reminded us that our journey had begun two days after the explosion in April 2010. We were finally seeing the Gulf of Mexico three years after the largest marine oil spill in the history of the petroleum industry. Nearly five million barrels of oil directly affected 57,700 square miles of ocean, leaving its mark in the form of oil slicks, tar balls, and gunk on the seafloor, wreaking havoc on the marine ecosystem for years to come.

Heading down the coast, we were back to the challenge of finding places to camp amid development until we reached the Everglades. Fortunately, we had people looking out for us along the way. We received a warm welcome in Tampa, thanks to another dogsledding connection. Trisha had arranged interviews with local news media, several school presentations, and even a chance to meet the mayor. Near Sarasota we had a brief reprieve at Dave's aunt and uncle's house. At Sanibel Island we reunited with John and Pat, who we had met way back in Maine. Each stop with these familiar faces provided a respite from the slog of finishing the journey, and we left with renewed enthusiasm for reaching Key West. The countdown toward the end had begun.

*　*　*

AS THE RANGER at the Gulf Coast station in the northwest corner of Everglades National Park issued us our backcountry camping permit, he casually mentioned that the ranger station would be closing for the summer in a couple of weeks. "The bugs are so bad in the summer it would be cruel to make people live and work here," he said with a knowing grin. As we were walking out the door, he added, "Make sure you're in your tent before dusk because this time of year, the mosquitoes will carry you away from dusk until dawn." We hurried off to fill our water containers and continue south, urged on by the desire to immerse ourselves in the largest wilderness area east of the Mississippi and reach our next campsite before the sun dipped below the horizon.

The Muscogee (Creek) call it Pa-hay-Okee (pah-HIGH-oh-geh), "grassy waters," and Marjory Stoneman Douglas called it the "river of grass." We soon understood why as we began paddling through millions of acres of saw grass swaying in the gentle breeze. We felt a sense of calm we had rarely felt since leaving Lake Superior's rugged, wild shores. The sounds, sights, and aromas of cars and industry were gone. For months we had been hopping between tiny pockets of wildness. There had been birds and trees, crabs and marshes, dolphins and sea turtles, but nothing on the scale of this vast, wet wilderness. The Everglades is basically a fifty-mile-wide slow-moving river that flows from north to south at a barely perceptible pace through a sea of grasses dotted with pockets of forest.

For five days we followed a serpentine water trail dotted with several dozen designated campsites. Most nights we camped on slivers of beaches covered in shells on the barrier islands separating the freshwater grasslands from the Gulf. Here we found a more reliable breeze to keep the bugs at bay, but the trade-off was raccoons in search of fresh water. Each night we carefully sealed our food and water inside the cargo hatches of our kayaks to keep it safe from the raccoons that inevitably invaded our campsite in the dark. They never got anything, but the presence of their glowing yellow-green eyes made for some fitful nights. The only evidence of their presence each morning were sandy miniature hand-shaped footprints on our kayaks.

The National Park Service has built a network of camping platforms called chickees that are elevated a few feet above the water. Looking for a break from the raccoons, we pulled up to a chickee, surrounded by open water, on our third day in the Everglades. It was only three o'clock, so we had the whole afternoon to fish, repair gear, read, and work on our next Wilderness Classroom update. We had slowed our pace considerably as we crept toward Key West. With only ten or fifteen miles to paddle each day, it was a real delight to soak in the uninterrupted hum of the natural world. As we sat on the edge of the platform, our feet dangling a foot above the water, a shark glided right under us, its tail rhythmically pulsing from side to side with exacting efficiency. An hour later a five-foot-long alligator floated by with its eyes and snout just piercing the water surface.

We felt torn between the joy brought on by these ancient creatures who were unfazed by our presence and the nagging reality that even this vast watery wilderness, which a third of all Floridians rely on for fresh water, is in peril. Since paddling away from the ranger station three days before, we hadn't been more than about ten feet above sea level. In the last thirty years the sea in southern Florida has risen close to six inches, and the rate is increasing. Scientists predict the ocean to rise another foot by 2050. As the alligator's undulating tail sent ripples across the smooth dark water, we were struck by both the breadth and the sheer flatness of this place. As humans, it is perhaps easier to focus on the billions of people who live along the world's coastlines who will be displaced and deeply impacted by rising waters, and the disruptive and destabilizing effects that will ripple through humanity. Trillions of dollars and a mobilization like none humanity has ever amassed will be needed to address this truly global crisis we have created. But in the moment, it was the Pa-hay-Okee we were concerned about. What will happen to the largest subtropical wetland in North America when the ocean infiltrates its waters? The Everglades are home to more than thirty endangered or threatened species, and early visitors described birds so numerous the sky would turn black when a large flock erupted into flight from a vast field of swaying saw grasses.

In *Rising*, Elizabeth Rush explains: "As sea levels rise, the interface between salt water and freshwater is pushing deeper and deeper into this fragile ecosystem, transforming the marsh from within. The saw grass found in the Florida Everglades is somewhat salt tolerant but, like many marsh grasses, has a threshold. When exposed to a salinity level beyond that threshold, it puts fewer roots into the soil, microbial activity kicks up, and the ground around the plant slumps and loses elevation."

However, she adds that today, "Topography is perhaps the single most important element contributing to Florida's profoundly precarious position. Southern Florida is so flat, so close to sea level, that a three-centimeter jump in the height of the ocean, as has occurred over the past decade, has already dramatically affected not only seaside human communities but the flora and fauna that have long called this place home."

* * *

FLORIDA BAY'S SHALLOW water clung to our kayaks as if it were trying to hold us in the Everglades a little while longer. In water less than two or three feet deep, it takes considerably more effort to propel a boat forward, not to mention frequent groundings as we misjudged the water depths. For miles we picked our way across shallow sand flats that stretched to the horizon. The Keys were so close, and we grew frustrated as we flailed away with our paddles trying to find a few more inches of water, momentarily distracted by three-foot bonnethead sharks cruising through the shallows with their fins piercing the surface. We laughed uncontrollably the first time we realized gulls were not floating on the water surface but standing in just an inch of water. But mostly we just stewed in our own mental juices, trying to digest the reality that our three-year honeymoon was coming to an end.

Halfway across the twenty-five-mile-wide bay, we pitched our tent on a tiny clump of land ringed with mangroves. Sadly, our frustrations brought on by the shallow water and our relatively slow progress didn't allow reality to sink in. Unbeknownst to us this would be our last wilderness campsite. From here on out we would be camping in state parks, private campgrounds, and mangroves disturbingly touched by civilization. The sky was dark, the wind and the rhythmic lapping of water were the only sounds, but rather than savoring this last nugget of wildness, we allowed time and schedules to overtake us. With the end of our journey looming near, we had both lost the ability to live in the moment. That—living in the moment—had been our reality for the greater part of three years, with intense focus on our own breaths, paddle strokes, footsteps, and the sights, sounds, and smells of our surroundings. Now our minds were suddenly elsewhere—imagining arriving home in Minnesota, scheduling school assemblies, working through what we would say in interviews—instead of savoring the final few days.

Paddling under one of the many US Route 1 bridges that connect the Keys to the mainland lifted our spirits. The shallows of Florida Bay were behind us, and Key West was less than fifty miles away. Shortly after this milestone, Bryan, who paddled with us in the Boundary Waters and on Lake Superior, joined us again to help document our final few days. It was nice to have his fresh prospective, reminding us how lucky we were to be on the water every day exercising our minds and bodies. Our three colorful kayaks glided past islands dotted with houses enveloped in the steady hum of US 1, but beneath the surface a whole new world appeared. The clear, shallow water revealed numerous spotted eagle rays and the occasional shark or turtle gliding silently underneath our kayaks. When we went snorkeling over the coral reef off Marathon, colorful fish pulsed through a forest of coral heads, and we all grinned for an hour after climbing from the water to warm up. This brief dive into the world beneath the surface reminded us how vast and intricate the earth is. Everywhere we look there is something new; we just have to remember to open our eyes and take the time to truly see.

On April 4, 2013, we packed up camp for the last time. We hadn't planned to reach the southernmost point in the continental United States until the following day, but our inertia was too great. It all seemed so surreal and abstract. A hundred people lined the Fort Zachary Taylor Historic State Park beach as we took our final paddle strokes and the bows of our kayaks slid onto the beach of coarse crushed coral, but these people were all just sunbathing, unaware of the transformative journey we were completing in that moment.

Amy's parents were going to be our only welcoming committee, but they were running a few minutes late. The anticlimactic nature of this journey's end didn't matter to us. We hugged each other and laughed while Bryan's shutter snapped away. The reality that we wouldn't be launching our kayaks again in the morning would not sink in for a while. As we pulled our lunch bag out, a very distraught public servant arrived to explain that this beach was for swimming only and that kayaks were not allowed, so lunch would have to wait. Our daydreams of our arrival in Key West while dogsledding across frozen expanses, or paddling far-flung waterways over the previous thirty-five months, had never been very concrete—just involving warmth, sunshine, and the ocean. They were really just a distraction from the monotony that comes with tens of millions of paddle strokes and footsteps, but being hurriedly shooed off the beach had never been part of the fantasy. We gave each other mirthful glances and winks as we quickly worked to haul our kayaks and all our gear off the beach so we could return to the sand with our lunch bag for one final meal by the sea.

* * *

WE WERE PROUD to finally reach our goal but also filled with anxiety. How would we find meaning and purpose "back in the real world" after years of intense focus on the arbitrary goal of Key West? The scars on the land we had witnessed, large and small, haunted us and left us confused and unsure. Would we seamlessly slip into a more "normal" sedentary life as the physical and emotional calluses of our journey softened? In some ways we craved that comfort and predictability, but we couldn't help but wonder if we would be like birds in a cage who quickly forget what it is like to roam the skies. We are drawn to this hard existence by some intangible force, continually in search of answers to questions that remain unclear. These journeys bring us closer to the land and help us feel whole.

If the land was speaking to the two of us in the subtle lapping of water against shore and the change of the seasons, then it really got our attention when we saw a remote beach so covered in plastic trash that the ground could not be found, when humpback whales approached us in our kayaks, when the grizzly bear and moose let us pass unscathed, when the blizzard encircled us in white, when caribou streamed past our campsite, and when the viscous sludge of blue-green algae on Lake Winnipeg gripped our paddle blades.

And the land was crying out—screaming even—to awaken those who might have been previously oblivious to her plight when the *Deepwater Horizon* exploded and millions of barrels of oil poured into the ocean, when the earthquake and tsunami hit Japan's coast and the Fukushima meltdowns unfolded, and when Hurricane Sandy ravaged the East Coast, causing over $70 billion worth of damage. The voice of the land has grown so loud that more and more people are hearing it—and responding. But will enough people hear it in time? And will those people possess the compassion, motivation, and political will necessary to bring about real change?

## Afterword

FROM THE MOMENT the hulls of our kayaks made contact with that beach in Key West, we were lost—struggling to regain a sense of purpose. The end of the journey had not felt as either of us expected. There was no elation or even really a sense of accomplishment. Sure, we had done what we set out to do; we had reached our goal, but it slowly dawned on us that it had been an arbitrary goal. We spent three years traveling across the continent by our own power. So what?

We tried to fill the hollow feeling in our guts with activity. The whirl-wind of interviews, school assemblies, and speaking engagements kept us distracted for a while. We struggled with determining where to live. Should we finally build a cabin on our land? Should we rent a house in town? The prospect of living in a building was daunting. Too confining. Too permanent. After three years living out of our tent, we couldn't bear the thought of a house that didn't move, and even the smallest of con-ventional homes seemed cavernous and intimidating. Our solution was to purchase an old twenty-seven-foot sailboat from a friend. We spent the summer guiding canoe and kayak trips, learning to sail, and living on the boat in the Grand Marais, Minnesota, harbor. For a couple thou-sand dollars we had a tiny floating house that, with a little elbow grease and practice, could take us anywhere.

In Grand Marais, we attempted to reinsert ourselves back into our old lives but found we had a lot of catching up to do. How does one begin to pick up the threads of a life that was put on hold three years previously? We lived in an odd time warp. People's lives had continued without us. Friends had gotten engaged, others married, while still others started families. Some couples had broken up. Some friends had moved away or started new jobs.

By the time our first summer back home came to a close, the seeds had been planted for a new journey. This time we would listen to our hearts and attempt something different. The countless environmental atrocities we had witnessed were welling up inside us, and we had to take action to defend our home wilderness—the Boundary Waters Canoe Area Wilderness.

The threat to our beloved BWCAW was (and still is, over ten years later) sulfide-ore copper mining proposed just upstream. If we—people who ply its waters by canoe in the summer and make tracks in the snow in the winter, who love it and know it intimately, whose livelihoods depend on it—did not speak for it, who would? We got involved with the Campaign to Save the Boundary Waters and launched Paddle to DC in the fall of 2014, followed by a Year in the Wilderness in 2015 and 2016, an experience that became our first book with the same title.

Our odyssey had led us to appreciate the patch of Laurentian mixed forest we call home and, ultimately, had awakened our environmental consciousness. When the wild space dearest to us was threatened, we stood up to speak for it. And we are still speaking for it. In all of our time listening to the land since, we have come to realize that conservation and fighting climate change are both needed if we are to stand a chance of maintaining a habitable planet. Forests are the most powerful and efficient carbon capture system on Earth. So, in addition to changing international and national policies and greatly simplifying our lifestyles to reduce carbon emissions, we need to keep enough mature trees around to clean up the mess we've made. The challenges we face as a global community seem so large that it is paralyzing at times to determine how to move forward, but if anything became clear as we climbed out of our kayaks in Key West, it was that every action, no matter how small, is a step forward, and as we all move forward, we must listen to the land and act on its behalf.

# *Notes*

INTRODUCTION

XI  *canoe country*  Tom Nehil, "Sig Olson's Wilderness Canoe Country," MinnPost, July 2, 2012, https://www.minnpost.com /minnclips/2012/07/sig-olsons-wilderness-canoe-country/.

1: KAYAKING THE INSIDE PASSAGE

4  *motivated by an understanding that*  Baba Dioum (presentation, General Assembly of the International Union for the Conservation of Nature and Natural Resources, New Delhi, India, 1968).

9  *According to the World Wildlife Fund*  "Temperate Coniferous Forest," World Wildlife Fund, accessed February 6, 2024, https://www.worldwildlife.org/biomes/temperate -coniferous-forest.

9  *North America's temperate rainforest*  Paul Koberstein and Jessica Applegate, "Where the Forest Has No Name," Mongabay, May 24, 2019, https://news.mongabay.com/2019/05/where-the -forest-has-no-name/.

9  *this coastal temperate rainforest*  "Forest Facts," TREE Foundation, accessed February 6, 2023, https://treefoundation.org /education/forest-facts/.

10      ***Robin Wall Kimmerer writes***  Robin Wall Kimmerer, *Braiding Sweetgrass: Indigenous Wisdom, Scientific Knowledge, and the Teachings of Plants* (Minneapolis, MN: Milkweed Editions), 278.

13      ***2.5 billion people produced***  "Feature: UN's Mission to Keep Plastics Out of Oceans and Marine Life," United Nations, April 27, 2017, https://news.un.org/en/story/2017/04/556132-feature-uns-mission-keep-plastics-out-oceans-and-marine-life.

13      ***14 million tons of plastic***  Issues Brief (International Union for Conservation of Nature: Gland, Switzerland, November 2021), https://www.iucn.org/resources/issues-brief/marine-plastic-pollution.

13      ***more than 5 trillion pieces***  Marcus Eriksen et al., "Plastic Pollution in the World's Oceans: More Than 5 Trillion Plastic Pieces Weighing over 250,000 Tons Afloat at Sea," *PLOS One* 9, no. 12 (December 2014): https://doi.org/10.1371/journal.pone.0111913.

17      ***at that temperature***  John A. Downing, "Hypothermia: Understanding and Prevention," University of Minnesota Duluth, accessed February 6, 2024, https://seagrant.umn.edu/programs/recreation-and-water-safety-program/hypothermia#graphics.

21      ***a Heiltsuk descriptive place name***  "Bella Bella," Our World, accessed February 6, 2024, https://www.ourworldlanguage.ca/bella-bella.

22      ***after the world's fair Expo '86***  Rae-Anne Guenther, "Indigenous Advocate to Receive Honorary Doctorate Degree from VIU," Vancouver Island University, May 8, 2019, https://news.viu.ca/indigenous-advocate-receive-honorary-doctorate-degree-viu; Traditional Canoes for Traditional Reasons (British Columbia, Canada: Great Bear Rainforest Education and Awareness Trust, November 8, 2019), https://greatbearrainforesttrust.org/wp-content/uploads/2019/11/8-Traditional-Canoes.pdf.

22    *issued a challenge*  Misao Dean, *Inheriting a Canoe Paddle: The Canoe in Discourses of English-Canadian Nationalism* (Toronto, Canada: University of Toronto Press, 2013), 168.

22    *More than thirty canoes*  Gilbert W. Arias, "S'Klallam canoe leaving Port Gamble, June 13, 1993," Museum of History and Industry, accessed February 6, 2024, https://digitalcollections.lib.washington.edu/digital/collection/imlsmohai/id/16846/.

23    *the fight against* Canadian Press, "B.C. Natives Protest Enbridge Pipeline," CBC News, December 2, 2010, https://web.archive.org/web/20101206071407/http://www.cbc.ca/canada/british-columbia/story/2010/12/02/bc-first-nations-enbridge-pipeline.html#ixzz650h3Fu9A.

23    *imposed a ban*  Ethan Lou, "Canada Introduces Law to Ban Tankers off North British Columbia," *Reuters*, May 12, 2017, https://www.reuters.com/article/canada-politics-tankers-idINL1N1IE1M3/.

23    *officially rejected plans*  Jason Proctor, "Northern Gateway Pipeline Approval Overturned," CBC News, June 30, 2016, https://www.cbc.ca/news/canada/british-columbia/northern-gateway-pipeline-federal-court-of-appeal-1.3659561.

23    *130 First Nations bands*  David P. Ball, "Nations Sign Save the Fraser Declaration," *Raven's Eye* 30, no. 5 (2012): https://ammsa.com/publications/ravens-eye/nations-sign-save-fraser-declaration.

23    *the largest oil spill*  Alejandra Borunda, "We Still Don't Know the Full Impacts of the BP Oil Spill, 10 Years Later," *National Geographic*, April 20, 2020, https://www.nationalgeographic.com/science/article/bp-oil-spill-still-dont-know-effects-decade-later.

31    *approximately seventeen million acres*  "Tongass National Forest," Alaska Wilderness League, accessed February 6, 2024, https://alaskawild.org/tongass-national-forest/.

31    *virgin temperate rainforest*  "Forest Facts."

35    *ban on commercial whaling*  "Humpback Whale," NOAA

Fisheries, accessed February 6, 2024, https://www.fisheries
.noaa.gov/species/humpback-whale.

35    *more than eighty thousand*   "Scientists Tag Humpback
      Whales in Southeast Pacific," Smithsonian Tropical Re-
      search Institute, April 13, 2017, https://stri.si.edu/story
      /tracking-humpback-whales.

36    *no longer be visible*   Sue Mitchell, "Study Says Alaska Could
      Lose Massive Icefield by 2200," University of Alaska Fair-
      banks, March 24, 2016, https://www.uaf.edu/news/archives
      /news-archives-2010-2021/62165-2.php.

36    *largest freshwater reservoir*   "How Much of Earth's Water
      Is Stored in Glaciers?," US Geological Survey, accessed Feb-
      ruary 6, 2024, https://www.usgs.gov/faqs/how-much-earths
      -water-stored-glaciers.

36    *the last 12.5 million years*   "Habitat of Steep Creek in Men-
      denhall Valley," US Department of Agriculture Forest Ser-
      vice, accessed February 6, 2024, https://www.fs.usda.gov
      /detail/r10/specialplaces/?cid=fsbdev2_038753.

37    *Earth is projected to warm*   H. Lee and J. Romero, eds., *Cli-
      mate Change 2023: Synthesis Report*, 6th Assessment Report
      (Geneva, Switzerland: Intergovernmental Panel on Climate
      Change, March 2023), 57, https://doi.org/ 10.59327/IPCC
      /AR6-9789291691647.

37    *limited to 1.5 degrees Celsius*   David R. Rounce et al., "Global
      Glacier Change in the 21st Century: Every Increase in Tem-
      perature Matters," *Science* 379, no. 6627 (January 2023):
      https://doi.org/10.1126/science.abo1324.

2: Hiking and Paddling to the Arctic

41    *John Muir described*   Samuel Hall Young, *Alaska Days with
      John Muir* (New York: Fleming H. Revell Company, 1915), 210,
      https://www.google.com/books/edition/Alaska_Days
      _with_John_Muir/hEZIAAAAMAAJ.

41     *the primary packers* "History: Chilkoot Trail National Historic Site," Parks Canada, last updated November 19, 2022, https://parks.canada.ca/lhn-nhs/yt/chilkoot/culture/hist.

41     *crossed the Chilkoot Pass* Glen Boles, "Chilkoot Pass," The Canadian Encyclopedia, February 6, 2006, https://www.thecanadianencyclopedia.ca/en/article/chilkoot-pass.

42     *weighed about one ton* "Ton of Goods," National Park Service, last updated May 1, 2018, https://www.nps.gov/klgo/learn/historyculture/tonofgoods.htm.

45     *only about thirty thousand* Amanda Onion et al., "Klondike Gold Rush," History, January 17, 2018, https://www.history.com/topics/19th-century/klondike-gold-rush.

45     *Gwich'in in origin* Ken S. Coates and William R. Morrison, *Land of the Midnight Sun: A History of the Yukon* (Edmonton: Hurtig, 1988), 21.

47     *famed Five Finger Rapids* *Yukon River Heritage: An Illustrated Introduction for River Travelers*, rev. ed. (Yukon, Canada: Government of Yukon, Department of Tourism and Culture, 2013), 23, https://yukon.ca/sites/yukon.ca/files/tc/tc-yukon-river-heritage.pdf.

47     *damaged the ecosystem in many ways* "Environmental Consequences of the Gold Rush," National Park Service, last updated February 5, 2024, https://www.nps.gov/klgo/learn/historyculture/environmental-impacts.htm.

48     *area comprised of* *A Guide to Tombstone Territorial Park* (Yukon, Canada: Government of Yukon, 2021), https://yukon.ca/sites/yukon.ca/files/env/env-guide-tombstone-territorial-park.pdf.

48     *The Hän name for this area* "Tombstone Territorial Park," Yukon, accessed February 7, 2024, https://yukon.ca/en/tombstone-territorial-park.

55     *the Tth'oh Zraii Njik* Gwich'in Place Names Atlas, s.v. "Tth'oh Zraii Njik," accessed February 7, 2024, https://atlas.gwichin.ca/index.html.

55    *Beringia, an ancient oasis*  "Beringia," Yukon Beringa In-
      terpretive Centre, accessed February 7, 2024, https://www
      .beringia.com/exhibits/beringia.

56    *roughly three-hundred-foot drop*  "Bering Land Bridge:
      Beringia," National Park Service, last updated June 21, 2023,
      https://www.nps.gov/bela/learn/beringia.htm.

56    *in their place*  "Beringia."

57    *twenty-six thousand square miles*  Tom Clynes, "Victory for
      Yukon Wilderness Is 'Game-Changer,'" *National Geographic*,
      December 6, 2014, https://www.nationalgeographic.com
      /science/article/141206-peel-watershed-yukon-canada-ruling
      -land-use-planning.

58    *Teetł'it Gwinjik*  Gwich'in Place Names Atlas, s.v. "Teetł'it
      Gwinjik," accessed February 7, 2024, https://atlas.gwichin.ca
      /index.html.

59    *Nan Zhak Nadhàdlaii*  Gwich'in Place Names Atlas, s.v.
      "Nan Zhak Nadhàdlaii," accessed February 7, 2024, https://
      atlas.gwichin.ca/index.html.

64    *working to protect 80 percent*  "Our Story," Protect the Peel,
      accessed March 4, 2024, http://protectpeel.ca/our-story.

66    *the watershed was finally protected*  "After 15 Years, Final Yukon
      Agreement Signed to Protect the Peel Watershed," CBC News,
      August 22, 2019, https://www.cbc.ca/news/canada/north
      /government-first-nations-agreement-peel-plan-1.5255446.

67    *Teetł'it Zheh*  Ingrid Kritsch, "Fort McPherson," The
      Canadian Encyclopedia, August 7, 2012, https://www
      .thecanadianencyclopedia.ca/en/article/fort-mcpherson.

68    *people of the headwaters*  "Fort McPherson," GTC Depart-
      ment of Cultural Heritage, accessed February 7, 2024, https://
      www.gwichin.ca/gwichin-settlement-region/fort-mcpherson.

68    *Nagwichoonjik*  Randy Freeman, *Nagwichoonjik, the
      "River through a Big Country"* (Yellowknife, Canada:
      Gwich'in Chapter, 2005), https://gwichin.ca/publications
      /nagwichoonjik-river-through-big-country.

68    *river of great significance*    Allison Chandler, "Mackenzie River Caused Global Cooling 13,000 Years Ago, Study Suggests," CBC News, July 13, 2018, https://www.cbc.ca/news/canada/north/mackenzie-river-global-cooling-1.4742707.

69    *Tsiigehtchic*    "Tsligehtchic," Spectacular Northwest Territories, accessed February 7, 2024, https://spectacularnwt.com/destinations/western-arctic/tsiigehtchic.

69    *Alexander Mackenzie*    Alexander Mackenzie, *Voyages from Montreal through the Continent of North America, to the Frozen and Pacific Oceans, 1789–1793*, vol. 2 (Whitefish, MT: Literary Licensing, LLC, 2014).

70    *first European to follow*    Kat Eschner, "How One Quest for the Northwest Passage Ended at the Icy Mouth of Disappointment River," *Smithsonian Magazine,* July 14, 2017, https://www.smithsonianmag.com/smart-news/how-one-quest-northwest-passage-ended-mouth-disappointment-river-180964005/.

### 3: Dogsledding to Great Slave Lake

97    *In Canada, "First Nations*    "Residential School History," National Centre for Truth and Reconciliation, accessed February 8, 2024, https://nctr.ca/education/teaching-resources/residential-school-history/.

97    *National Centre for Truth and Reconciliation*    "Residential School History."

97    *The United States opened*    Zach Levitt et al., "War Against Children," *New York Times*, August 30, 2023, https://www.nytimes.com/interactive/2023/08/30/us/native-american-boarding-schools.html.

97    *Canada's Truth and Reconciliation Commission*    "Truth and Reconciliation Commission of Canada," Government of Canada, last updated September 29, 2022, https://www.rcaanc-cirnac.gc.ca/eng/1450124405592/1529106060525.

98    *Truth and Healing Commission*    Truth and Healing

Commission on Indian Boarding School Policies Act, S. 1723, 118th Cong. (2023), https://www.govtrack.us/congress/bills /118/s1723.

104  *two times more likely* Gianna Melillo, "First Nations Women of Canada Have Higher Diabetes Rates, Study Finds," American Journal of Managed Care, February 11, 2020, https:// www.ajmc.com/view/first-nations-women-of-canada-have -higher-diabetes-rates-study-finds.

110  *Deline would become* Garrett Hinchey and Kate Kyle, "Deline Set to Launch Historic Self-Government, 20 Years in the Making," CBC News, August 31, 2016, https://www.cbc.ca/news /canada/north/deline-to-sign-historic-agreement-1.3742178.

110  *Tsá Tué Biosphere Reserve* Kate Kyle, "'We'll Speak for the Lake': Deline Celebrates UNESCO Biosphere Reserve Designation," CBC News, August 13, 2016, https://www.cbc.ca/news /canada/north/deline-unesco-biosphere-celebration -1.3719445.

110  *Leeroy was elected* "Deline Residents Choose New Chief and Council in First Self-Government Election," CBC News, July 13, 2018, https://www.cbc.ca/news/canada/north/first -deline-election-results-1.4746190.

110  *highest honest leader* "Leader Ship & Councils," Délı̨nę Got'ı̨nęGovernment, accessed February 8, 2024, https://www .deline.ca/leader-ship-councils/.

114  *estimated to be 120,000 caribou* Barren-Ground Caribou in the NWT: Bluenose-East Herd (Yellowknife, Canada: Government of Northwest Territories, 2018), https://www.gov.nt.ca/ecc/sites /ecc/files/resources/fact_sheet_bluenose-east_caribou_en.pdf.

114  *an estimated 6,240 caribou left* Yereth Rosen, "Climate Change Seen as Suspected Factor in Western Arctic Caribou Herd Decline," Alaska Beacon, December 30, 2022, https:// alaskabeacon.com/2022/12/30/climate-change-seen-as -suspected-factor-in-western-arctic-caribou-herd-decline/.

114  *caribou numbers have plummeted* Bob McDonald, "Mining

Activities, Not Hunting, Responsible for Northern Caribou Declines," *Quirks and Quarks* (blog), CBC Radio, March 2, 2018, https://www.cbc.ca/radio/quirks/blog/mining-activities -not-hunting-responsible-for-northern-caribou-declines -1.4559410.

114 ***A study conducted by NOAA*** Cody Sullivan, "2018 Arctic Report Card: Reindeer and Caribou Populations Continue to Decline," NOAA Climate.gov, December 11, 2018, https://www.climate.gov/news-features/featured-images /2018-arctic-report-card-reindeer-and-caribou-populations -continue.

115 ***caribou populations have declined*** Sullivan.

115 ***A recent study predicts*** "George River Caribou Herd in Critical State as Unprecedented Population Decline Continues," Fisheries and Land Resources, Newfoundland Labrador, September 21, 2018, https://www.gov.nl.ca/releases/2018 /flr/0921n03/.

116 ***In 2022 the George River herd's*** Susan Bell, "Quebec Cree and Innu Leaders Agree to Reduce Caribou Harvest After Summer Wildfires," CBC News, January 23, 2024, https://www.cbc.ca/news/canada/north/cree-innu-caribou -northern-quebec-leaf-river-1.7092301.

116 ***climate modeling suggest*** Peter Varga, "Warming Climate Threatens Caribou in Nunavik, Labrador, Baffin," Nunatsiaq News, December 20, 2013, https://nunatsiaq.com/stories /article/65674warming_climate_threatens_caribou_in _nunavik_labrador_baffin/.

117 ***Barges ran from east to west*** "Uranium And The Sahtúot'ine," Sahtú Renewable Resources Board, accessed March 5, 2024, https://www.srrb.nt.ca/people-and-places/sahtu-atlas/102 -sahtu-atlas/resources-and-development/201-uranium-and -the-sahtuot-ine.

118 ***reported concentrations of radioactivity*** Bliss L. Tracy, "Radiation Effects on Caribou and Reindeer," *Encyclopedia*

of *Sustainability Science and Technology* (2012): https://doi
.org/10.1007/978-1-4419-0851-3_283.

122 ***three communities*** "Behchokǫ̀," Tłı̨chǫ Ndek'àowo Government, accessed February 11, 2024, https://tlicho.ca
/community/behchoko.

125 ***polluted the surrounding landscape*** Meghan Pearson, "The
City of Yellowknife, Canada, Is Sitting on Enough Arsenic to
Kill Every Human on Earth," Vice, April 16, 2014, https://
www.vice.com/en/article/xd5gw7/yellowknife-is-sitting-on
-enough-arsenic-to-kill-every-human-on-earth.

125 ***four-billion-dollar, taxpayer-funded program*** Sidney Co-
hen, "Cost of Cleaning Up Yellowknife's Giant Mine Now
Pegged at $4.38B, up from $1B," CBC News, November
10, 2022, https://www.cbc.ca/news/canada/north/giant
-mine-remediation-cost-4-billion-1.6647952.

125 ***melting permafrost in the Northwest Territories*** "State
Permafrost," *NWT State of the Environment Report,* 2022,
accessed March 5, 2024, https://www.gov.nt.ca/ecc/en
/services/nwt-state-environment-report/13-state-permafrost.

125 ***fifteen underground chambers*** "Safeguarding Health And
Safety At Canada's Giant Mine," Parsons, January 26, 2020,
https://www.parsons.com/2020/01/safeguarding-health
-and-safety-at-canadas-giant-mine/.

## 4: CANOEING TO LAKE SUPERIOR

133 ***also known as oil sands*** David J. Tenenbaum, "Oil Sands
Development: A Health Risk Worth Taking?," *Environmental
Health Perspectives* 117, no. 4 (April 2009): https://doi.org
/10.1289/ehp.117-a150.

133 ***Earth's largest-known oil sands deposits*** Stephen Leahy,
"This Is the World's Most Destructive Oil Operation—
and It's Growing," *National Geographic,* April 11, 2019,
https://www.nationalgeographic.com/environment/article

/alberta-canadas-tar-sands-is-growing-but-indigenous-people
-fight-back.

133 *fifty-four thousand square miles* Dr. Liz Kimbrough, "More
Trouble with Tar Sands: Oil Extraction Leading to Big Forest
Loss in Alberta," Mongabay, August 29, 2014, https://news
.mongabay.com/2014/08/more-trouble-with-tar-sands-oil
-extraction-leading-to-big-forest-loss-in-alberta/.

133 *According to National Geographic* Leahy, "This Is the
World's Most Destructive Oil Operation."

133 *The oil sands produce* Kyle Bakx, "Oilsands Companies Have
an Emissions Problem and a Plan to Fix It—But Who's Listening?," CBC News, April 29, 2022, https://www.cbc.ca/news
/business/bakx-pathways-oilsands-ghg-ccs-ccus-1.6431428.

144 *every fifty to two hundred years* "Forest Fires and Climate
Change" (Ottawa, Canada: Sierra Club of Canada, July 1996),
https://www.sierraclub.ca/national/programs/atmosphere
-energy/climate-change/climfire.html.

144 *In Eaarth* Bill McKibben, *Eaarth: Making a Life on a Tough
New Planet* (New York: Times Books, 2010), 41–42.

144 *Canada's 2023 wildfire season* "Canada's Record-Break-
ing Wildfires in 2023: A Firey Wake-Up Call," Government
of Canada, last updated September 8, 2013, https://natural
-resources.canada.ca/simply-science/canadas-record-breaking
-wildfires-2023-fiery-wake-call/25303.

144 *the 2023 Canadian fire season* Adam Voiland, "Relentless
Wildfires in Canada," NASA Earth Observatory, August 8, 2023,
https://earthobservatory.nasa.gov/images/151696/relentless
-wildfires-in-canada.

144 *the wildfire season ended* "2023: A Year of Intense Global Wildfire Activity," Copernicus, December 12, 2023, https://atmosphere
.copernicus.eu/2023-year-intense-global-wildfire-activity.

145 *The Richardson fire* Martina Igini, "Top 12 Largest Wildfires in History," Earth.org, September 4, 2022, https://earth
.org/largest-wildfires-in-history/.

146    ***2,500 people lived there in 1982*** "Western Provinces and the Territories," 1981 Census of Canada, Statistics Canada, May 1983, https://publications.gc.ca/collections/collection _2017/statcan/CS94-904-1981.pdf.

152    ***Thompson, trying to find a shortcut*** David Thompson, *David Thompson's Narrative of His Explorations in Western America, 1784–1812* (Toronto: The Champlain Society, 1916), http://www.americanjourneys.org/aj-138/print.

153    ***a bifurcation lake*** "Wollaston Lake—Hatchet Lake First Nation," accessed February 9, 2024, https://www .cameconorth.com/community/community-profiles/wollaston -lake-hatchet-lake-first-nation.

153    ***Rabbit Lake uranium mine*** "Rabbit Lake," Cameco, last updated December 31, 2023, https://www.cameco.com /businesses/uranium-operations/suspended/rabbit-lake.

153    ***the mine was shuttered*** Alex MacPherson, "Rabbit Lake Mine Closure Bad News for Workers, Northern Saskatchewan: Grand Chief," *Saskatoon StarPhoenix*, April 23, 2016, https:// thestarphoenix.com/business/local-business/rabbit-lake-mine -closure-bad-news-for-workers-northern-saskatchewan-grand -chief.

160    ***government formally apologized*** "Manitoba Apologizes to First Nation for Environmental Damage," CBC News, January 20, 2015, https://www.cbc.ca/news/canada/manitoba /manitoba-apologizes-to-first-nation-for-environmental -damage-1.2919768.

160    ***eviction of Manitoba Hydro employees*** Ian Graham, "Hydro Employees Evicted from Jenpeg by Pimicikamak First Nation Members," *Thompson Citizen*, October 17, 2014, https://www .thompsoncitizen.net/nickel-belt-news/hydro-employees -evicted-from-jenpeg-by-pimicikamak-first-nation-members -4282223.

160    ***In addition to the apology*** "Occupation of Manitoba Hydro Dam Ends After Deal Reached," Global News, November

28, 2014, https://globalnews.ca/news/1698236/occupation-of
-manitoba-hydro-dam-ends-after-deal-reached.

160  *devastating effects on the surrounding ecosystem* Kazim Ali,
*Northern Light: Power, Land, and the Memory of Water* (Minneapolis, MN: Milkweed Editions, 2021), 63.

160  *told author Kazim Ali* Ali, 68.

160  *since the spring thaw* Manitoba *2011 Flood Review Task Force
Report,* April 2013, https://www.gov.mb.ca/asset_library/en
/2011flood/flood_review_task_force_report.pdf.

160  *In all, 7,100 Manitobans* "1. Historic Flood Fights in the
West," Top Ten Weather Stories for 2011, Government of
Canada, last updated August 9, 2017, https://www.ec.gc.ca
/meteo-weather/default.asp?lang=En&n=0397DE72-1.

161  *diverted floodwaters onto reserve land* Ali, *Northern
Light,* 68.

171  *As **Northern Wilds** describes* Joe Friedrichs, "Wilderness
Rangers Survive the Pagami Creek Fire," *Northern Wilds,*
December 27, 2016, http://northernwilds.com/wilderness
-rangers-survive-pagami-creek-fire/.

171  *The primary reasons* US Department of Agriculture
Forest Service, *Pagami Creek Wildfire,* January 2012,
https://www.fs.usda.gov/Internet/FSE_DOCUMENTS
/stelprdb5346343.pdf.

171  *$23 million* "Forest Service Changes Policy on Letting Some
Forest Fires Burn," *Bemidji Pioneer,* August 6, 2012, https://
www.bemidjipioneer.com/news/forest-service-changes
-policy-on-letting-some-forest-fires-burn.

172  *drastically increased in size* "Wildfires and Acres," National
Interagency Fire Center, accessed February 11, 2024, https://
www.nifc.gov/fire-information/statistics/wildfires.

172  *an eight-fold increase* American Geophysical Union, "Area
Burned by Severe Fire Increased 8-Fold in Western US over Past
Four Decades," ScienceDaily, November 30, 2020, "https://
www.sciencedaily.com/releases/2020/11/201130131400.htm.

172   *The US government spent* "Suppression Costs," National Interagency Fire Center, accessed February 12, 2024, https://
www.nifc.gov/fire-information/statistics/suppression-costs.

## 5: KAYAKING TO KEY WEST

181   *As Dan Egan says* Dan Egan, *The Death and Life of the Great
Lakes* (New York: W. W. Norton & Company, 2017),
282–284.

182   *as many as 650 caribou* "Assessment of Impacts on Woodland Caribou," from *Environmental Assessment for the
Marathon PGM-Cu Project at Marathon, Ontario,* July 19,
2012, 62, https://iaac-aeic.gc.ca/050/documents_staticpost
/54755/80504/Supporting_Document_26_-_Woodland
_Caribou_Report.pdf.

182   *in the spring of 2012* "Lake Superior Caribou," *Lake Superior
Magazine,* April 7, 2022, https://www.lakesuperior.com/the-lake
/natural-world/lake-superior-caribou/.

183   *Caribou Island is very small* "Relocated Caribou Have Bred
on Lake Superior Island," CBC News, October 11, 2019,
https://www.cbc.ca/news/canada/thunder-bay/lake-superior
-caribou-successfully-bred-1.5316691.

185   *many of the pits were made* "Executive Summary,"
from *Pukaskwa National Park of Canada: State of the
Park Report, 2008,* Government of Canada, 5, https://
parks.canada.ca/pn-np/on/pukaskwa/info/index/~/media
/1299F9F60130420485FA3CEB93B7183E.ashx.

185   *it was called Bahweting* "Oldest City in Michigan," Sault
Ste. Marie, accessed February 12, 2024, https://saultstemarie
.com/soo-area-and-great-waters-region/our-local-history/.

186   *North America's surface fresh water* "Great Lakes Facts and
Figures," United States Environmental Protection Agency, last
updated November 2, 2023, https://www.epa.gov/greatlakes
/great-lakes-facts-and-figures.

187   *time of its completion in 1825*  Andy Riga, "St. Lawrence Seaway at 60: Timeline of an Engineering Marvel," *Montreal Gazette*, April 26, 2019, https://montrealgazette.com/news/local -news/seaway-at-60/st-lawrence-seaway-at-60-timeline-of-an -engineering-marvel.

189   *For nearly fifty years*  Ingrid Peritz, "Bombs Lie on Bed of Serene Quebec Lake," *Globe and Mail*, August 19, 2005, https:// www.theglobeandmail.com/news/national/bombs-lie-on -bed-of-serene-quebec-lake/article20425191/.

189   *also a UNESCO biosphere reserve*  Peritz.

191   *Grand Communications Route*  W. E. Campbell, "Establishing the Route: The Beginnings to 1760," chap. 1 in *The Road to Canada: The Grand Communications Route from Saint John to Quebec* (Fredericton, Canada: Goose Lake Editions, 2005).

194   *long road to recovery*  Roy MacGregor, "Fishing for Answers," *Globe and Mail*, August 27, 2017, https://www.theglobeandmail .com/life/travel/charting-the-future-of-canadas-historic-saint -johnriver/article36097707/.

196   *ascend the Saint John River*  Micah A. Pawling, "*Wəlastəkwey* (Maliseet) Homeland: Waterscapes and Community within the Lower St. John River Valley, 1784–1900," *Acadiensis* 46, no. 2 (2017): https://journals.lib.unb.ca/index.php /acadiensis/article/view/25946/30150.

197   *Rock walls of billion-year-old*  "Dishing the Dirt on the Elusive Stonehammer Geopark," CBC News, April 25, 2021, https:// www.cbc.ca/news/canada/new-brunswick/stonehammer -geopark-1.5999706.

203   *Inmates from Rikers Island*  Nina Bernstein, "Unearthing the Secrets of New York's Mass Graves," *New York Times*, May 15, 2016, https://www.nytimes.com/interactive/2016/05/15 /nyregion/new-york-mass-graves-hart-island.html.

205   *describes in* **Storm Surge**  Adam Sobel, *Storm Surge: Hurricane Sandy, Our Changing Climate, and Extreme Weather of the Past and Future* (New York: Harper Wave, 2014), xv–xvi.

211   **As Elizabeth Rush writes**   Elizabeth Rush, *Rising: Dispatches from the New American Shore* (Minneapolis, MN: Milkweed Editions, 2018), 258.

211   **largest estuary in the United States**   "Where Is the Largest Estuary in the United States?," National Ocean Service, accessed February 12, 2024, https://oceanservice.noaa.gov/facts/chesapeake.html.

217   **Between the 1880s and 1930s**   "Jekyll Island Club Resort History," Jekyll Island Club Resort, accessed March 5, 2024, https://www.jekyllclub.com/about/jekyll-island-history/.

218   **More than 309,000 acres burned**   Russ Bynum, "Wildfire Burns 250 Acres, Destroys Home in Southeast Georgia," AP News, March 29, 2017, https://apnews.com/general-news-caaf3f8edd064f85a2fcc58d8bb28eed.

219   **In this passage from Eaarth**   McKibben, *Eaarth*, 22.

219   **One study estimated**   Adam C. Watts and Leda N. Kobziar, "Smoldering Combustion and Ground Fires: Ecological Effects and Multi-Scale Significance," *Fire Ecology* 9 (2013): https://doi.org/10.4996/fireecology.0901124. Watts and Kobziar reference B. Langmann and A. Heil, "Release and Dispersion of Vegetation and Peat Fire Emissions in the Atmosphere over Indonesia 1997/1998," *Atmospheric Chemistry and Physics* 4, no. 8 (2004): https://doi.org/10.5194/acp-4-2145-2004.

222   **Nearly five million barrels**   Richard Pallardy, "Deepwater Horizon Oil Spill," Encyclopedia Britannica, December 29, 2023, https://www.britannica.com/event/Deepwater-Horizon-oil-spill.

222   **The Muscogee (Creek) call it**   Robert H. Keller and Michael F. Turek, "Everglades National Park and the Seminole Problem," chap. 10 in *American Indians and National Parks* (Tuscon, Arizona: University of Arizona Press, 1998), 216.

222   **Marjory Stoneman Douglas called it**   Marjory Stoneman Douglas, *The Everglades: River of Grass* (1947; repr. Sarasota, FL: Pineapple Press, 2007).

223    *The Everglades is basically*    "Florida: Everglades National Park," National Park Service, last updated August 7, 2017, https://www.nps.gov/articles/everglades.htm.

224    *risen close to six inches*    *Sea Level Rise and Coastal Risk* (Tallahassee, FL: Florida Climate Center, 2016), https://climatecenter .fsu.edu/topics/sea-level-rise.

224    *rise another foot by 2050*    Christina Nunez, "Sea Levels Are Rising at an Extraordinary Pace. Here's What to Know," *National Geographic*, April 10, 2023, https://www.nationalgeographic .com/environment/article/sea-level-rise-1.

224    *The Everglades are home*    "Threatened and Endangered Species," National Parks Service, accessed March 5, 2024, https://www.nps.gov/ever/learn/nature/techecklist.htm.

224    *Elizabeth Rush explains*    Rush, *Rising*, 80–81.

224    *she adds that today*    Rush, 82.

# Acknowledgments

IT IS HARD to put into words how grateful we are for the support that we received from so many individuals, schools, organizations, and businesses, which made this life-changing odyssey possible. We will try to acknowledge as many of you here as we can, but honestly, from every person we met along the way to every student who emailed us questions, artwork, or words of encouragement—thank you. You made this journey possible and our lives richer.

The resources required to feed, clothe, and equip ourselves and to effectively share our experiences with tens of thousands of students and teachers throughout the journey were substantial. We would like to thank the following companies, organizations, and foundations for their support: The Brinson Foundation, Shedd Aquarium (Joy Kubarek-Sandor), Wild Gift, Clif Family Foundation, The New York Stock Exchange, Adventure Scientists, 1% for the Planet, Wenonah Canoe, Current Designs Kayaks, Wintergreen Dogsled Lodge, Wintergreen Northern Wear, MTI Adventurewear (acquired by Mustang Survival), Mitchell Paddles, Snowtrekker Tents, North Water, Granite Gear, ExOfficio, Palm Equipment, Goal Zero, GoMacro, Lärabar, Clif Bar, Petzl, Midwest Mountaineering, Tamarack Media Cooperative, Vermont Farm Tours, Kondos Outdoors, Crapola, Hodgson Mill, Cabot Creamery, and Steger Mukluks.

While the Wilderness Classroom and the educational nature

of the North American Odyssey plays a relatively small part in this book, the students and teachers emailing us questions, voting each week to decide where we would go and what we would study, and inviting us into their schools for assemblies were the main reason we undertook this adventure and were the glue that held this journey together. We owe a huge thank-you to all the students, teachers, and administrators who participated in this learning adventure as well as the Wilderness Classroom board members, past and present, who have helped guide the Wilderness Classroom Organization for the past twenty-two years.

The people who joined us for days, weeks, or even several months at a time made the journey so much more interesting, and we really appreciate all the time and effort you poured into planning and preparing as well as all the camp chores, campfires, sunsets, and memories shared. Thank you, John Amren and Clayton White, for putting up with our slow paddling; Ellen Root and Van Conrad, for sharing a tent with us for a whole winter; Dan Modal, for doing his summer-long outdoor-education internship with us; Bryan Hansel, for all the beautiful images from the Boundary Waters and Florida Keys; Kate Ford, for paddling with us in Quebec and hosting us in Vermont; Scott McPherson, for joining us in the Yukon; as well as Melissa Williams from the Shedd Aquarium, for organizing a group of educators and students who joined us for a week on the Yukon River (Maureen, Kelsey, Konrad, and Kevin). Thank you to Sue and Paul Schurke and all the Wintergreen guides who made our wedding possible; Bernard Herrmann, for making a miraculous wedding cake; Eric Frost for marrying us; and Terrence, Marge, Laura, and Jeff, for the music and calling the dance. Thank you to Chris Maher, for loaning us six sled dogs; Krystal Hagstrom, for loaning us four sled dogs; Van's parents, for the use of their lake house; Ellen's mom, for knitting our wristlets; Molly Breslin, for writing the first grant proposal for the Brinson Foundation and donating tons of beans from Breslin Farms.

When we set out from Bellingham, we assumed the wild, untrammeled spaces would be the highlight of our journey, but the people we met—many of whom opened their homes, hosted us in their communities, stored food and gear for us, and shared meals and stories, knowledge and glimpses into their lives—blew us away and showed us how kind and generous humans can be. We can't possibly thank all of you by name, but we will try to acknowledge as many of you as we can.

Larry in Bellingham; Stu, Adriel, and Julius in the San Juan Islands; Ken on M/V *Westcoast Spirit*; Jaret Slipp in Whitehorse; Ben Learmont on the Yukon River; Miranda Currie and Judy and Michael Fredrick at their fish camp on the Mackenzie River; W. and Frank and Adeline Peirrot in Fort Good Hope; Keith Hickling, Peter, Erik Koopman, and Julie Logie in Norman Wells; Ron Doctor in Tulita; Leeroy Andre in Deline; Bruce and Verna in Deline; Joe Zoe in Gameti; José and Mauricio in Rae; Jeremy MacIver, principal in Whati; Matt Clements in Gameti; Max in Yellowknife; Linda and Wayne, along the Taltson River; Yves at the Twin Gorges dam; Tim on Hill Island Lake; Ed in Stony Rapids; Joe and Joe in Cross Lake; Edgar, Doreen, Lynda, and Richard in Loon Strait; Jason Zabokrtsky in Ely; Darrell Makin in Thunder Bay; David Wells and everyone at Naturally Superior in Wawa; Steve and Joyce Humphrey in Marathon; Conor Mihell in Sault Ste. Marie; Andy Thompson along the Ottawa River; Louis and Julie Brunet in Ottawa; Chris Howell, Erik Hoekstra, and Pete Land in Burlington; Martin in Pohenegamook; Paul Huestis in Saint John; John and Pat in Lubec; Glenn Charles in Maine; Jeff and Steph Frigon in Exeter; the Starr family in Swampscott; Anna and Andy Devereaux in Beverly; Ari Ofsevit in Boston; Lili and Gordon Colby in Plymouth; Hugh, Nancy, and Bill Manke in New Haven; Eugene, Mira, and Liza Shats in Sea Gate; Todd, Nina, Devin, Avery, and Ian Hohman in Morristown; Erich Umar and Jim Hyde in New York City; Bill and Carmen Stage and John and Joan Ritchie in Barnegat Bay; Andrew Grossman in Ocean City; Kathleen and Tom Wright on Kiawah Island; Lyn Law, Jim Marron, and Jordan Law-Marion on Saint Simons Island; and Trisha Gallagher and Buddy in Tampa Bay.

We started writing this book in 2018, and Milkweed Editions has stuck with us through thick and thin. We would specifically like to thank Daniel Slager, Whitney Bak, Lauren Langston Klein, Helen Whybrow, and Mary Austin Speaker for the editing and layout expertise, which makes our story shine in ways we never could.

Finally, we would like to thank our parents for fostering our love of the outdoors and their unwavering support as we have followed a somewhat unconventional path. We also owe a huge thank-you to all of our family and friends who have bid us farewell and welcomed us home so many times over the years. We miss weddings and births, birthdays, surgeries, funerals, and many other life events great and small during the course of our endless wanderings. Thank you for always being there when we return. We miss you and appreciate you more than you could possibly know.

**AMY AND DAVE FREEMAN** have traveled over fifty thousand miles through some of the world's wildest places, from the Amazon to the Arctic. They were named Adventurers of the Year by *National Geographic* in 2014, and they are also the authors of *A Year in the Wilderness*, an award-winning book about the year they spent in the Boundary Waters Canoe Area Wilderness. When they aren't on expeditions, their sailboat, or speaking tours, they are based in Ely, Minnesota, where they organize and lead canoe and dogsled trips.

milkweed
EDITIONS

Founded as a nonprofit organization in 1980, Milkweed Editions is an independent publisher. Our mission is to identify, nurture, and publish transformative literature, and build an engaged community around it.

Milkweed Editions is based in Bdé Óta Othúŋwe (Minneapolis) within Mní Sota Makhóčhe, the traditional homeland of the Dakhóta people. Residing here since time immemorial, Dakhóta people still call Mní Sota Makhóčhe home, with four federally recognized Dakhóta nations and many more Dakhóta people residing in what is now the state of Minnesota. Due to continued legacies of colonization, genocide, and forced removal, generations of Dakhóta people remain disenfranchised from their traditional homeland. Presently, Mní Sota Makhóčhe has become a refuge and home for many Indigenous nations and peoples, including seven federally recognized Ojibwe nations. We humbly encourage our readers to reflect upon the historical legacies held in the lands they occupy.

milkweed.org

Milkweed Editions, an independent nonprofit literary publisher, gratefully acknowledges sustaining support from our board of directors, the McKnight Foundation, the National Endowment for the Arts, and many generous contributions from foundations, corporations, and thousands of individuals—our readers. This activity is made possible by the voters of Minnesota through a Minnesota State Arts Board Operating Support grant, thanks to a legislative appropriation from the arts and cultural heritage fund.

Interior design by Mary Austin Speaker
Typeset in Arno

Arno was designed by Robert Slimbach. Slimbach named
this typeface after the river that runs through Florence, Italy.
Arno draws inspiration from a variety of typefaces created
during the Italian Renaissance; its italics were inspired by
the calligraphy and printing of Ludovico degli Arrighi.